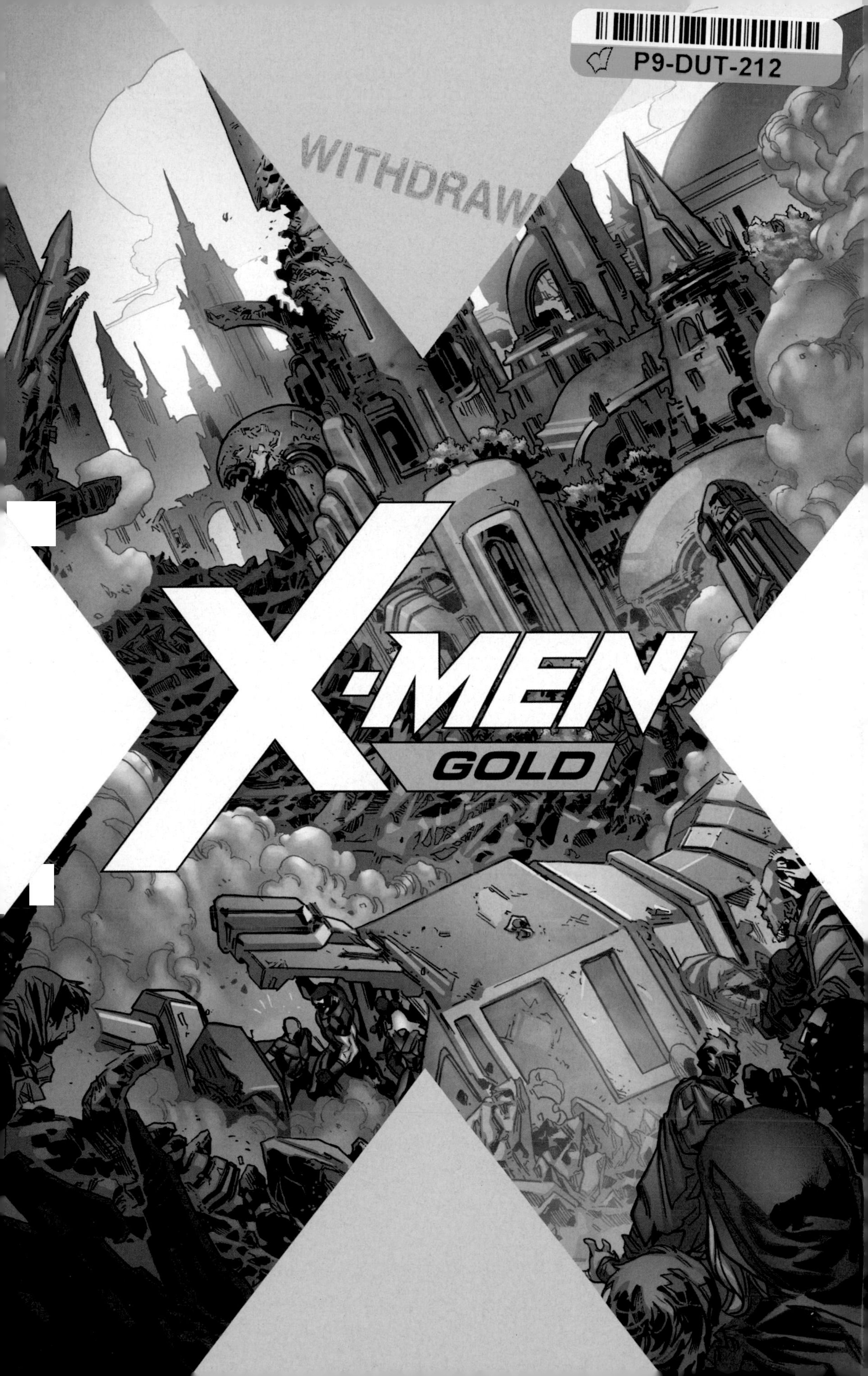
X-MEN
GOLD

THE X-MEN HAVE BEEN RECOVERING FROM THEIR SKIRMISH IN THE NEGATIVE ZONE, BUT THEIR RECOVERY MAY BE SHORT-LIVED. THE TEAM HAD PREVIOUSLY DISCOVERED THAT ANTI-MUTANT POLITICIAN LYDIA NANCE EMPLOYED THE TELEPATHIC VILLAIN KNOWN AS MESMERO TO CREATE A NEW "BROTHERHOOD OF EVIL MUTANTS."

KITTY PRYDE AND HER X-MEN THOUGHT THEY'D DEFEATED THE PHONY "BROTHERHOOD," BUT YOU CAN'T KEEP A GOOD VILLAIN DOWN...

Collection Editor/**JENNIFER GRÜNWALD** • Assistant Editor/**CAITLIN O'CONNELL**
Associate Managing Editor/**KATERI WOODY** • Editor, Special Projects/**MARK D. BEAZLEY**
VP Production & Special Projects/**JEFF YOUNGQUIST** • SVP Print, Sales & Marketing/**DAVID GABRIEL**
Book Designer/**JAY BOWEN**

Editor in Chief/**C.B. CEBULSKI** • Chief Creative Officer/**JOE QUESADA**
President/**DAN BUCKLEY** • Executive Producer/**ALAN FINE**

X-MEN GOLD VOL. 5: CRUEL AND UNUSUAL. Contains material originally published in magazine form as X-MEN GOLD #21-25. First printing 2018. ISBN 978-1-302-90975-8. Published by MARVEL WORLDWIDE, INC., a subsidiary of MARVEL ENTERTAINMENT, LLC. OFFICE OF PUBLICATION: 135 West 50th Street, New York, NY 10020. **Printed in Canada.** DAN BUCKLEY, President, Marvel Entertainment; JOHN NEE, Publisher; JOE QUESADA, Chief Creative Officer; TOM BREVOORT, SVP of Publishing; DAVID BOGART, SVP of Business Affairs & Operations, Publishing & Partnership; DAVID GABRIEL, SVP of Sales & Marketing, Publishing; JEFF YOUNGQUIST, VP of Production & Special Projects; DAN CARR, Executive Director of Publishing Technology; ALEX MORALES, Director of Publishing Operations; DAN EDINGTON, Managing Editor; SUSAN CRESPI, Production Manager; STAN LEE, Chairman Emeritus. For information regarding advertising in Marvel Comics or on Marvel.com, please contact Vit DeBellis, Custom Solutions & Integrated Advertising Manager, at vdebellis@marvel.com. For Marvel subscription inquiries, please call 888-511-5480. **Manufactured between 4/6/2018 and 5/8/2018 by SOLISCO PRINTERS, SCOTT, QC, CANADA.**

10 9 8 7 6 5 4 3 2 1

X-MEN GOLD

CRUEL AND UNUSUAL

Writer/**MARC GUGGENHEIM**

ISSUES #21-22
Penciler/**DIEGO BERNARD**
Inker/**JP MEYER**
Colorists/**ARIF PRIANTO** WITH JAVA TARTAGLIA (#22)
Cover Art/**MIKE DEODATO JR.** & **NOLAN WOODARD** (#21)
AND **DAN MORA** & **JUAN FERANDEZ** (#22)

ISSUES #23-24
Artist/**THONY SILAS**
Colorists/**ARIF PRIANTO** WITH MARCIO MENYZ (#24)
Cover Art/**DAVID NAKAYAMA**

ISSUE #25
Pencilers/**PAULO SIQUEIRA** & **JOSÉ LUIS**
Inkers/**CAM SMITH** & **VICTOR OLAZABA**
WITH **PAULO SIQUEIRA**
Colorists/**ARIF PRIANTO**, **JAVA TARTAGLIA**
& **JUAN FERNANDEZ**
Cover Art/**RYAN STEGMAN** & **EDGAR DELGADO**

Letterer/**VC's CORY PETIT**

Assistant Editors/**CHRISTINA HARRINGTON**
& **CHRIS ROBINSON**
Editor/**MARK PANICCIA**

SPECIAL THANKS TO **MIKE O'SULLIVAN**

X-MEN CREATED BY **STAN LEE** & **JACK KIRBY**

21

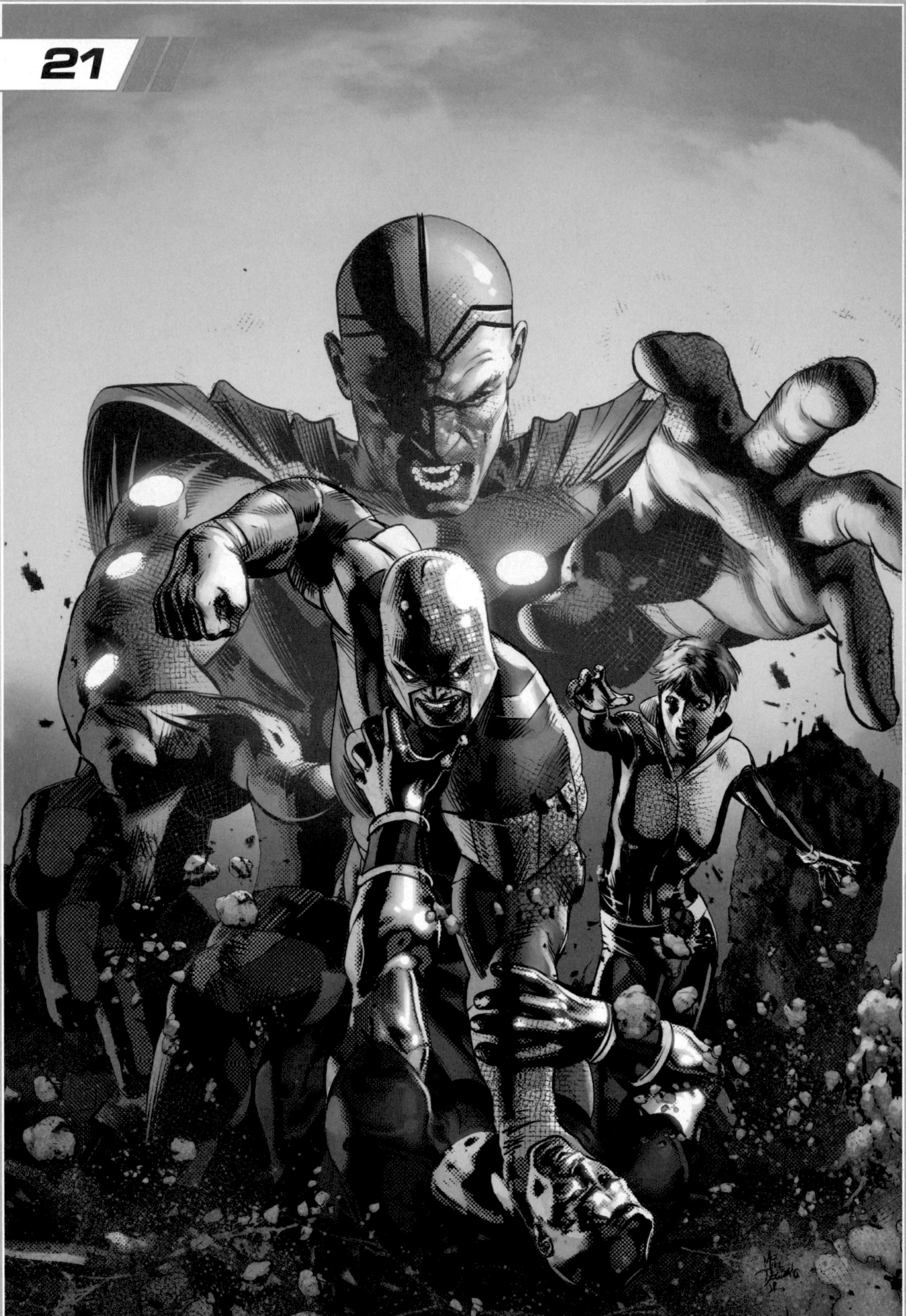

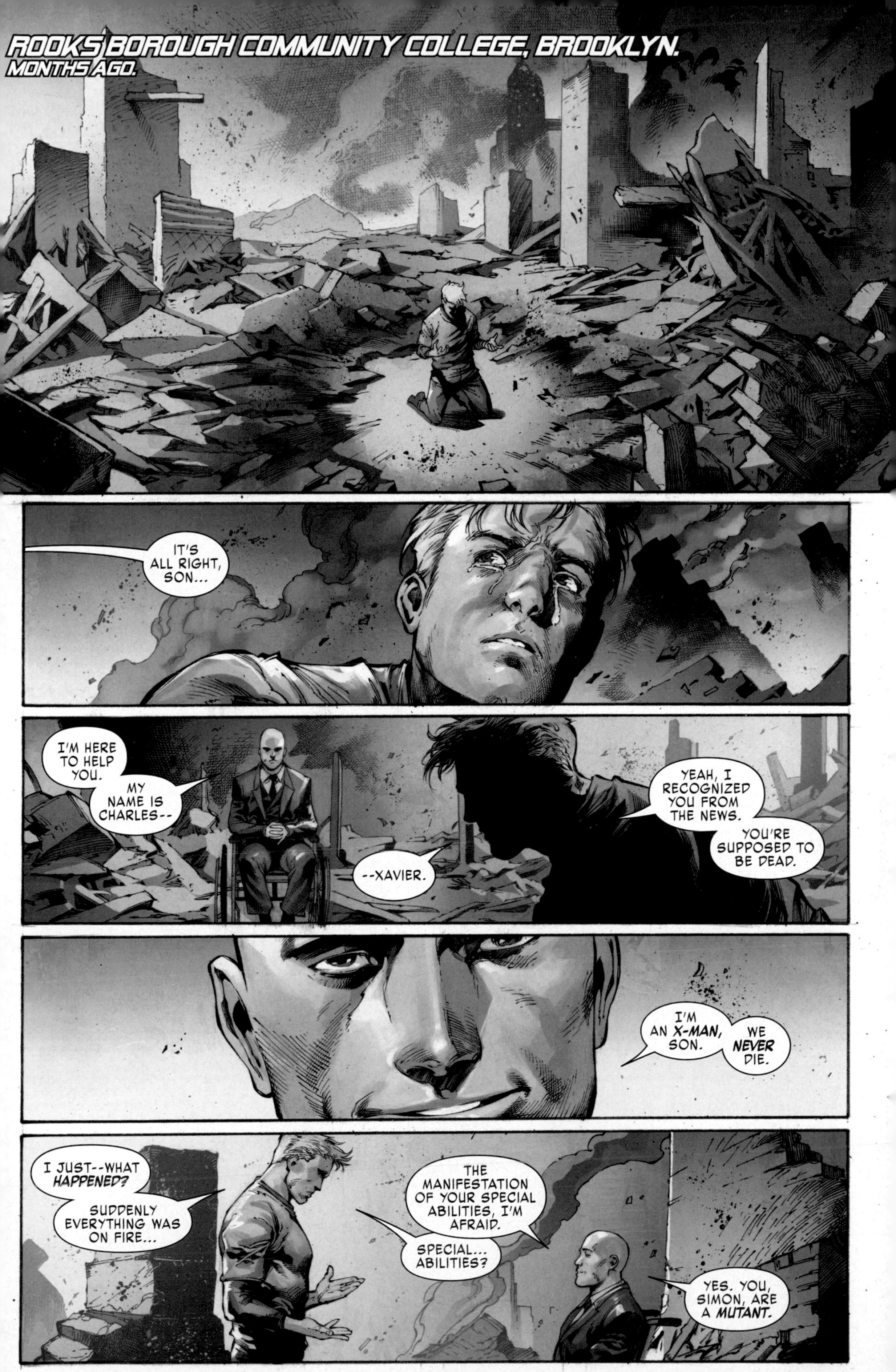
ROOKS BOROUGH COMMUNITY COLLEGE, BROOKLYN.
MONTHS AGO.
IT'S ALL RIGHT, SON...
I'M HERE TO HELP YOU.
MY NAME IS CHARLES--
--XAVIER.
YEAH, I RECOGNIZED YOU FROM THE NEWS.
YOU'RE SUPPOSED TO BE DEAD.
I'M AN X-MAN, SON.
WE NEVER DIE.
I JUST--WHAT HAPPENED?
SUDDENLY EVERYTHING WAS ON FIRE...
THE MANIFESTATION OF YOUR SPECIAL ABILITIES, I'M AFRAID.
SPECIAL... ABILITIES?
YES. YOU, SIMON, ARE A MUTANT.

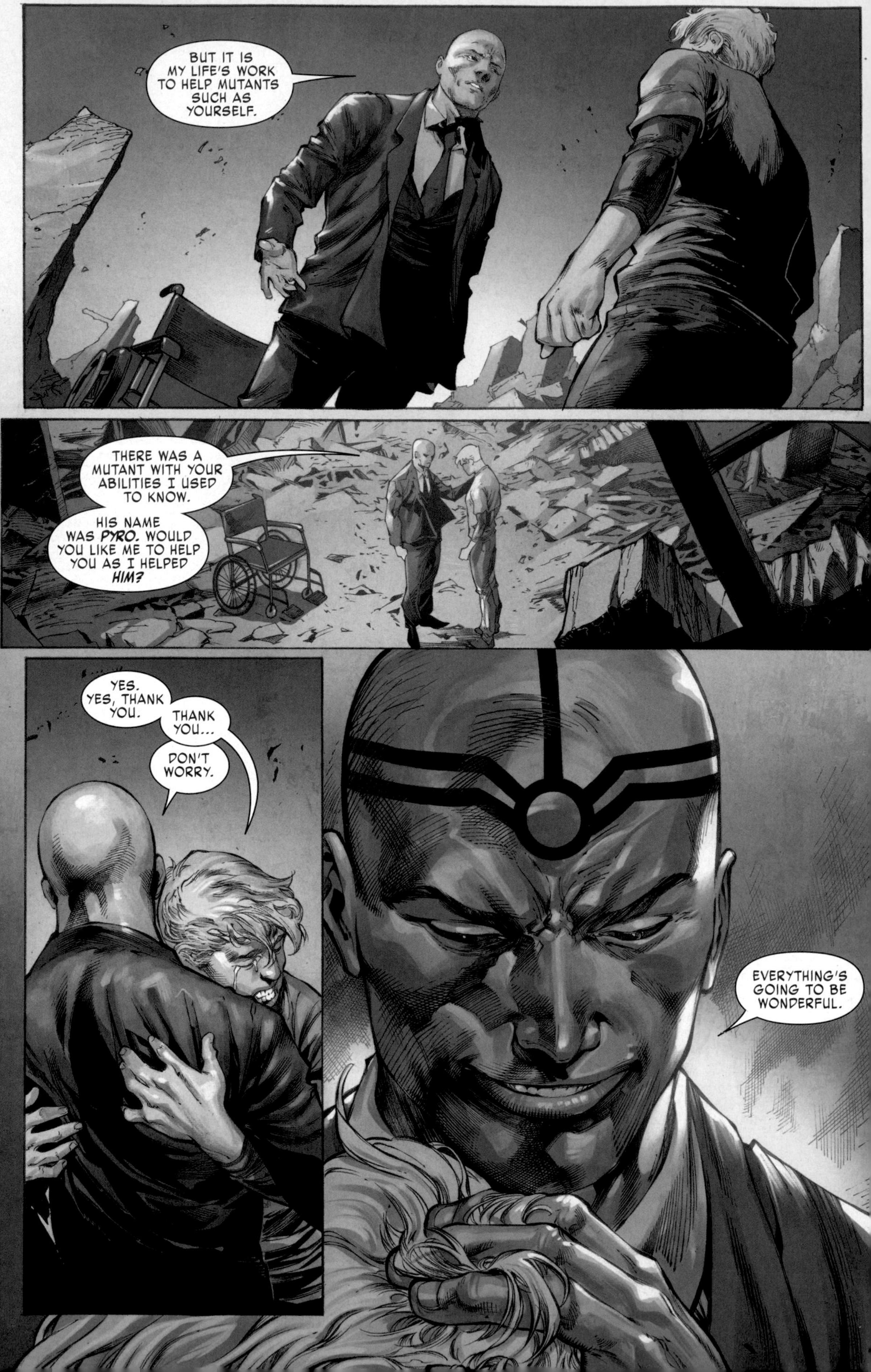
BUT IT IS MY LIFE'S WORK TO HELP MUTANTS SUCH AS YOURSELF.
THERE WAS A MUTANT WITH YOUR ABILITIES I USED TO KNOW.
HIS NAME WAS **PYRO.** WOULD YOU LIKE ME TO HELP YOU AS I HELPED **HIM?**
YES. YES, THANK YOU.
THANK YOU...
DON'T WORRY.
EVERYTHING'S GOING TO BE WONDERFUL.

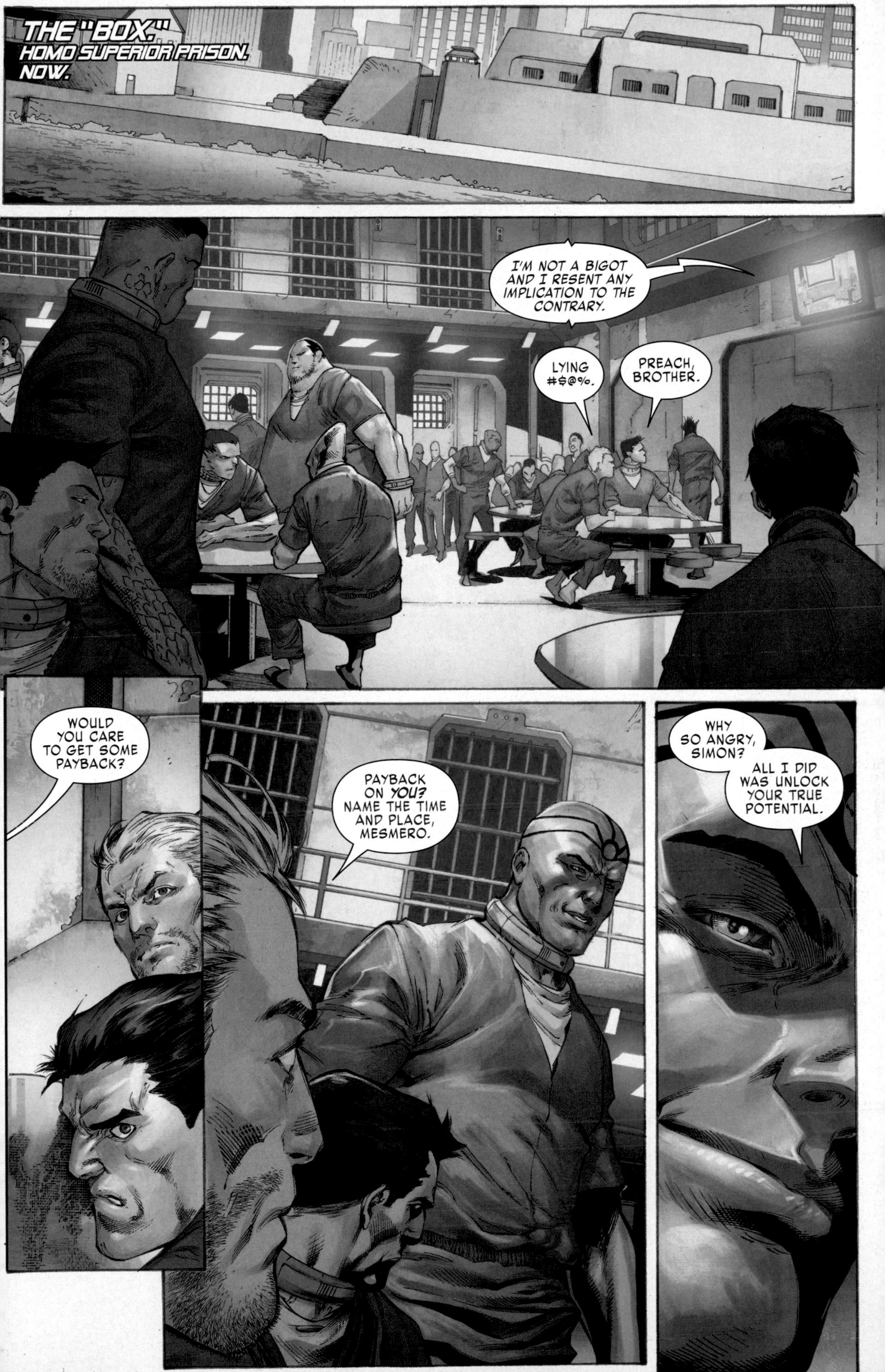
THE "BOX." HOMO SUPERIOR PRISON. NOW.
I'M NOT A BIGOT AND I RESENT ANY IMPLICATION TO THE CONTRARY.
LYING #$@%.
PREACH, BROTHER.
WOULD YOU CARE TO GET SOME PAYBACK?
PAYBACK ON YOU? NAME THE TIME AND PLACE, MESMERO.
WHY SO ANGRY, SIMON?
ALL I DID WAS UNLOCK YOUR TRUE POTENTIAL.

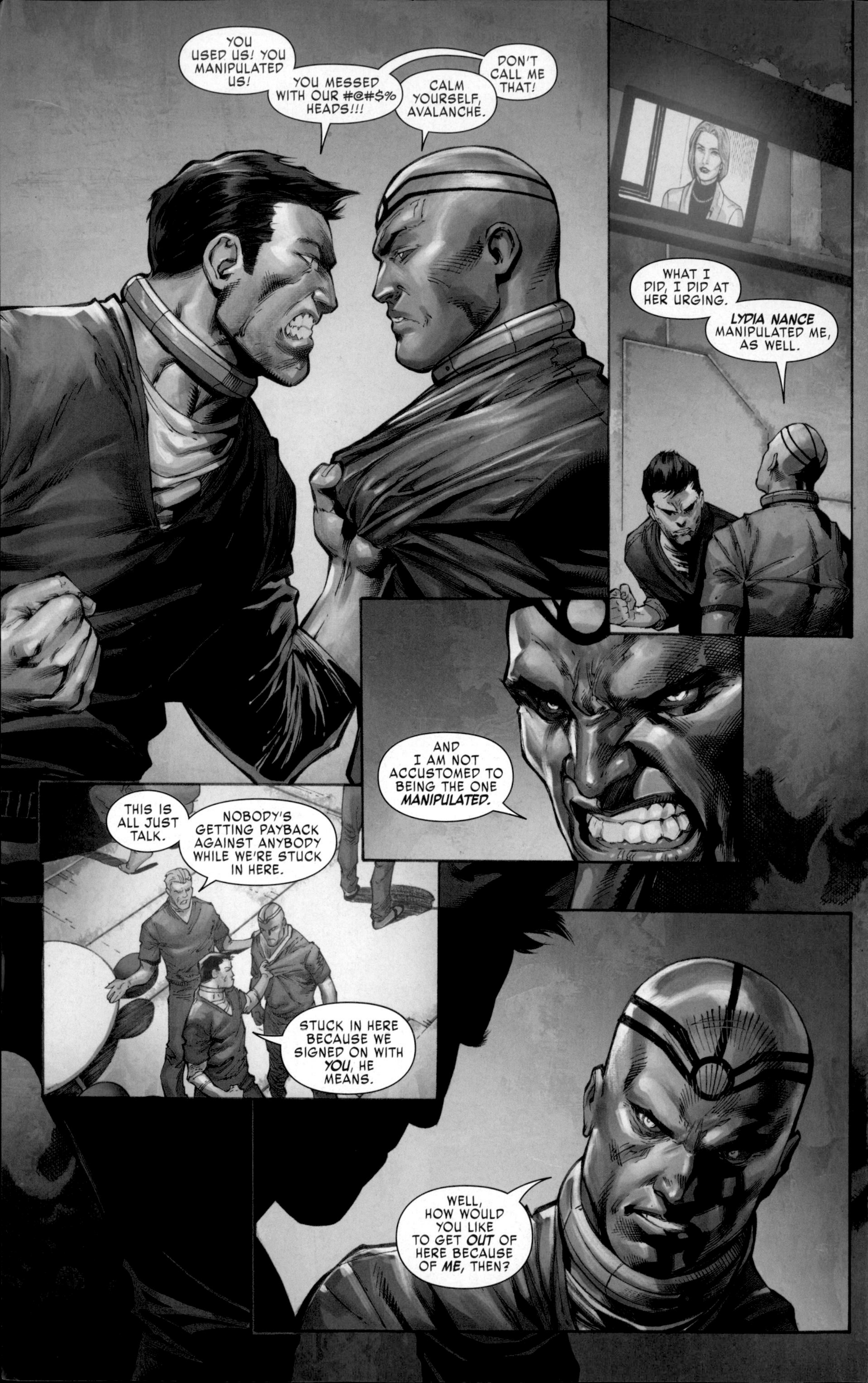
YOU USED US! YOU MANIPULATED US!
YOU MESSED WITH OUR #@#$% HEADS!!!
CALM YOURSELF, AVALANCHE.
DON'T CALL ME THAT!
WHAT I DID, I DID AT HER URGING.
LYDIA NANCE MANIPULATED ME, AS WELL.
AND I AM NOT ACCUSTOMED TO BEING THE ONE MANIPULATED.
THIS IS ALL JUST TALK.
NOBODY'S GETTING PAYBACK AGAINST ANYBODY WHILE WE'RE STUCK IN HERE.
STUCK IN HERE BECAUSE WE SIGNED ON WITH YOU, HE MEANS.
WELL, HOW WOULD YOU LIKE TO GET OUT OF HERE BECAUSE OF ME, THEN?

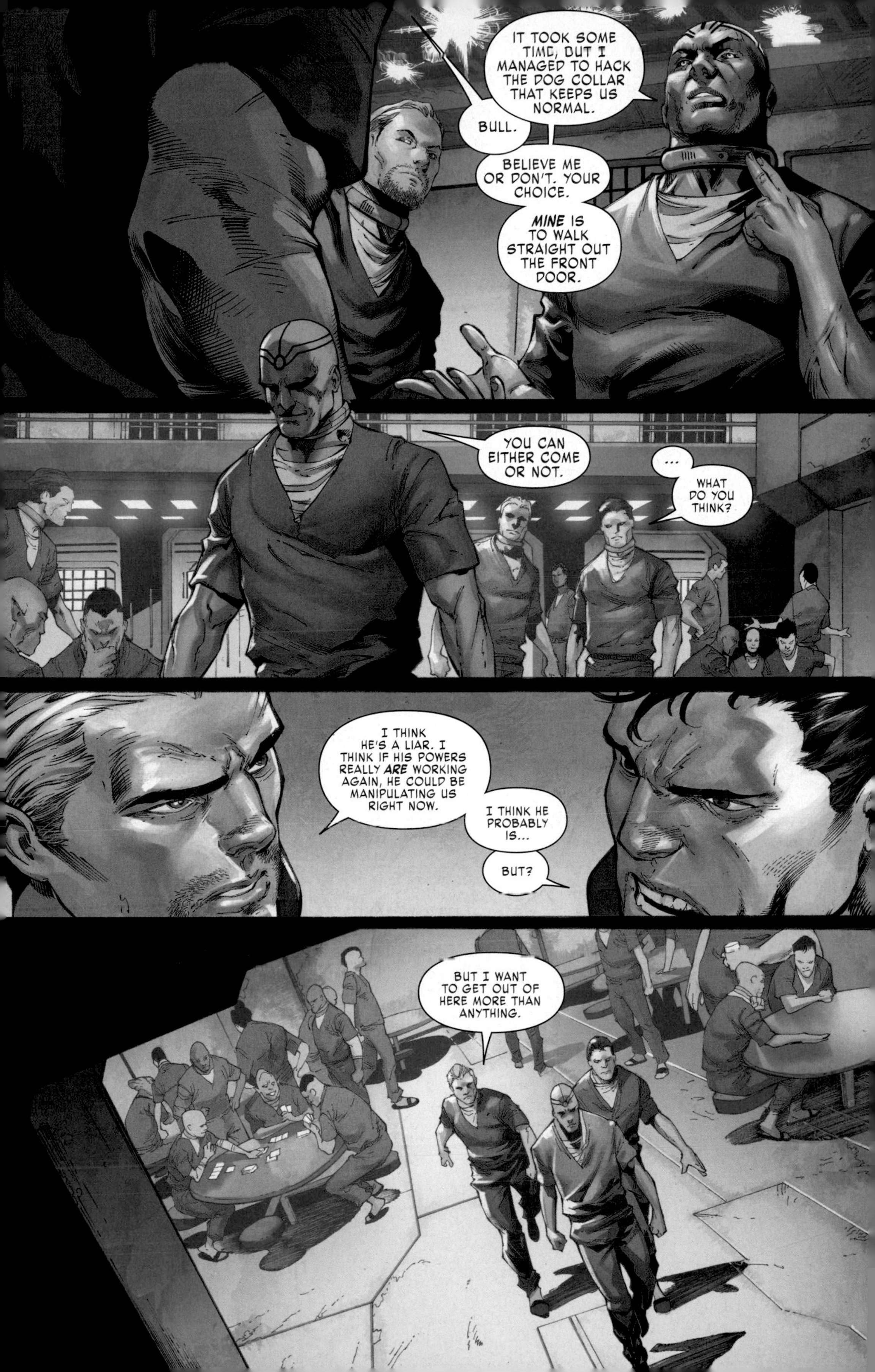
IT TOOK SOME TIME, BUT I MANAGED TO HACK THE DOG COLLAR THAT KEEPS US NORMAL.
BULL.
BELIEVE ME OR DON'T. YOUR CHOICE.
MINE IS TO WALK STRAIGHT OUT THE FRONT DOOR.
YOU CAN EITHER COME OR NOT.
...
WHAT DO YOU THINK?
I THINK HE'S A LIAR. I THINK IF HIS POWERS REALLY ARE WORKING AGAIN, HE COULD BE MANIPULATING US RIGHT NOW.
I THINK HE PROBABLY IS...
BUT?
BUT I WANT TO GET OUT OF HERE MORE THAN ANYTHING.

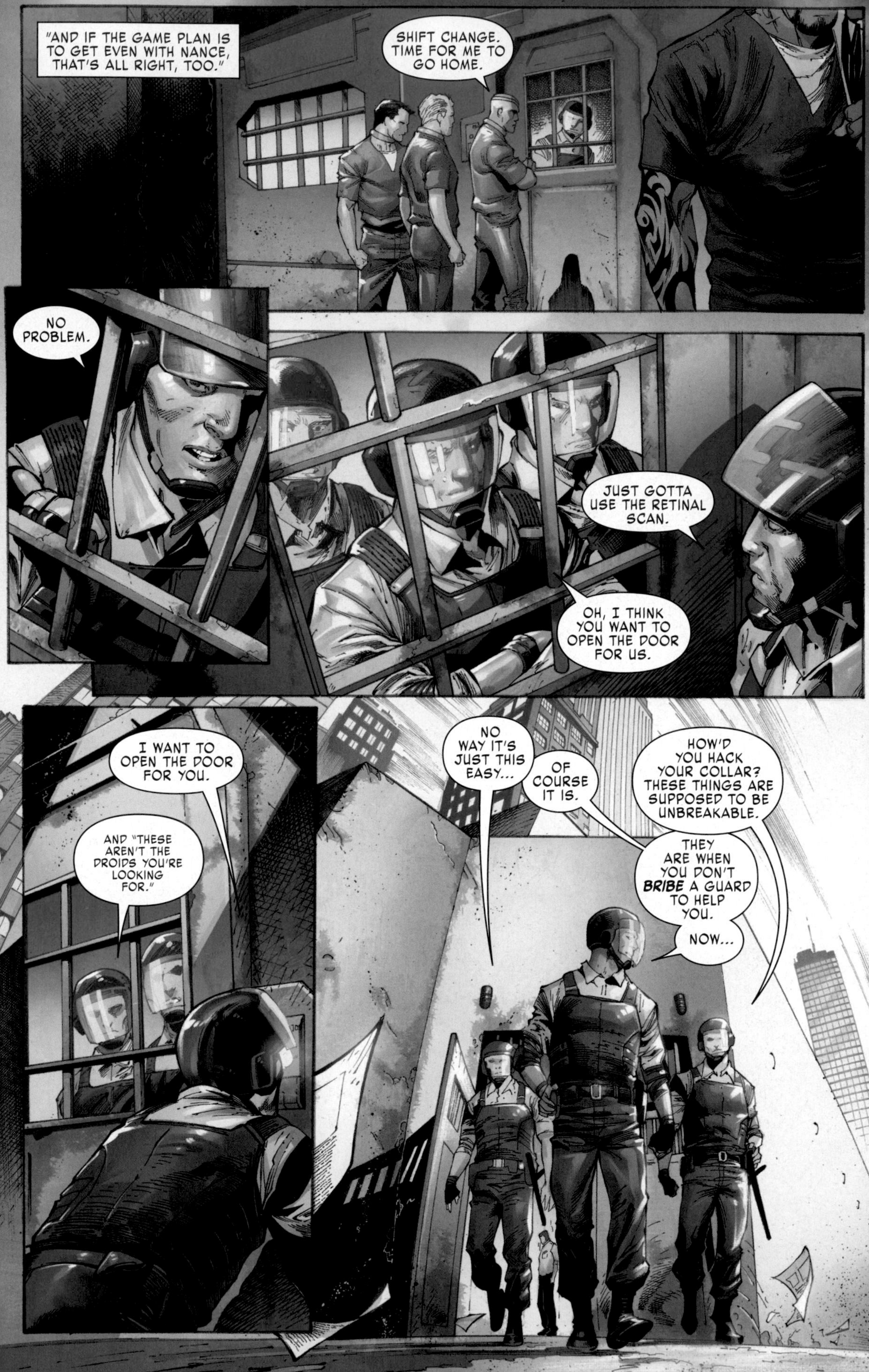
"AND IF THE GAME PLAN IS TO GET EVEN WITH NANCE, THAT'S ALL RIGHT, TOO."
SHIFT CHANGE. TIME FOR ME TO GO HOME.
NO PROBLEM.
JUST GOTTA USE THE RETINAL SCAN.
OH, I THINK YOU WANT TO OPEN THE DOOR FOR US.
I WANT TO OPEN THE DOOR FOR YOU.
AND "THESE AREN'T THE DROIDS YOU'RE LOOKING FOR."
NO WAY IT'S JUST THIS EASY...
OF COURSE IT IS.
HOW'D YOU HACK YOUR COLLAR? THESE THINGS ARE SUPPOSED TO BE UNBREAKABLE.
THEY ARE WHEN YOU DON'T **BRIBE** A GUARD TO HELP YOU.
NOW...

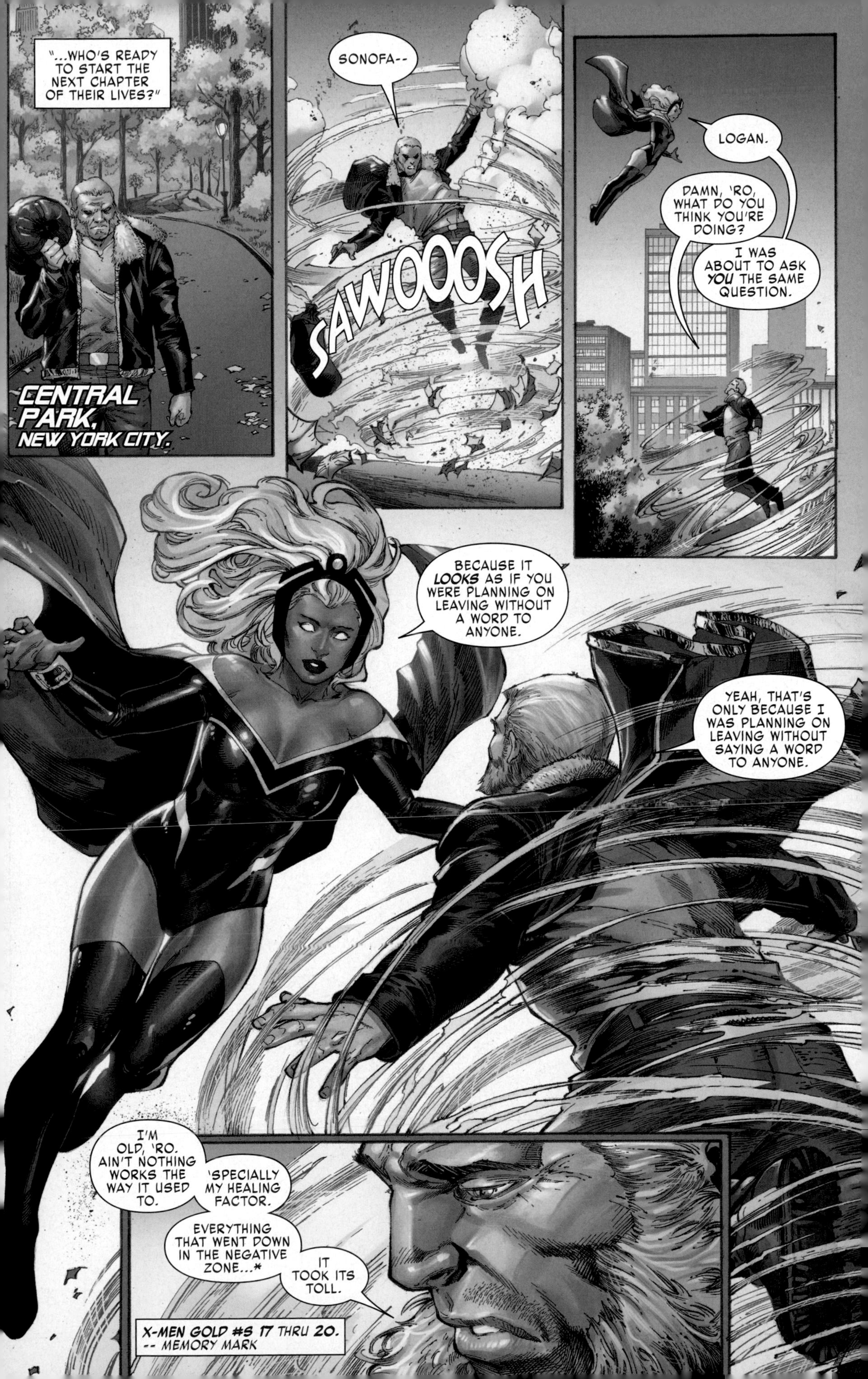
"...WHO'S READY TO START THE NEXT CHAPTER OF THEIR LIVES?"
CENTRAL PARK, NEW YORK CITY.
SONOFA--
SAWOOOSH
LOGAN.
DAMN, 'RO, WHAT DO YOU THINK YOU'RE DOING?
I WAS ABOUT TO ASK YOU THE SAME QUESTION.
BECAUSE IT LOOKS AS IF YOU WERE PLANNING ON LEAVING WITHOUT A WORD TO ANYONE.
YEAH, THAT'S ONLY BECAUSE I WAS PLANNING ON LEAVING WITHOUT SAYING A WORD TO ANYONE.
I'M OLD, 'RO. AIN'T NOTHING WORKS THE WAY IT USED TO.
'SPECIALLY MY HEALING FACTOR.
EVERYTHING THAT WENT DOWN IN THE NEGATIVE ZONE...*
IT TOOK ITS TOLL.
*X-MEN GOLD #S 17 THRU 20. -- MEMORY MARK

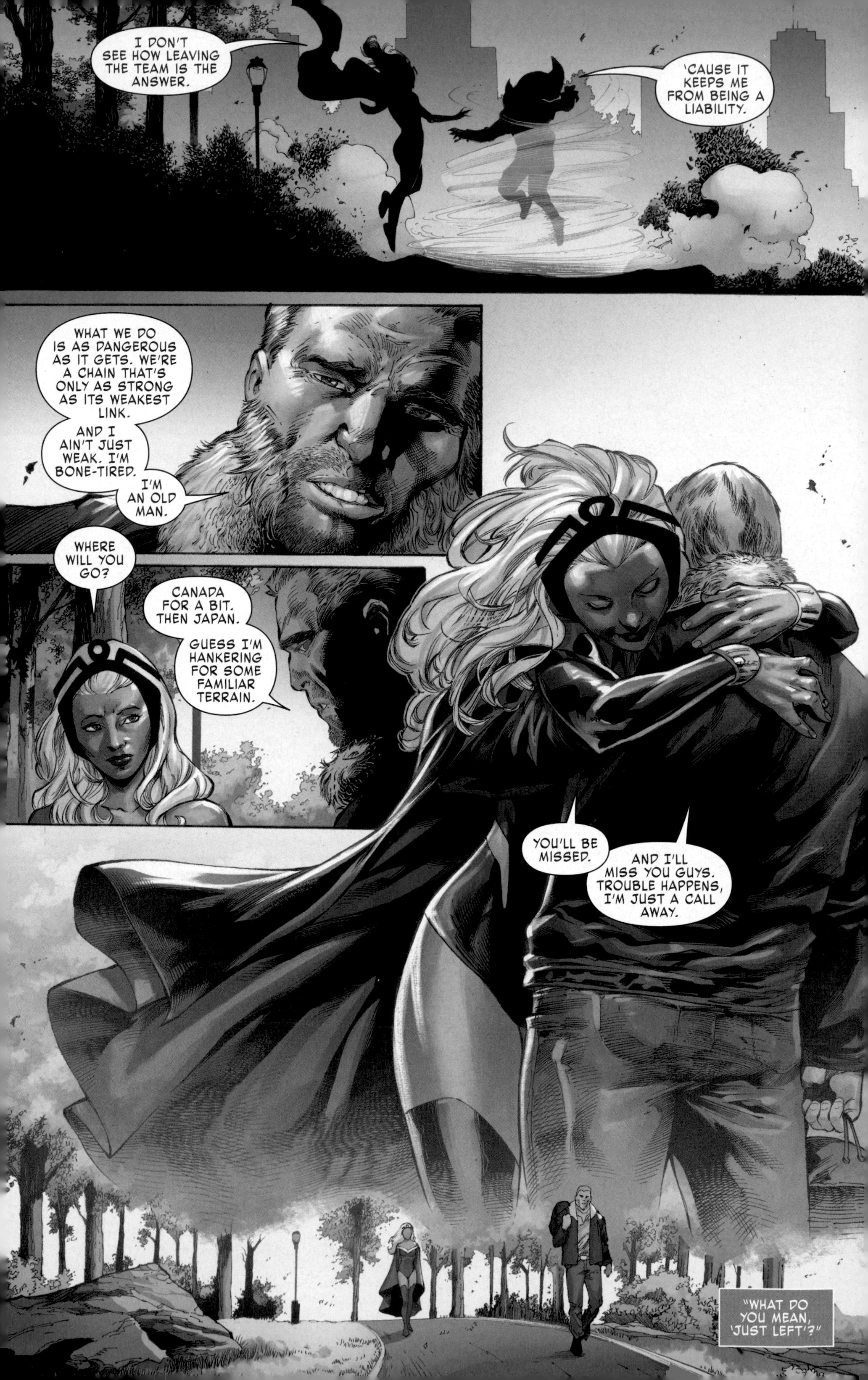

I DON'T SEE HOW LEAVING THE TEAM IS THE ANSWER.
'CAUSE IT KEEPS ME FROM BEING A LIABILITY.
WHAT WE DO IS AS DANGEROUS AS IT GETS. WE'RE A CHAIN THAT'S ONLY AS STRONG AS ITS WEAKEST LINK.
AND I AIN'T JUST WEAK. I'M BONE-TIRED.
I'M AN OLD MAN.
WHERE WILL YOU GO?
CANADA FOR A BIT. THEN JAPAN.
GUESS I'M HANKERING FOR SOME FAMILIAR TERRAIN.
YOU'LL BE MISSED.
AND I'LL MISS YOU GUYS. TROUBLE HAPPENS, I'M JUST A CALL AWAY.
"WHAT DO YOU MEAN, 'JUST LEFT'?"

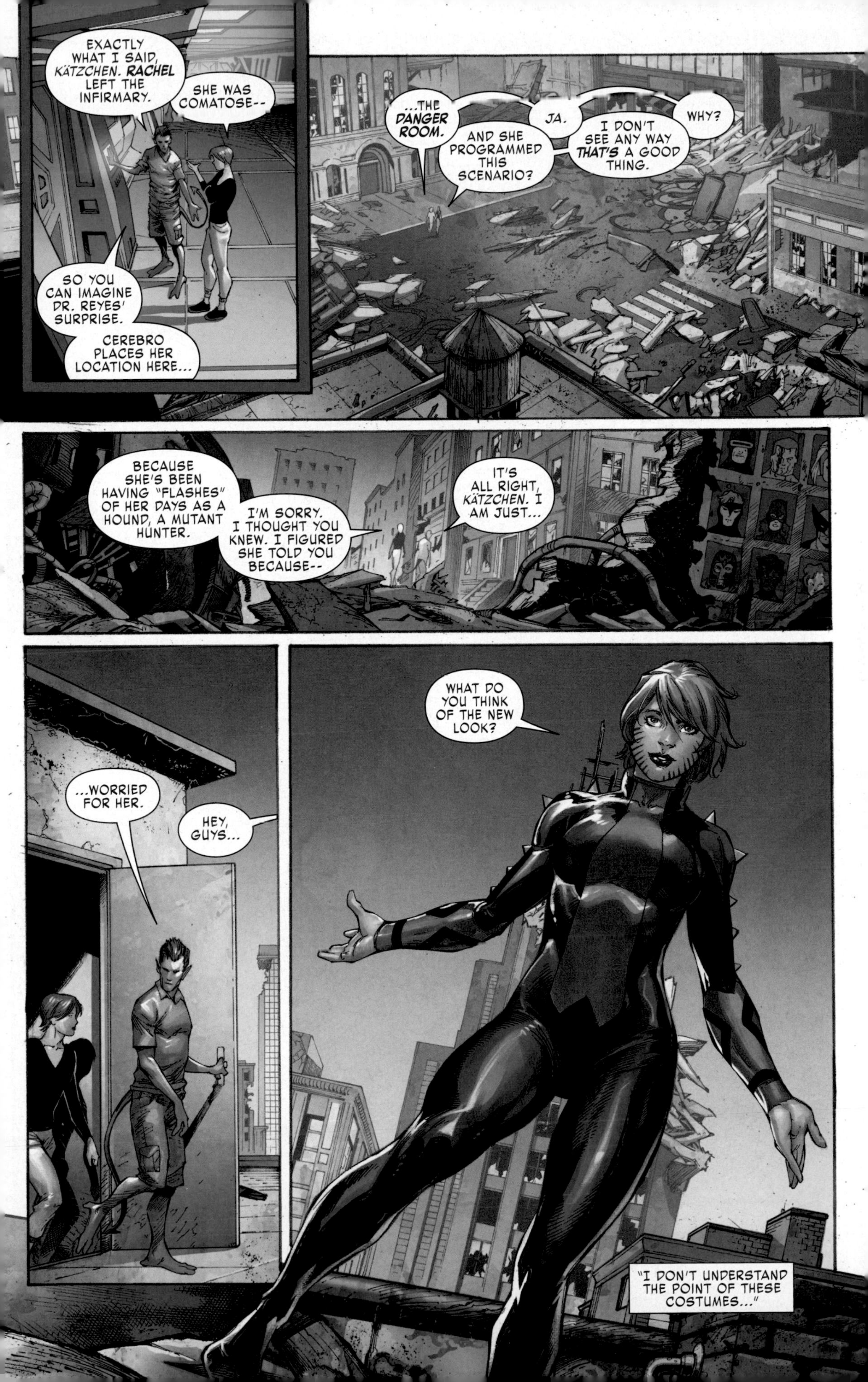
EXACTLY WHAT I SAID, KÄTZCHEN. **RACHEL** LEFT THE INFIRMARY.
SHE WAS COMATOSE--
SO YOU CAN IMAGINE DR. REYES' SURPRISE.
CEREBRO PLACES HER LOCATION HERE...
...THE **DANGER ROOM.**
AND SHE PROGRAMMED THIS SCENARIO?
JA.
I DON'T SEE ANY WAY **THAT'S** A GOOD THING.
WHY?
BECAUSE SHE'S BEEN HAVING "FLASHES" OF HER DAYS AS A HOUND, A MUTANT HUNTER.
I'M SORRY. I THOUGHT YOU KNEW. I FIGURED SHE TOLD YOU BECAUSE--
IT'S ALL RIGHT, *KÄTZCHEN.* I AM JUST...
...WORRIED FOR HER.
HEY, GUYS...
WHAT DO YOU THINK OF THE NEW LOOK?
"I DON'T UNDERSTAND THE POINT OF THESE COSTUMES..."

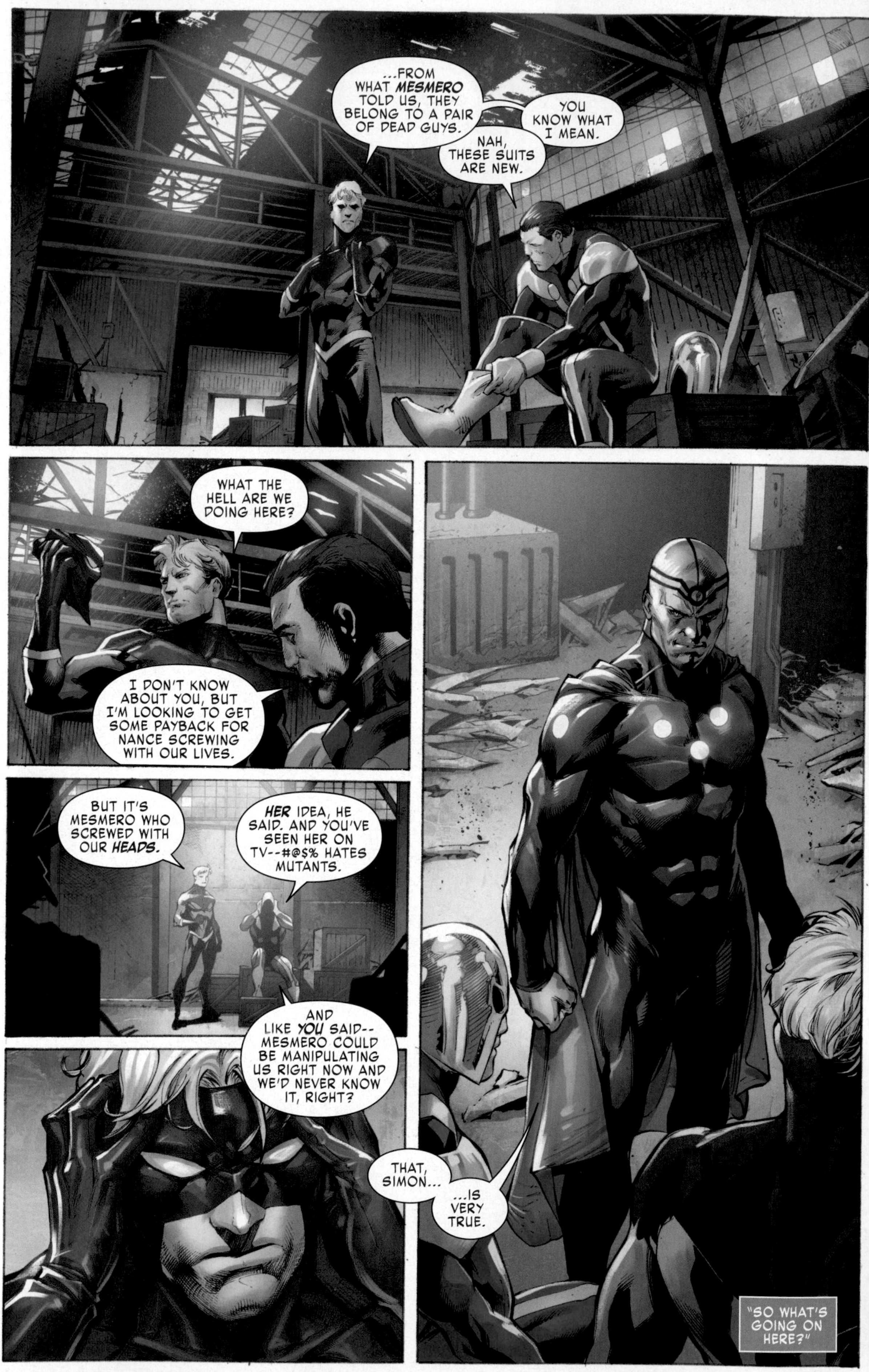
...FROM WHAT MESMERO TOLD US, THEY BELONG TO A PAIR OF DEAD GUYS.
NAH, THESE SUITS ARE NEW.
YOU KNOW WHAT I MEAN.
WHAT THE HELL ARE WE DOING HERE?
I DON'T KNOW ABOUT YOU, BUT I'M LOOKING TO GET SOME PAYBACK FOR NANCE SCREWING WITH OUR LIVES.
BUT IT'S MESMERO WHO SCREWED WITH OUR HEADS.
HER IDEA, HE SAID. AND YOU'VE SEEN HER ON TV--#@$% HATES MUTANTS.
AND LIKE YOU SAID--MESMERO COULD BE MANIPULATING US RIGHT NOW AND WE'D NEVER KNOW IT, RIGHT?
THAT, SIMON...
...IS VERY TRUE.
"SO WHAT'S GOING ON HERE?"

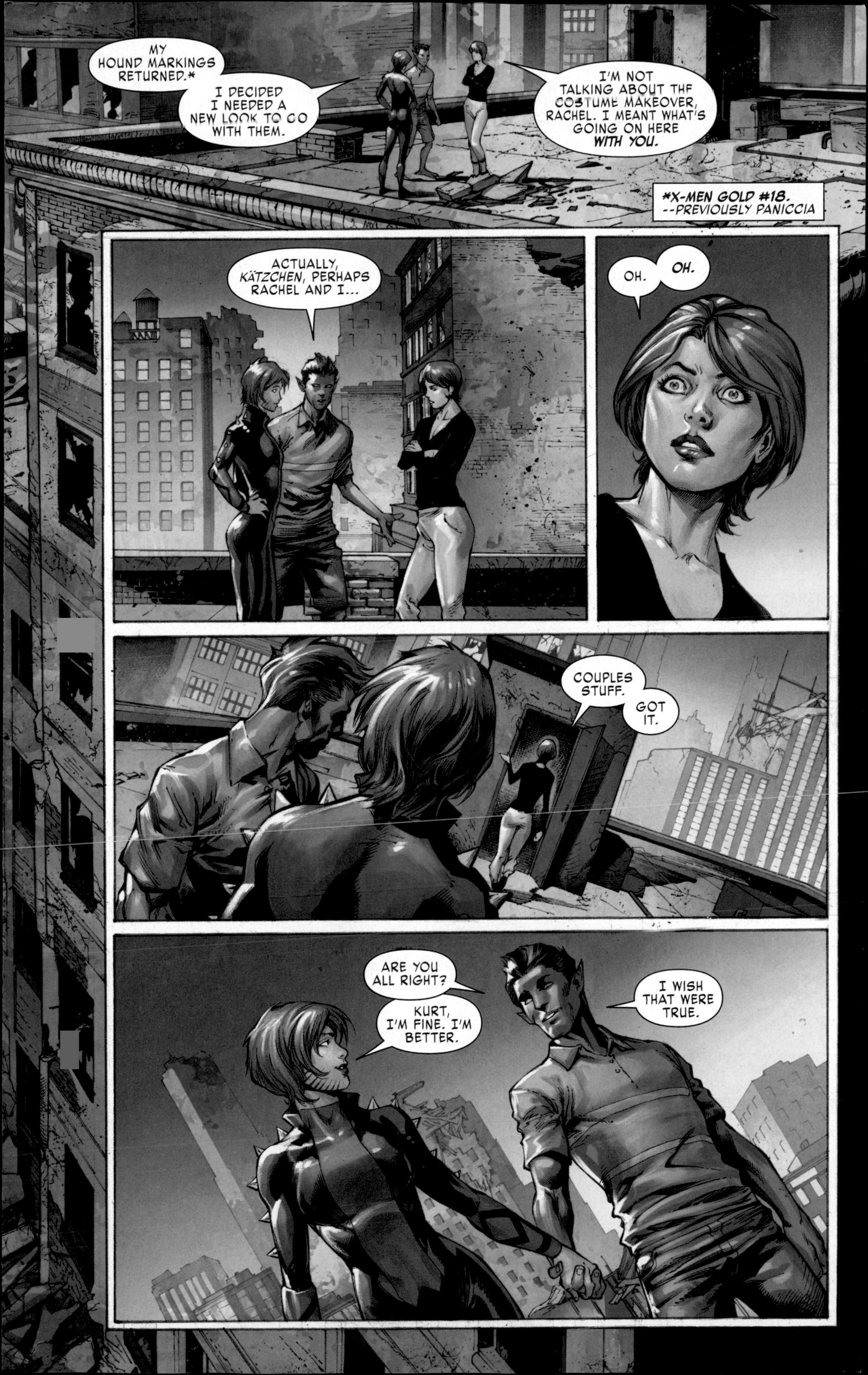
MY HOUND MARKINGS RETURNED.*
I DECIDED I NEEDED A NEW LOOK TO GO WITH THEM.
I'M NOT TALKING ABOUT THE COSTUME MAKEOVER, RACHEL. I MEANT WHAT'S GOING ON HERE WITH YOU.
*X-MEN GOLD #18. --PREVIOUSLY PANICCIA
ACTUALLY, KÄTZCHEN, PERHAPS RACHEL AND I...
OH.
OH.
COUPLES STUFF.
GOT IT.
ARE YOU ALL RIGHT?
KURT, I'M FINE. I'M BETTER.
I WISH THAT WERE TRUE.

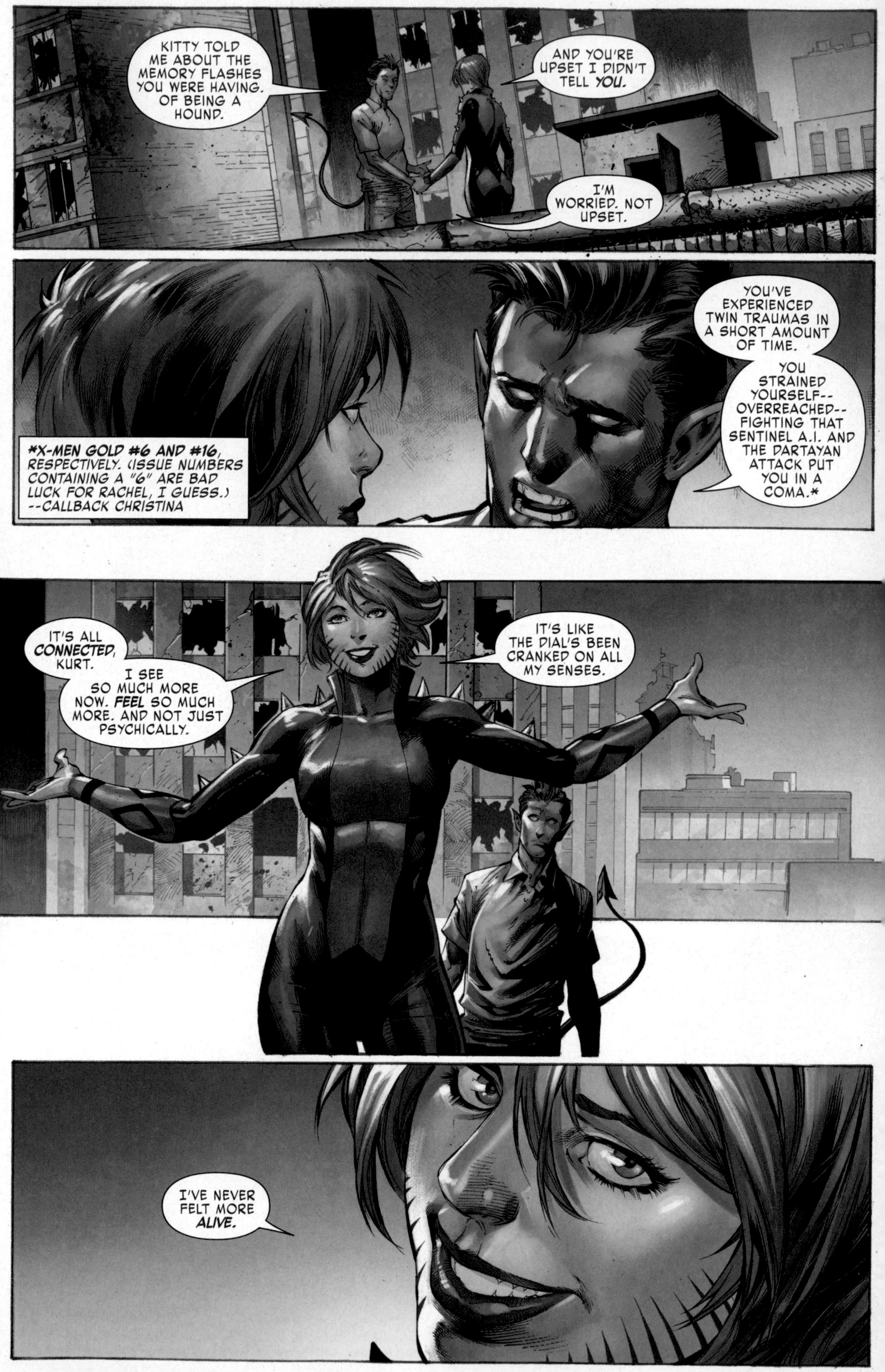
KITTY TOLD ME ABOUT THE MEMORY FLASHES YOU WERE HAVING. OF BEING A HOUND.
AND YOU'RE UPSET I DIDN'T TELL ***YOU.***
I'M WORRIED. NOT UPSET.
YOU'VE EXPERIENCED TWIN TRAUMAS IN A SHORT AMOUNT OF TIME.
YOU STRAINED YOURSELF--OVERREACHED--FIGHTING THAT SENTINEL A.I. AND THE DARTAYAN ATTACK PUT YOU IN A COMA.*
*X-MEN GOLD #6 AND #16, RESPECTIVELY. (ISSUE NUMBERS CONTAINING A "6" ARE BAD LUCK FOR RACHEL, I GUESS.) --CALLBACK CHRISTINA
IT'S ALL ***CONNECTED,*** KURT.
I SEE SO MUCH MORE NOW. ***FEEL*** SO MUCH MORE. AND NOT JUST PSYCHICALLY.
IT'S LIKE THE DIAL'S BEEN CRANKED ON ALL MY SENSES.
I'VE NEVER FELT MORE ***ALIVE.***

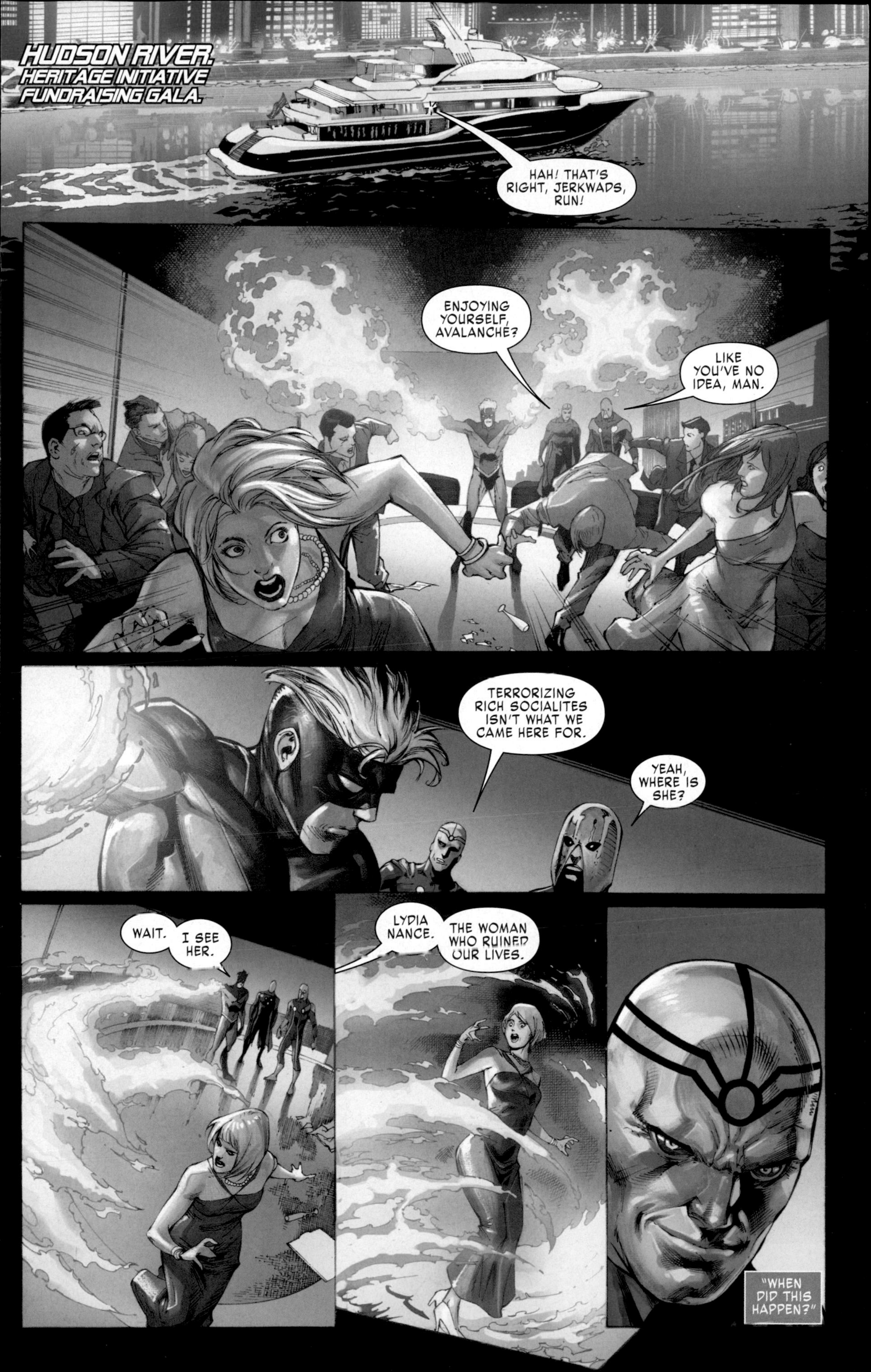
HUDSON RIVER.
HERITAGE INITIATIVE
FUNDRAISING GALA.
HAH! THAT'S RIGHT, JERKWADS, RUN!
ENJOYING YOURSELF, AVALANCHE?
LIKE YOU'VE NO IDEA, MAN.
TERRORIZING RICH SOCIALITES ISN'T WHAT WE CAME HERE FOR.
YEAH, WHERE IS SHE?
WAIT.
I SEE HER.
LYDIA NANCE.
THE WOMAN WHO RUINED OUR LIVES.
"WHEN DID THIS HAPPEN?"

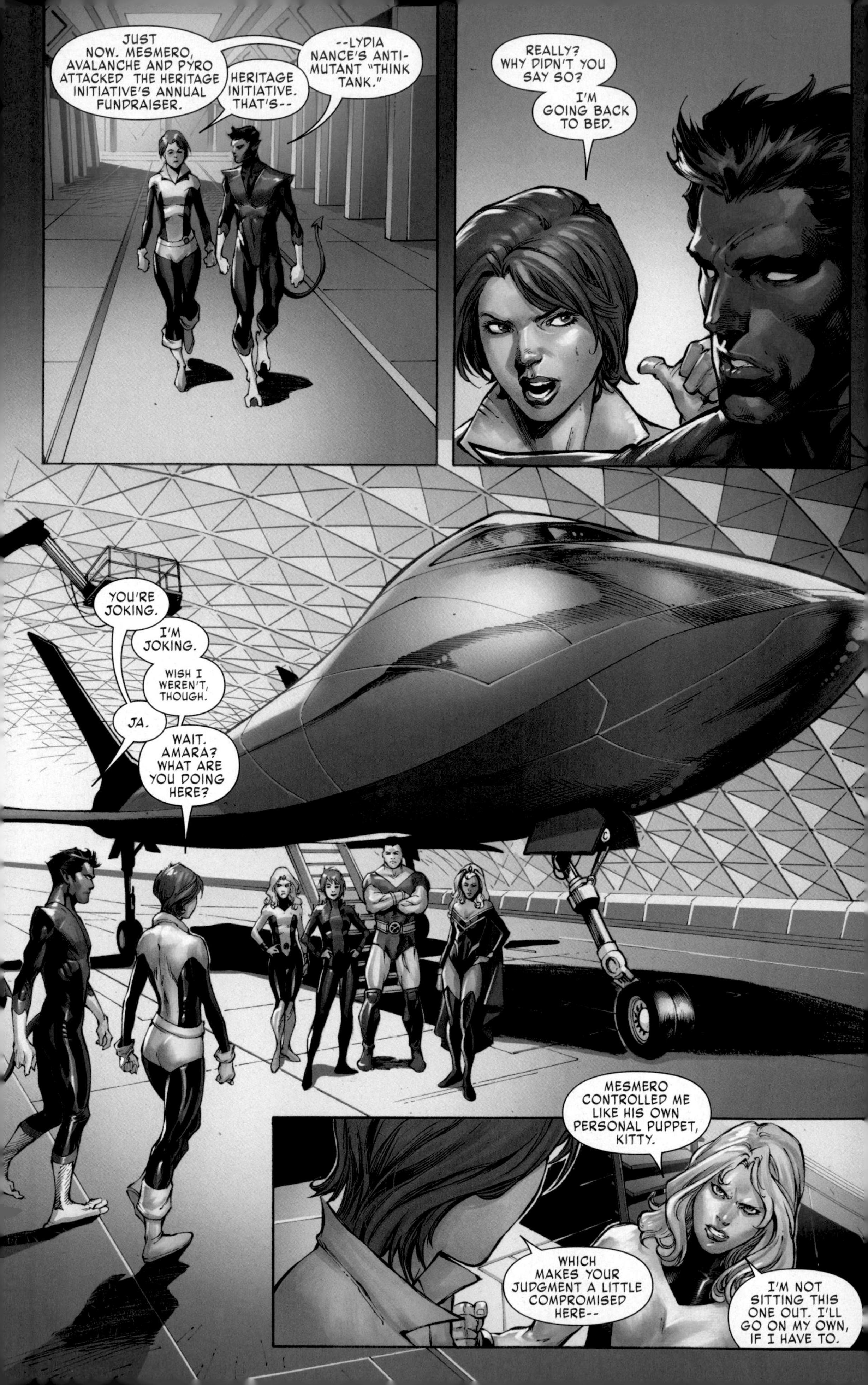
JUST NOW. MESMERO, AVALANCHE AND PYRO ATTACKED THE HERITAGE INITIATIVE'S ANNUAL FUNDRAISER.
HERITAGE INITIATIVE. THAT'S--
--LYDIA NANCE'S ANTI-MUTANT "THINK TANK."
REALLY? WHY DIDN'T YOU SAY SO?
I'M GOING BACK TO BED.
YOU'RE JOKING.
I'M JOKING.
WISH I WEREN'T, THOUGH.
JA.
WAIT. AMARA? WHAT ARE YOU DOING HERE?
MESMERO CONTROLLED ME LIKE HIS OWN PERSONAL PUPPET, KITTY.
WHICH MAKES YOUR JUDGMENT A LITTLE COMPROMISED HERE--
I'M NOT SITTING THIS ONE OUT. I'LL GO ON MY OWN, IF I HAVE TO.

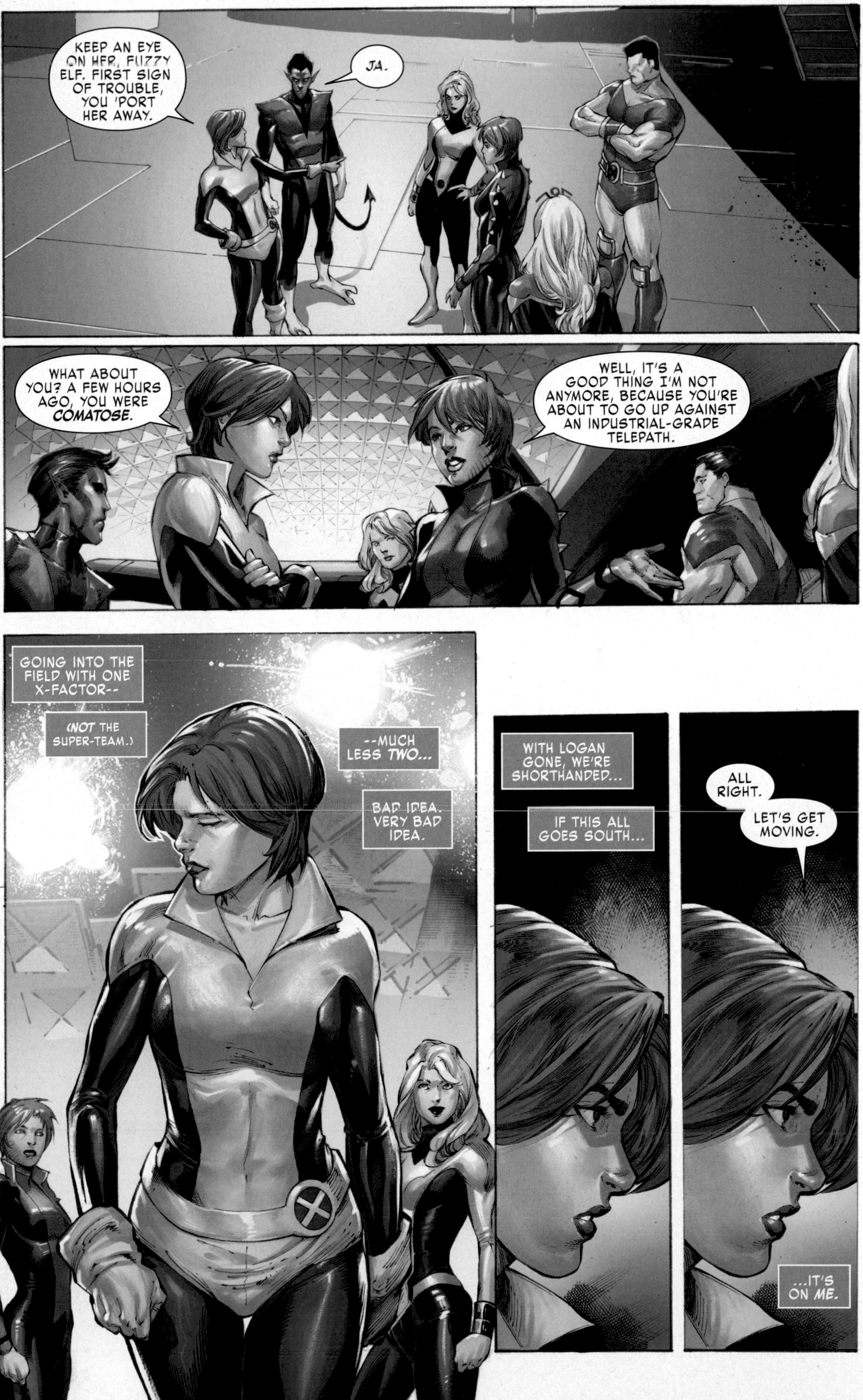
KEEP AN EYE ON HER, FUZZY ELF. FIRST SIGN OF TROUBLE, YOU 'PORT HER AWAY.
JA.
WHAT ABOUT YOU? A FEW HOURS AGO, YOU WERE COMATOSE.
WELL, IT'S A GOOD THING I'M NOT ANYMORE, BECAUSE YOU'RE ABOUT TO GO UP AGAINST AN INDUSTRIAL-GRADE TELEPATH.
GOING INTO THE FIELD WITH ONE X-FACTOR--
(NOT THE SUPER-TEAM.)
--MUCH LESS TWO...
BAD IDEA. VERY BAD IDEA.
WITH LOGAN GONE, WE'RE SHORTHANDED...
IF THIS ALL GOES SOUTH...
ALL RIGHT.
LET'S GET MOVING.
...IT'S ON ME.

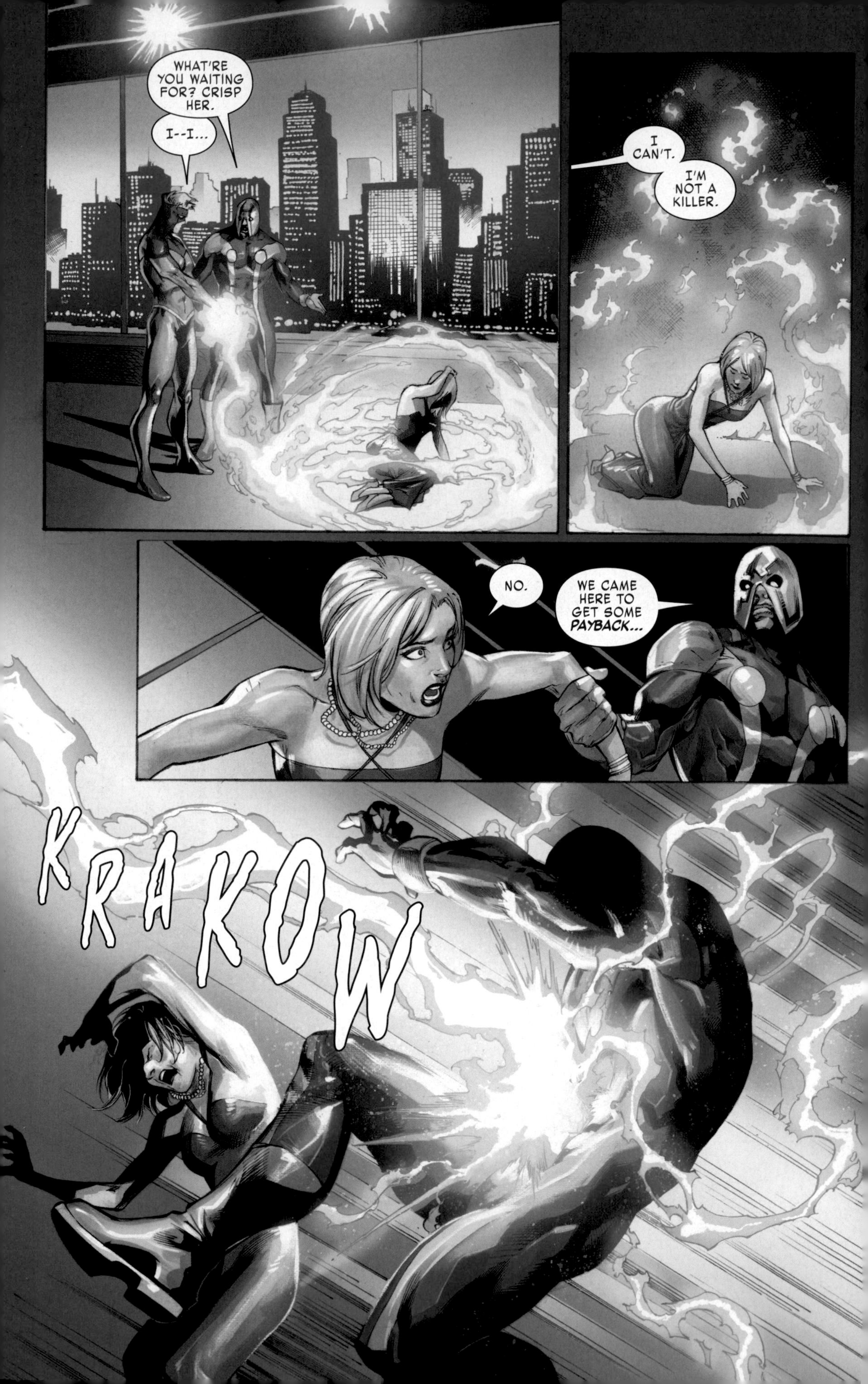
WHAT'RE YOU WAITING FOR? CRISP HER.
I--I...
I CAN'T.
I'M NOT A KILLER.
NO.
WE CAME HERE TO GET SOME PAYBACK...
KRAKOW

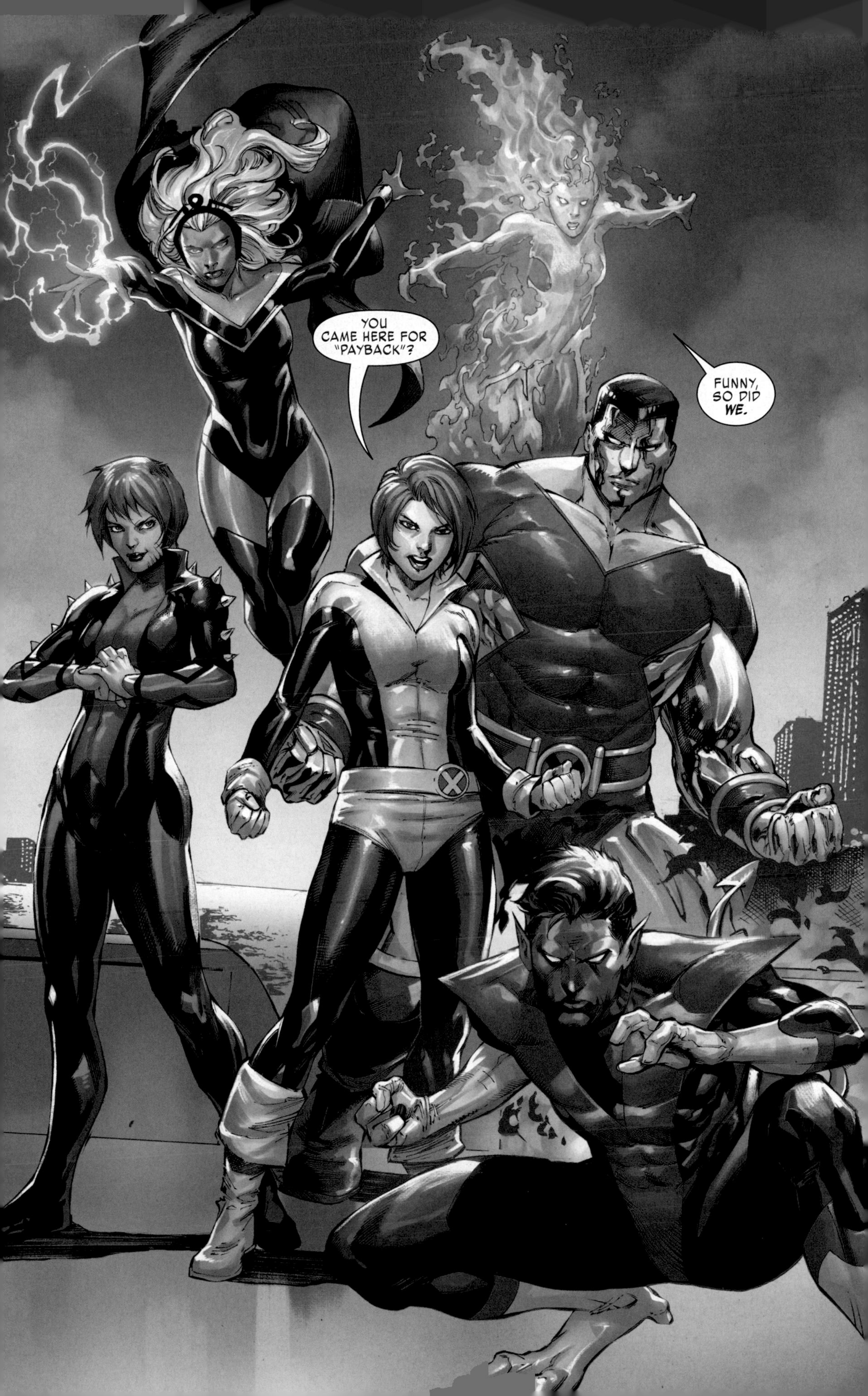
YOU CAME HERE FOR "PAYBACK"?
FUNNY, SO DID *WE.*

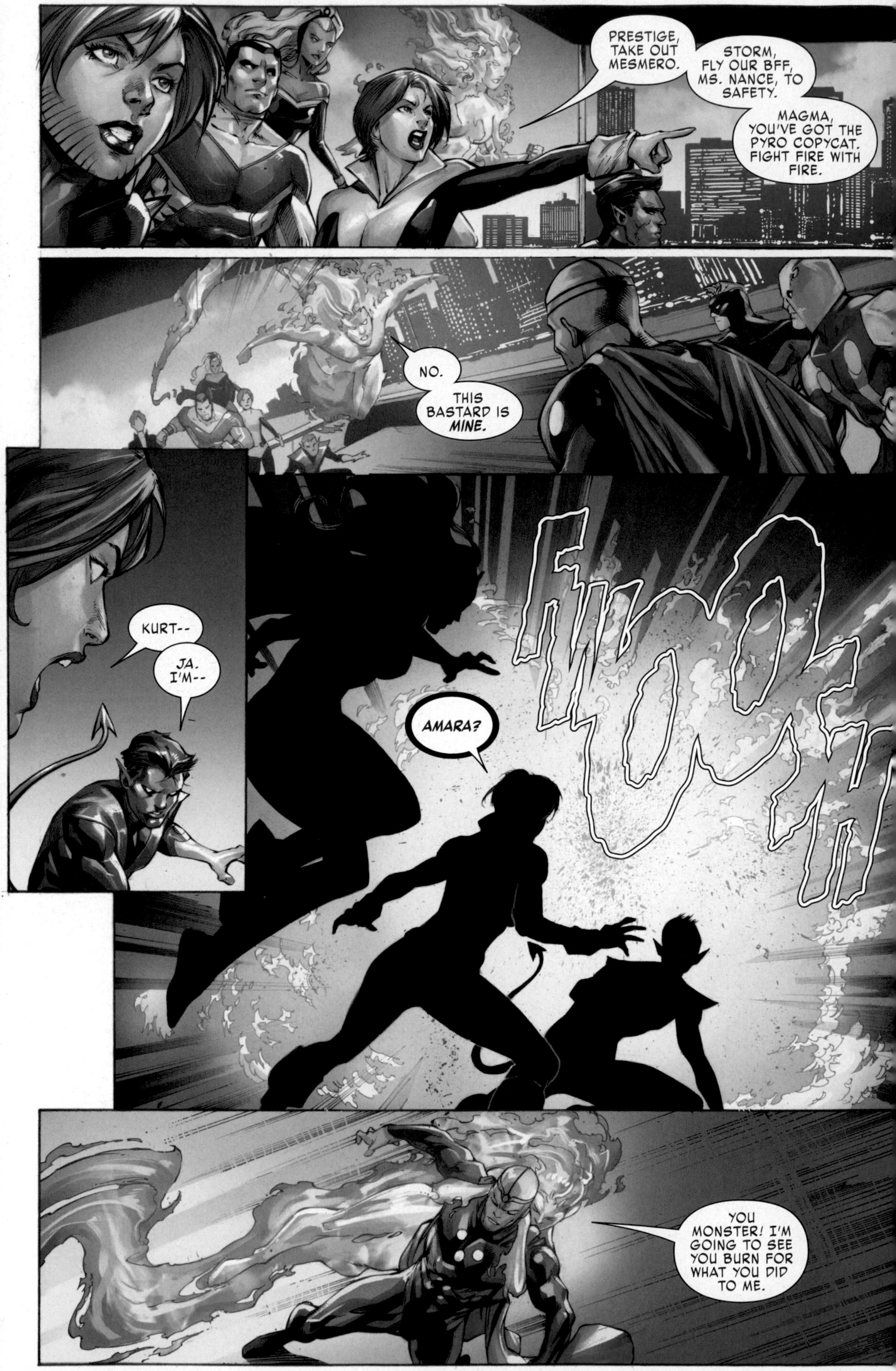
PRESTIGE, TAKE OUT MESMERO.
STORM, FLY OUR BFF, MS. NANCE, TO SAFETY.
MAGMA, YOU'VE GOT THE PYRO COPYCAT. FIGHT FIRE WITH FIRE.
NO.
THIS BASTARD IS *MINE.*
KURT--
JA. I'M--
AMARA?
YOU MONSTER! I'M GOING TO SEE YOU BURN FOR WHAT YOU DID TO ME.

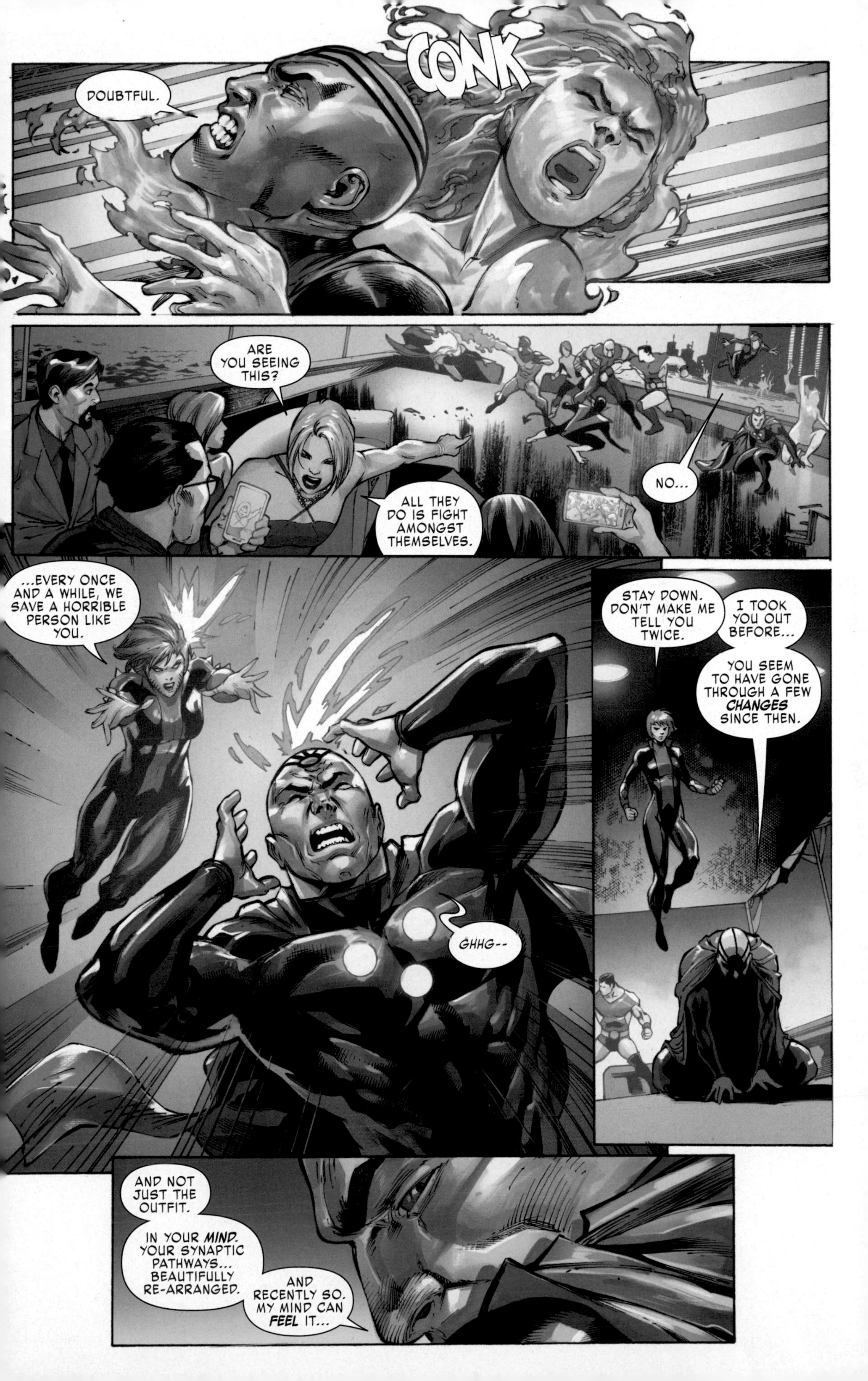
CONK
DOUBTFUL.
ARE YOU SEEING THIS?
ALL THEY DO IS FIGHT AMONGST THEMSELVES.
NO...
...EVERY ONCE AND A WHILE, WE SAVE A HORRIBLE PERSON LIKE YOU.
GHHG--
STAY DOWN. DON'T MAKE ME TELL YOU TWICE.
I TOOK YOU OUT BEFORE...
YOU SEEM TO HAVE GONE THROUGH A FEW CHANGES SINCE THEN.
AND NOT JUST THE OUTFIT.
IN YOUR MIND. YOUR SYNAPTIC PATHWAYS... BEAUTIFULLY RE-ARRANGED.
AND RECENTLY SO. MY MIND CAN FEEL IT...

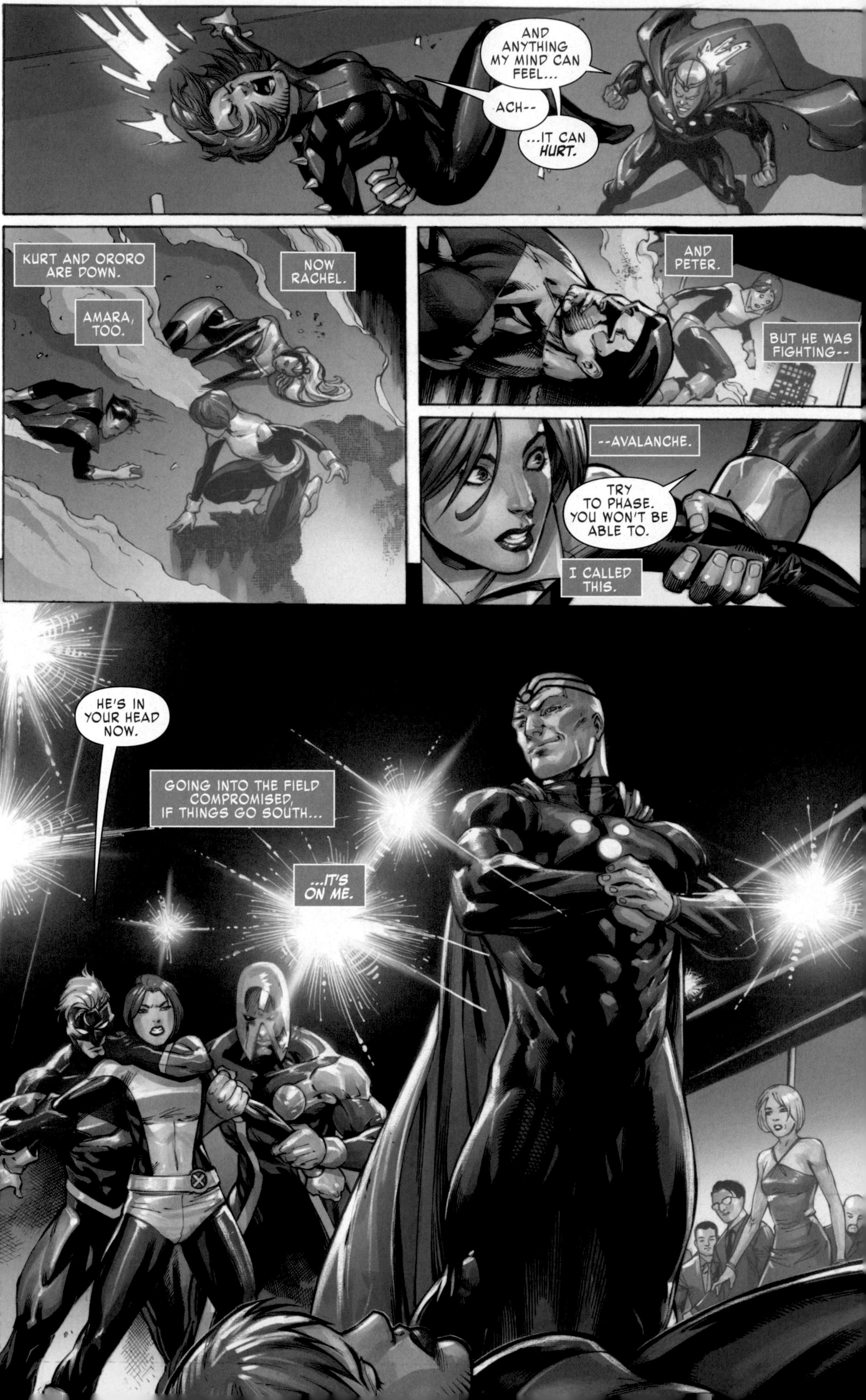
AND ANYTHING MY MIND CAN FEEL...
ACH--
...IT CAN HURT.
KURT AND ORORO ARE DOWN.
AMARA, TOO.
NOW RACHEL.
AND PETER.
BUT HE WAS FIGHTING--
--AVALANCHE.
TRY TO PHASE. YOU WON'T BE ABLE TO.
I CALLED THIS.
HE'S IN YOUR HEAD NOW.
GOING INTO THE FIELD COMPROMISED, IF THINGS GO SOUTH...
...IT'S ON ME.

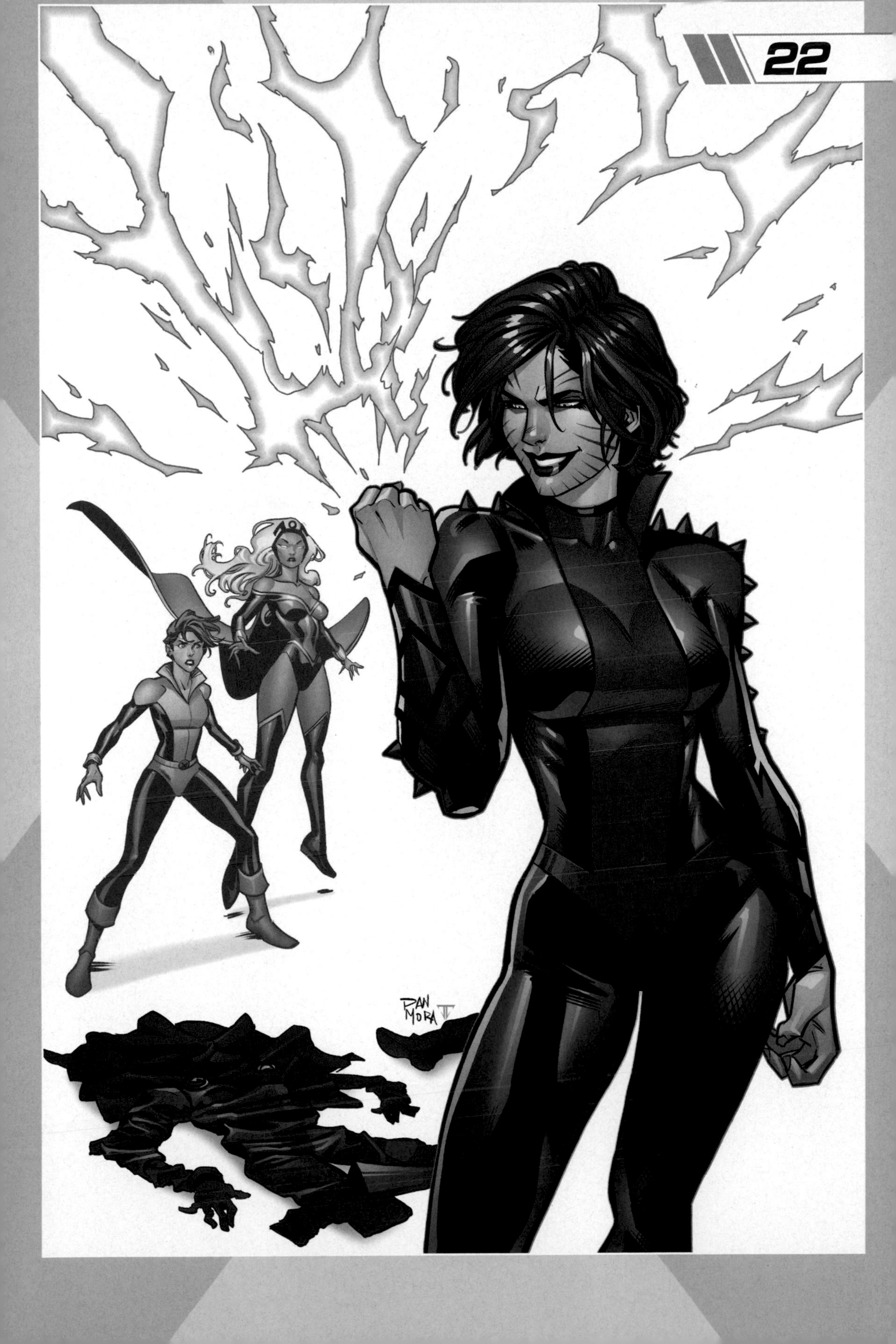
22
DAN MORA

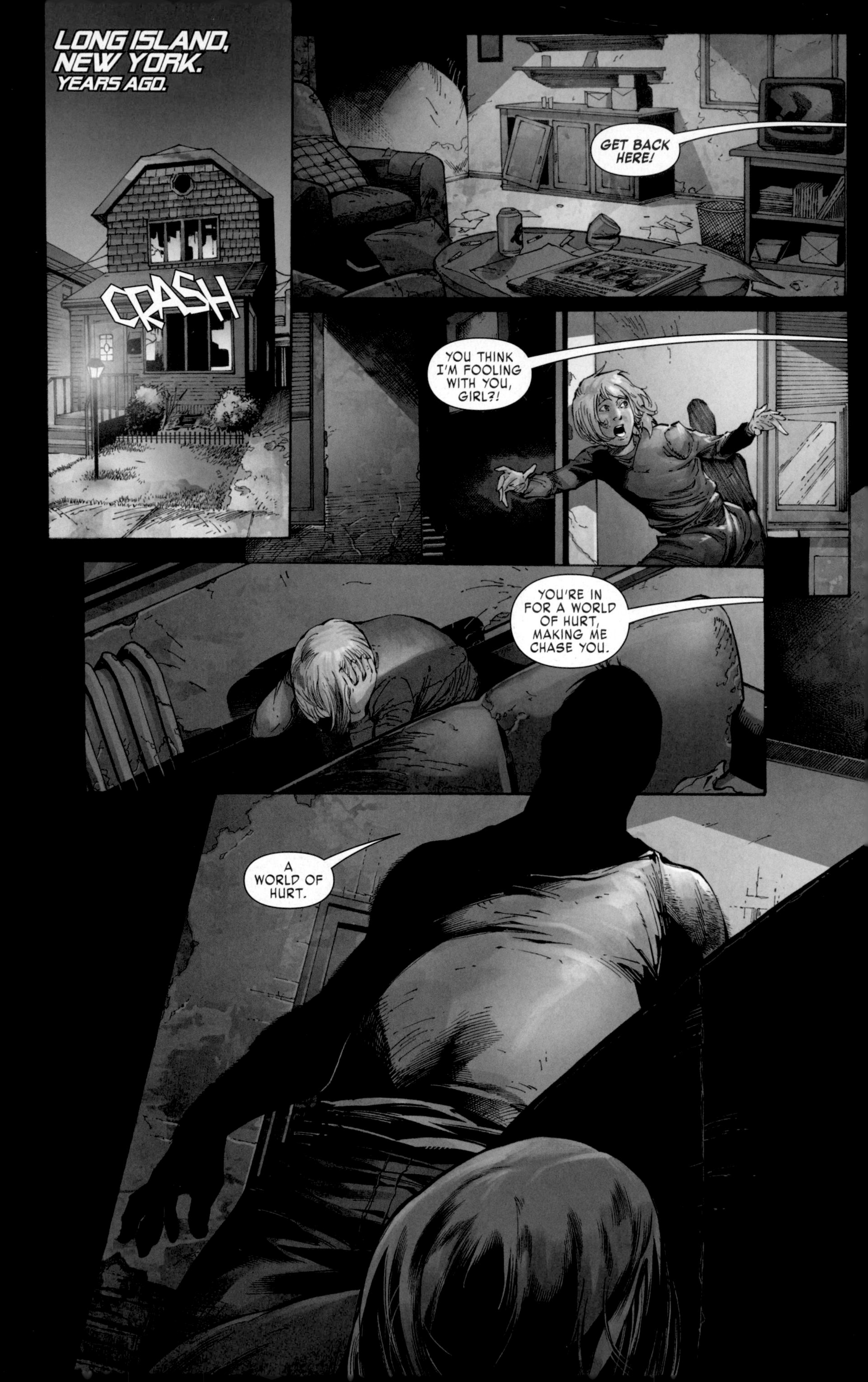
LONG ISLAND, NEW YORK. YEARS AGO.
CRASH
GET BACK HERE!
YOU THINK I'M FOOLING WITH YOU, GIRL?!
YOU'RE IN FOR A WORLD OF HURT, MAKING ME CHASE YOU.
A WORLD OF HURT.

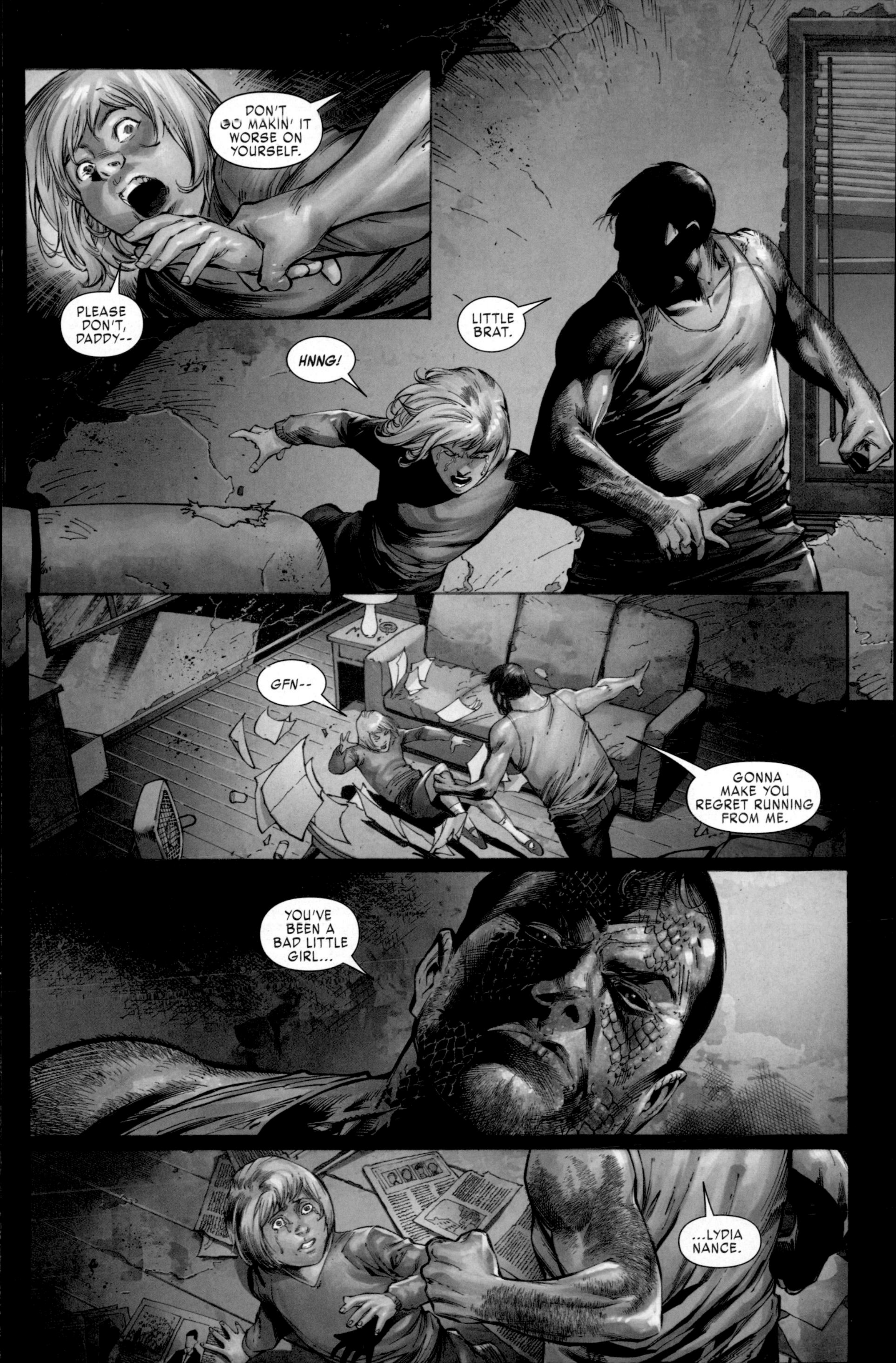
DON'T GO MAKIN' IT WORSE ON YOURSELF.
PLEASE DON'T, DADDY--
LITTLE BRAT.
HNNG!
GFN--
GONNA MAKE YOU REGRET RUNNING FROM ME.
YOU'VE BEEN A BAD LITTLE GIRL...
...LYDIA NANCE.

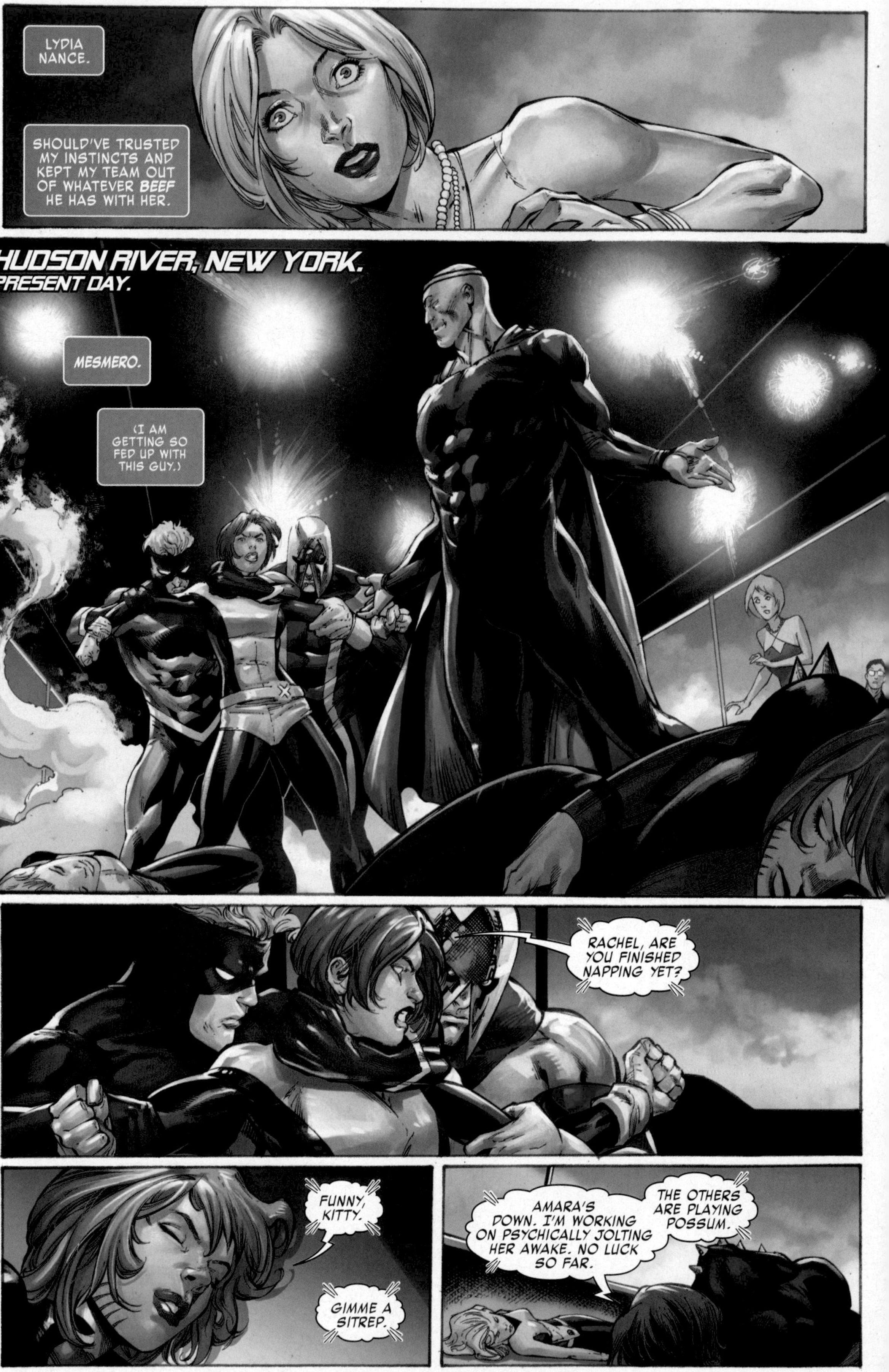

LYDIA NANCE.
SHOULD'VE TRUSTED MY INSTINCTS AND KEPT MY TEAM OUT OF WHATEVER BEEF HE HAS WITH HER.
HUDSON RIVER, NEW YORK.
PRESENT DAY.
MESMERO.
(I AM GETTING SO FED UP WITH THIS GUY.)
RACHEL, ARE YOU FINISHED NAPPING YET?
FUNNY, KITTY.
GIMME A SITREP.
AMARA'S DOWN. I'M WORKING ON PSYCHICALLY JOLTING HER AWAKE. NO LUCK SO FAR.
THE OTHERS ARE PLAYING POSSUM.

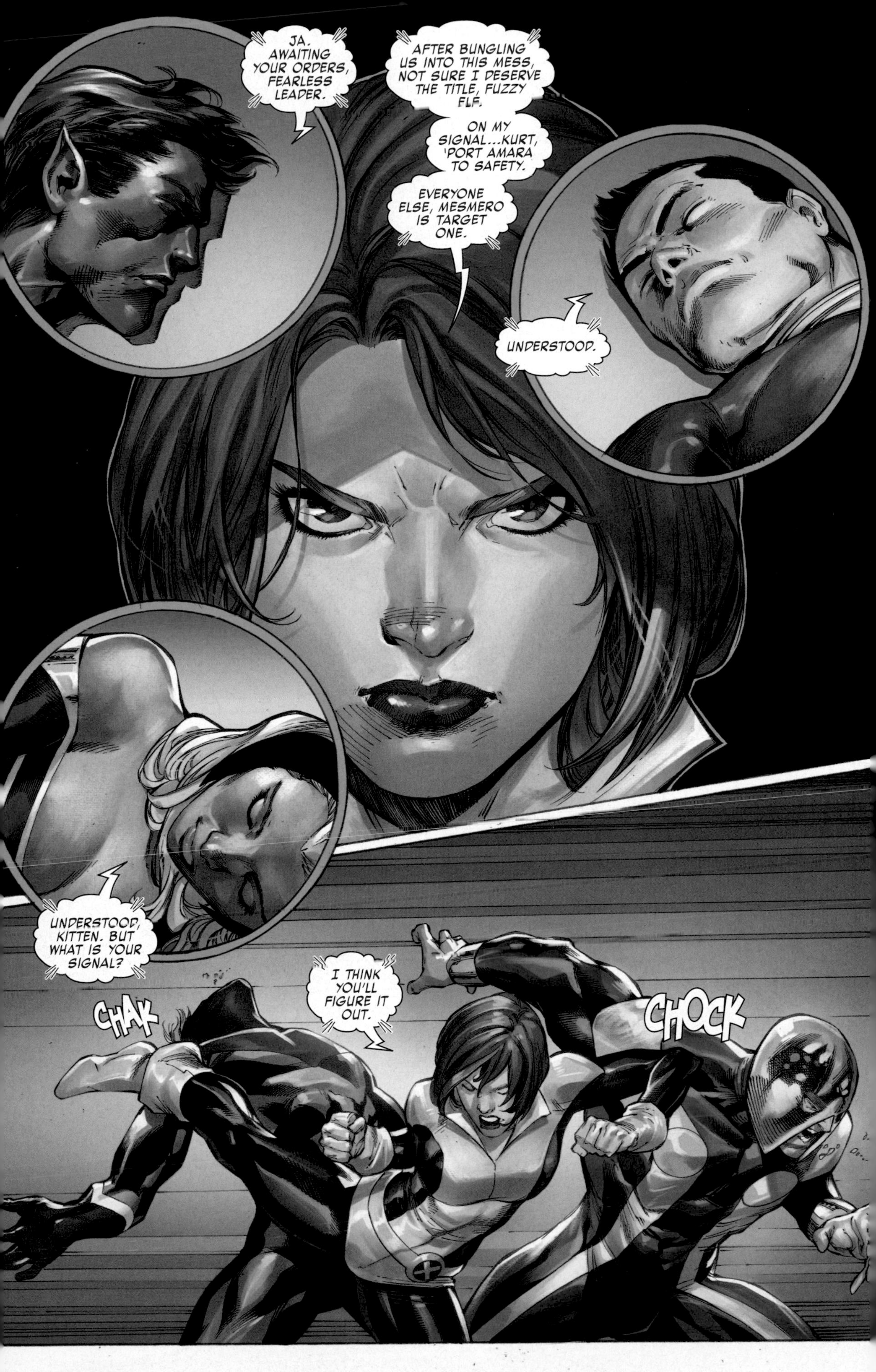
JA. AWAITING YOUR ORDERS, FEARLESS LEADER.
AFTER BUNGLING US INTO THIS MESS, NOT SURE I DESERVE THE TITLE, FUZZY ELF.
ON MY SIGNAL...KURT, 'PORT AMARA TO SAFETY.
EVERYONE ELSE, MESMERO IS TARGET ONE.
UNDERSTOOD.
UNDERSTOOD, KITTEN. BUT WHAT IS YOUR SIGNAL?
I THINK YOU'LL FIGURE IT OUT.
CHAK
CHOCK

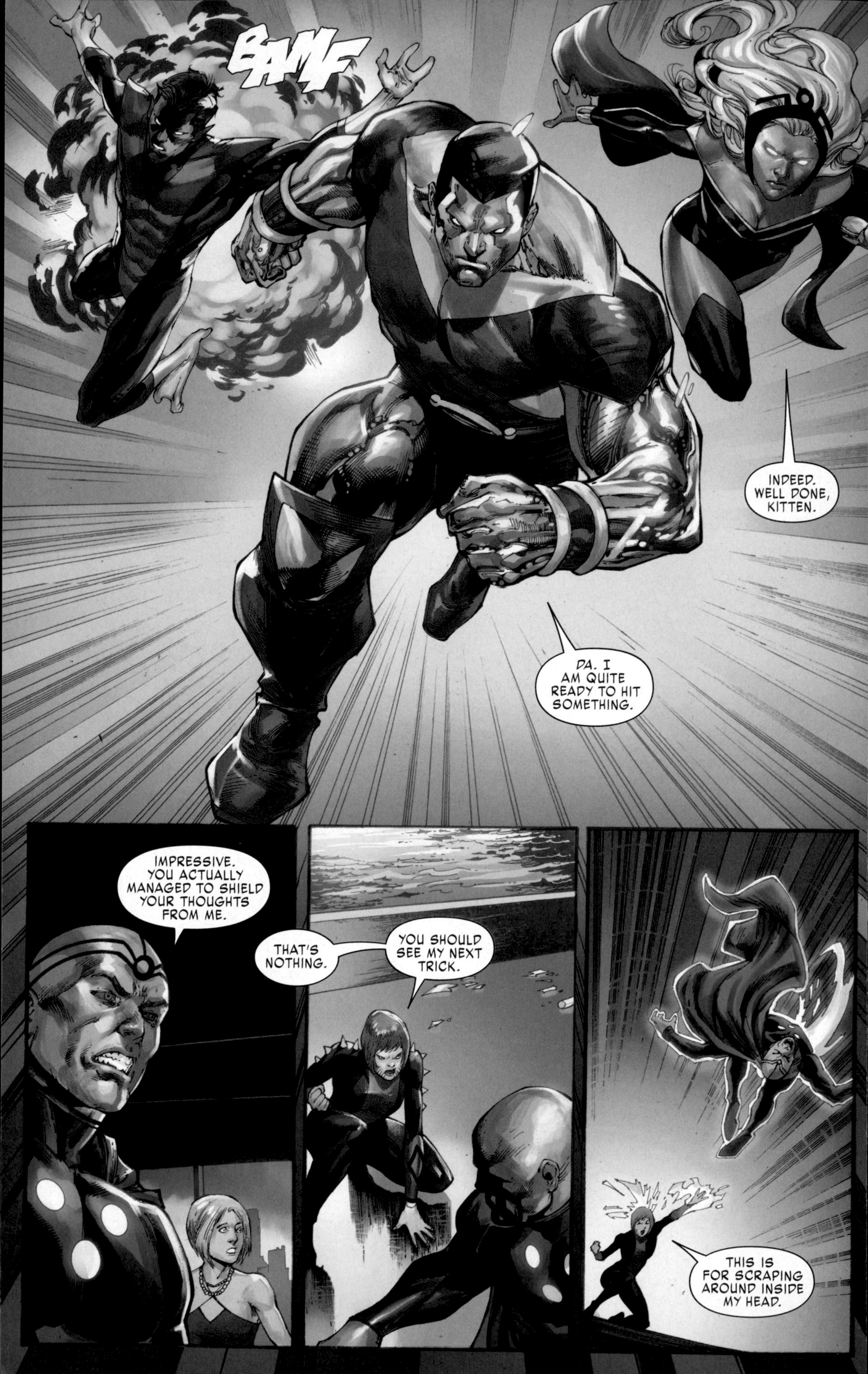
BAMF
INDEED. WELL DONE, KITTEN.
DA. I AM QUITE READY TO HIT SOMETHING.
IMPRESSIVE. YOU ACTUALLY MANAGED TO SHIELD YOUR THOUGHTS FROM ME.
THAT'S NOTHING.
YOU SHOULD SEE MY NEXT TRICK.
THIS IS FOR SCRAPING AROUND INSIDE MY HEAD.

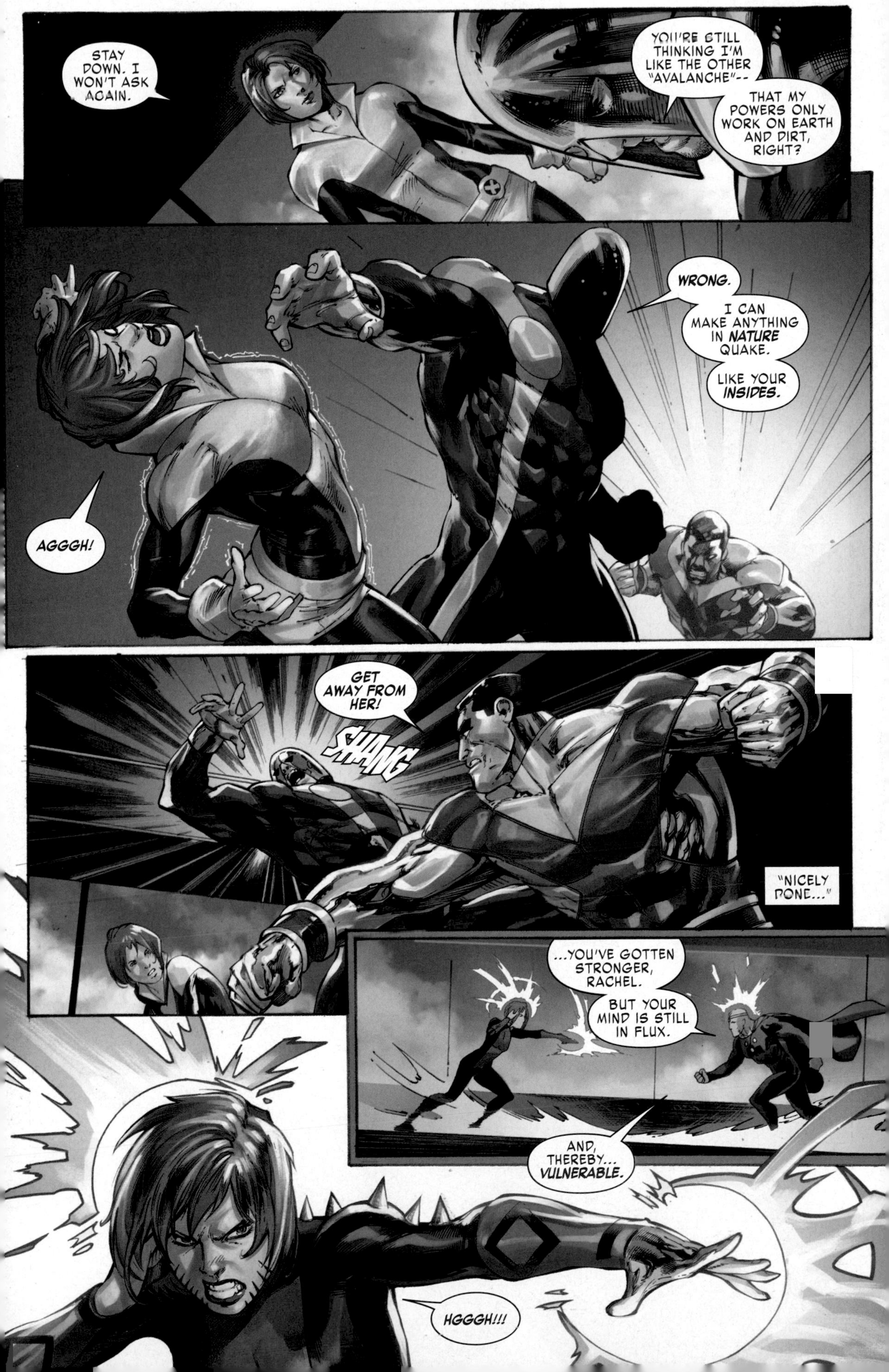

STAY DOWN. I WON'T ASK AGAIN.
YOU'RE STILL THINKING I'M LIKE THE OTHER "AVALANCHE"--
THAT MY POWERS ONLY WORK ON EARTH AND DIRT, RIGHT?
WRONG.
I CAN MAKE ANYTHING IN NATURE QUAKE.
LIKE YOUR INSIDES.
AGGGH!
GET AWAY FROM HER!
SHANG
"NICELY DONE..."
...YOU'VE GOTTEN STRONGER, RACHEL.
BUT YOUR MIND IS STILL IN FLUX.
AND, THEREBY... VULNERABLE.
HGGGH!!!

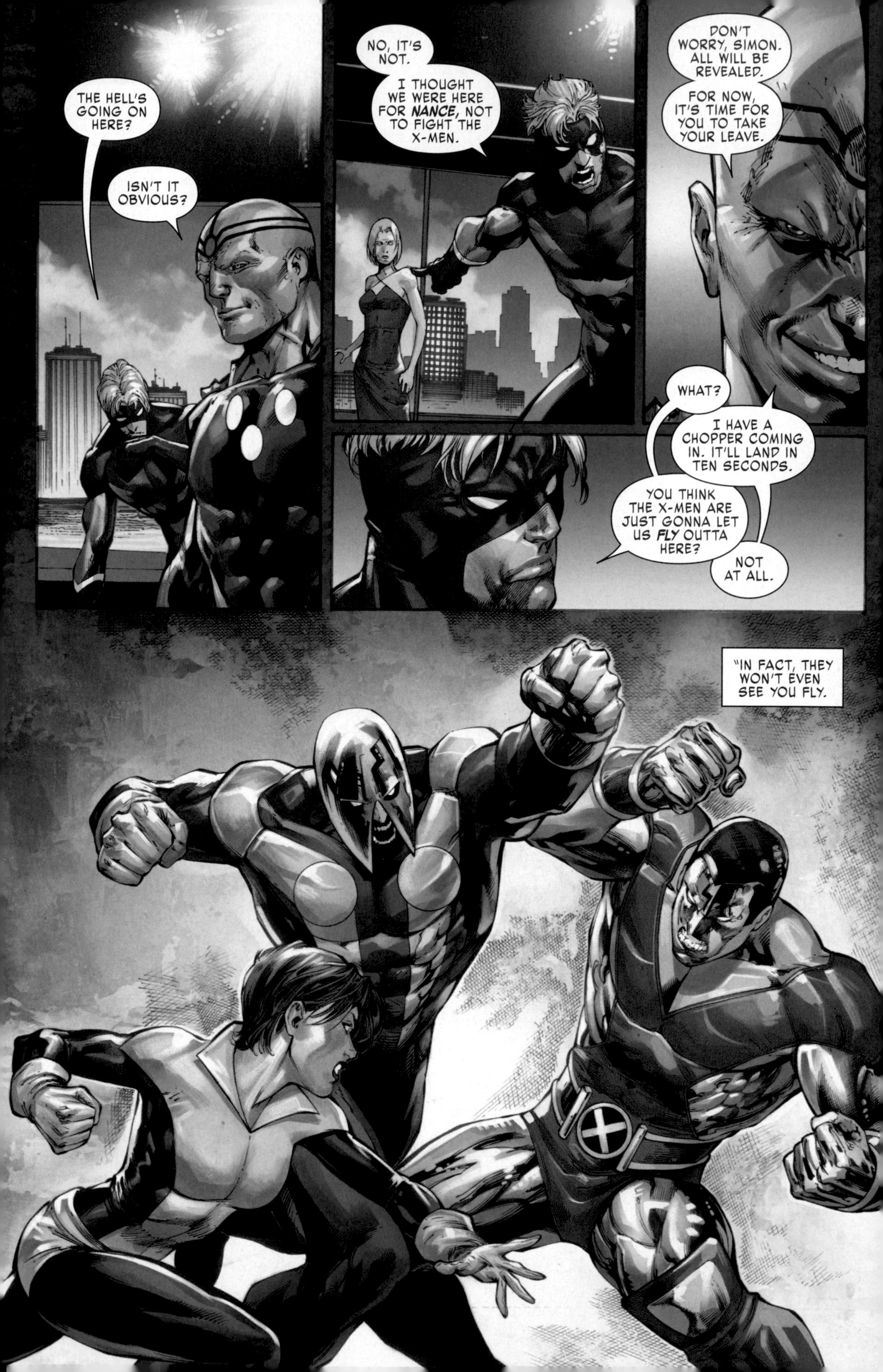
THE HELL'S GOING ON HERE?
ISN'T IT OBVIOUS?
NO, IT'S NOT.
I THOUGHT WE WERE HERE FOR NANCE, NOT TO FIGHT THE X-MEN.
DON'T WORRY, SIMON. ALL WILL BE REVEALED.
FOR NOW, IT'S TIME FOR YOU TO TAKE YOUR LEAVE.
WHAT?
I HAVE A CHOPPER COMING IN. IT'LL LAND IN TEN SECONDS.
YOU THINK THE X-MEN ARE JUST GONNA LET US FLY OUTTA HERE?
NOT AT ALL.
"IN FACT, THEY WON'T EVEN SEE YOU FLY.

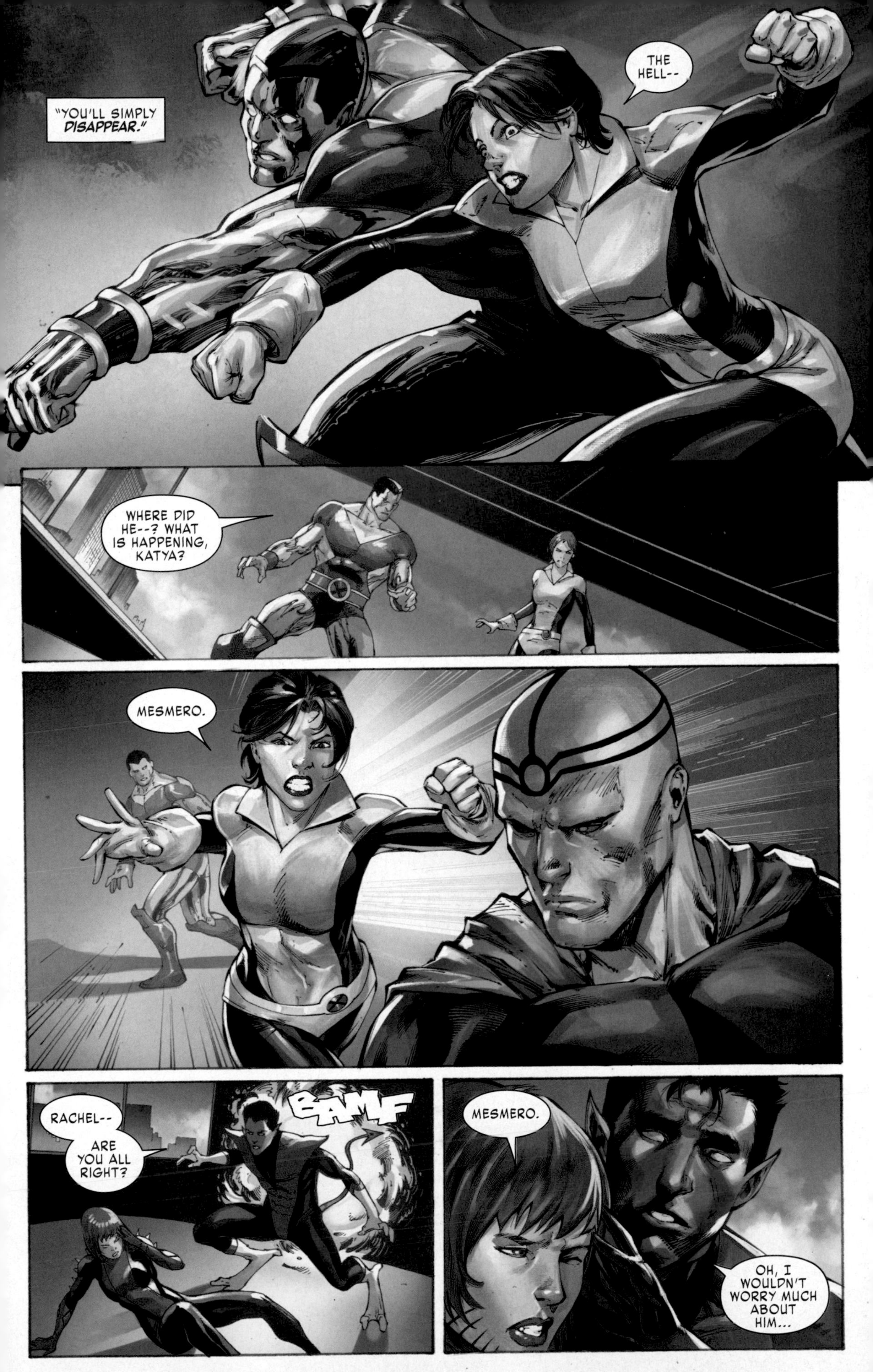
"YOU'LL SIMPLY DISAPPEAR."
THE HELL--
WHERE DID HE--? WHAT IS HAPPENING, KATYA?
MESMERO.
RACHEL--
ARE YOU ALL RIGHT?
BAMF
MESMERO.
OH, I WOULDN'T WORRY MUCH ABOUT HIM...

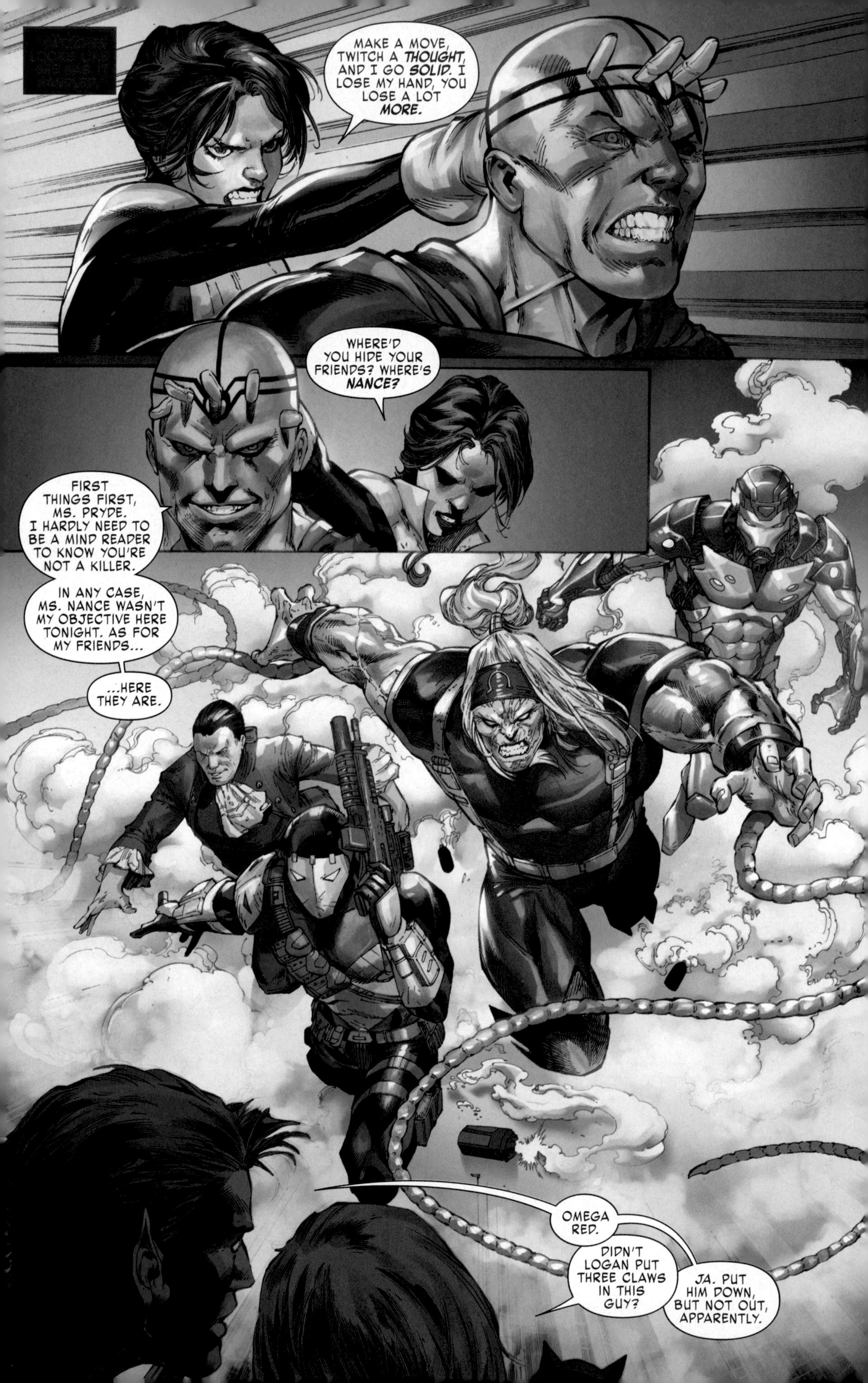
MAKE A MOVE, TWITCH A THOUGHT, AND I GO SOLID. I LOSE MY HAND, YOU LOSE A LOT MORE.
WHERE'D YOU HIDE YOUR FRIENDS? WHERE'S NANCE?
FIRST THINGS FIRST, MS. PRYDE. I HARDLY NEED TO BE A MIND READER TO KNOW YOU'RE NOT A KILLER.
IN ANY CASE, MS. NANCE WASN'T MY OBJECTIVE HERE TONIGHT. AS FOR MY FRIENDS...
...HERE THEY ARE.
OMEGA RED.
DIDN'T LOGAN PUT THREE CLAWS IN THIS GUY?
JA. PUT HIM DOWN, BUT NOT OUT, APPARENTLY.

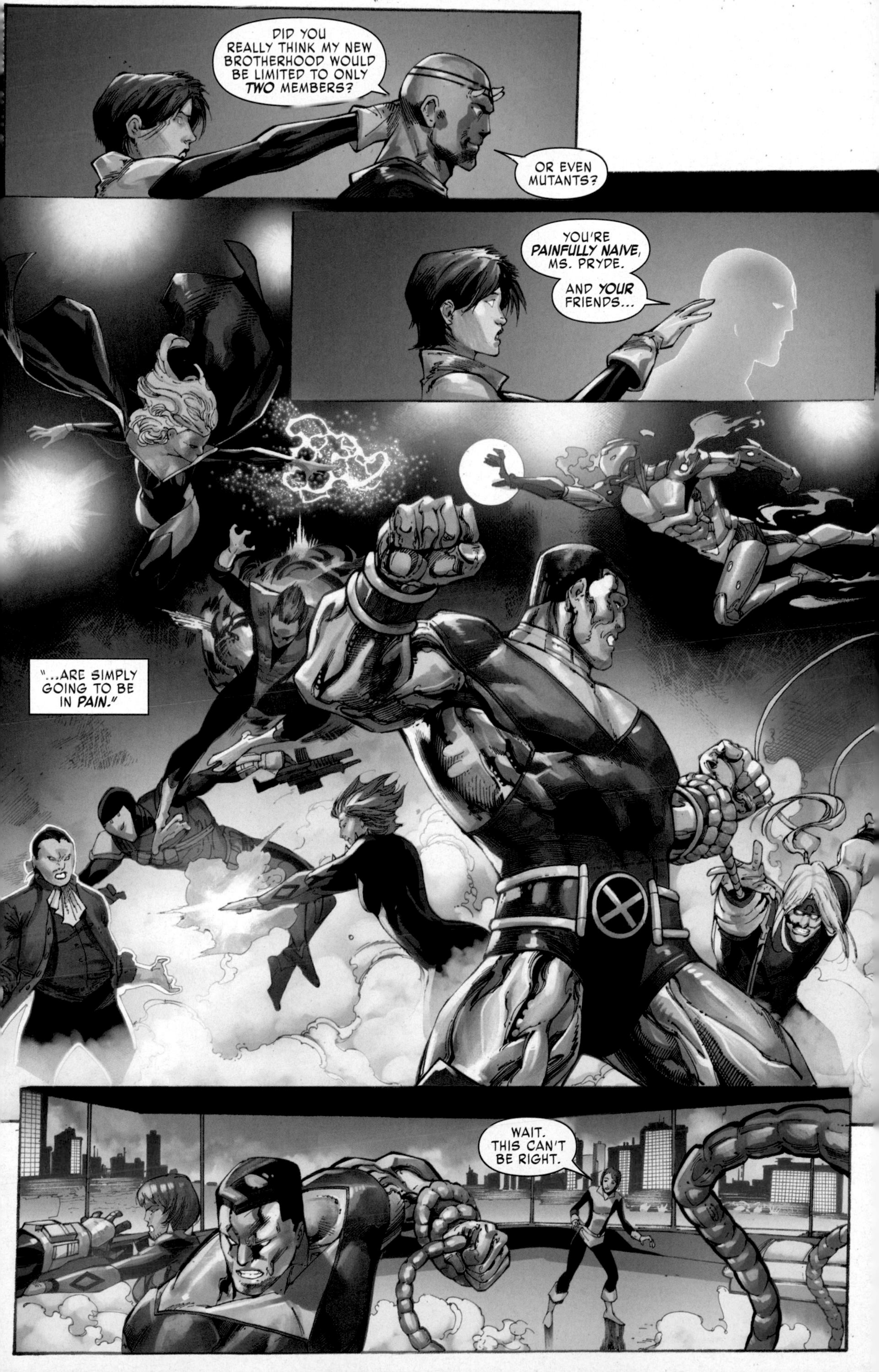
DID YOU REALLY THINK MY NEW BROTHERHOOD WOULD BE LIMITED TO ONLY TWO MEMBERS?
OR EVEN MUTANTS?
YOU'RE PAINFULLY NAIVE, MS. PRYDE.
AND YOUR FRIENDS...
"...ARE SIMPLY GOING TO BE IN PAIN."
WAIT. THIS CAN'T BE RIGHT.

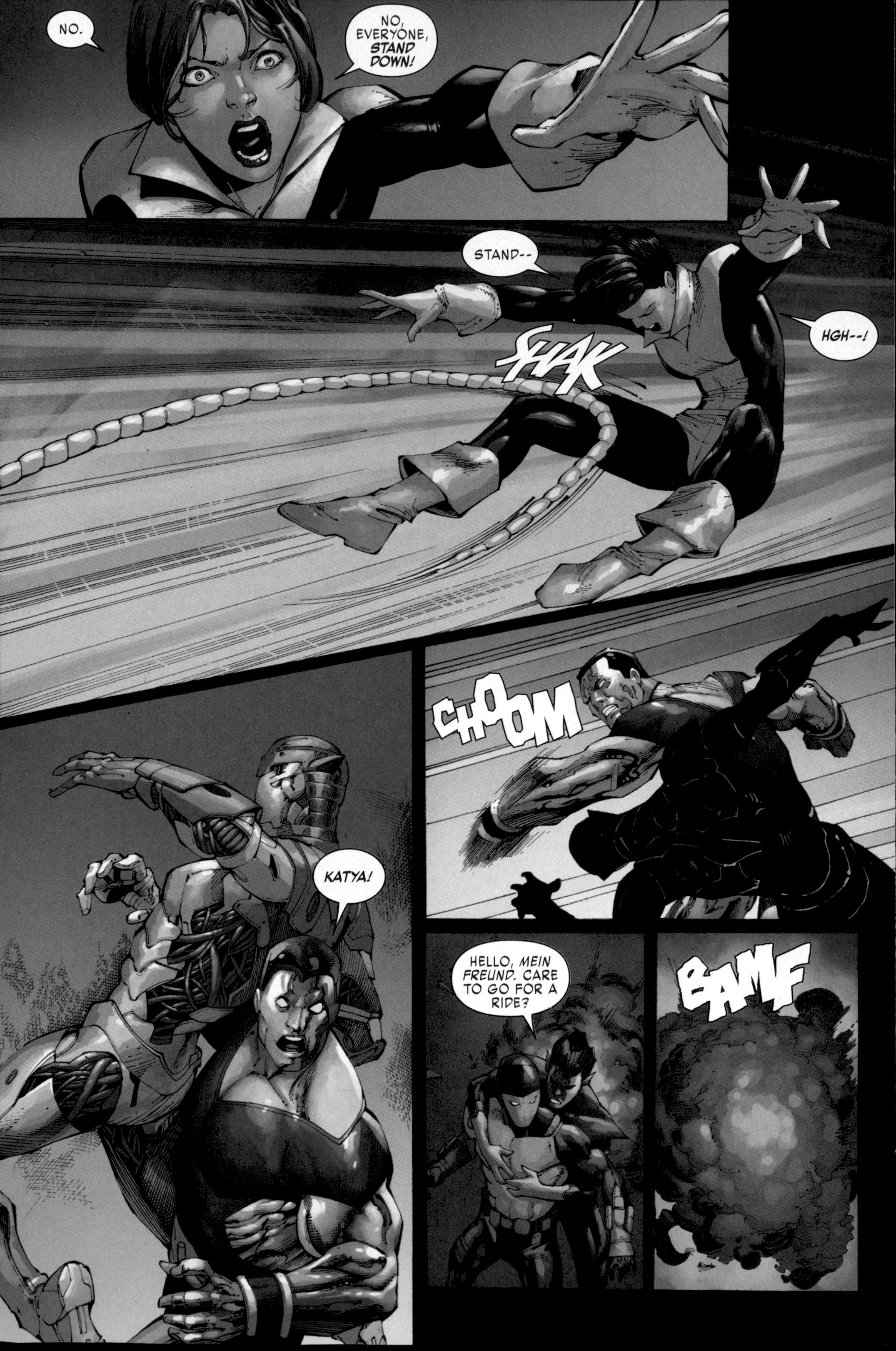
NO.
NO, EVERYONE, STAND DOWN!
STAND--
HGH--!
SHAK
CHOOM
KATYA!
HELLO, MEIN FREUND. CARE TO GO FOR A RIDE?
BAMF

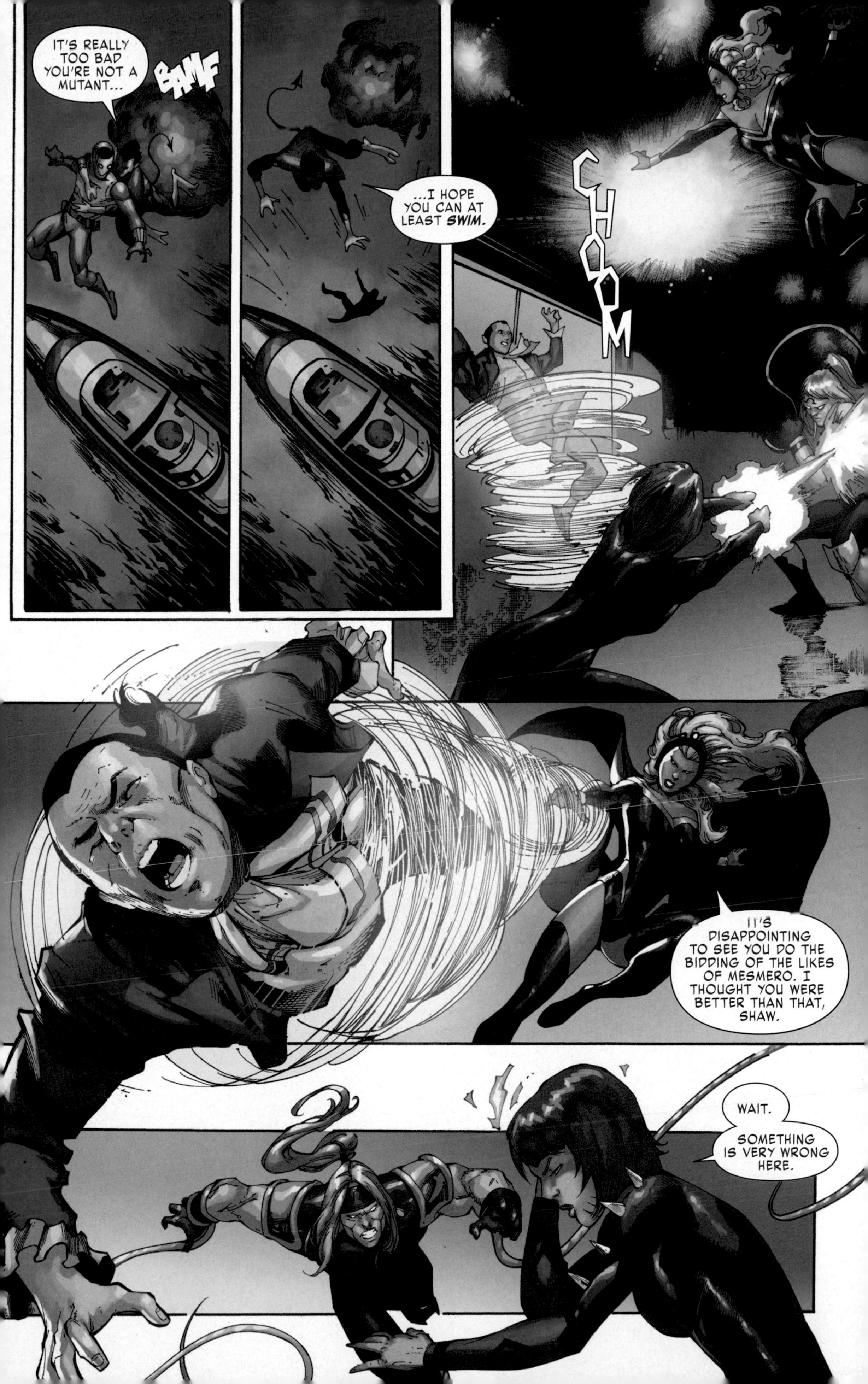
IT'S REALLY TOO BAD YOU'RE NOT A MUTANT...
BAMF
...I HOPE YOU CAN AT LEAST SWIM.
CHOOOM
IT'S DISAPPOINTING TO SEE YOU DO THE BIDDING OF THE LIKES OF MESMERO. I THOUGHT YOU WERE BETTER THAN THAT, SHAW.
WAIT.
SOMETHING IS VERY WRONG HERE.

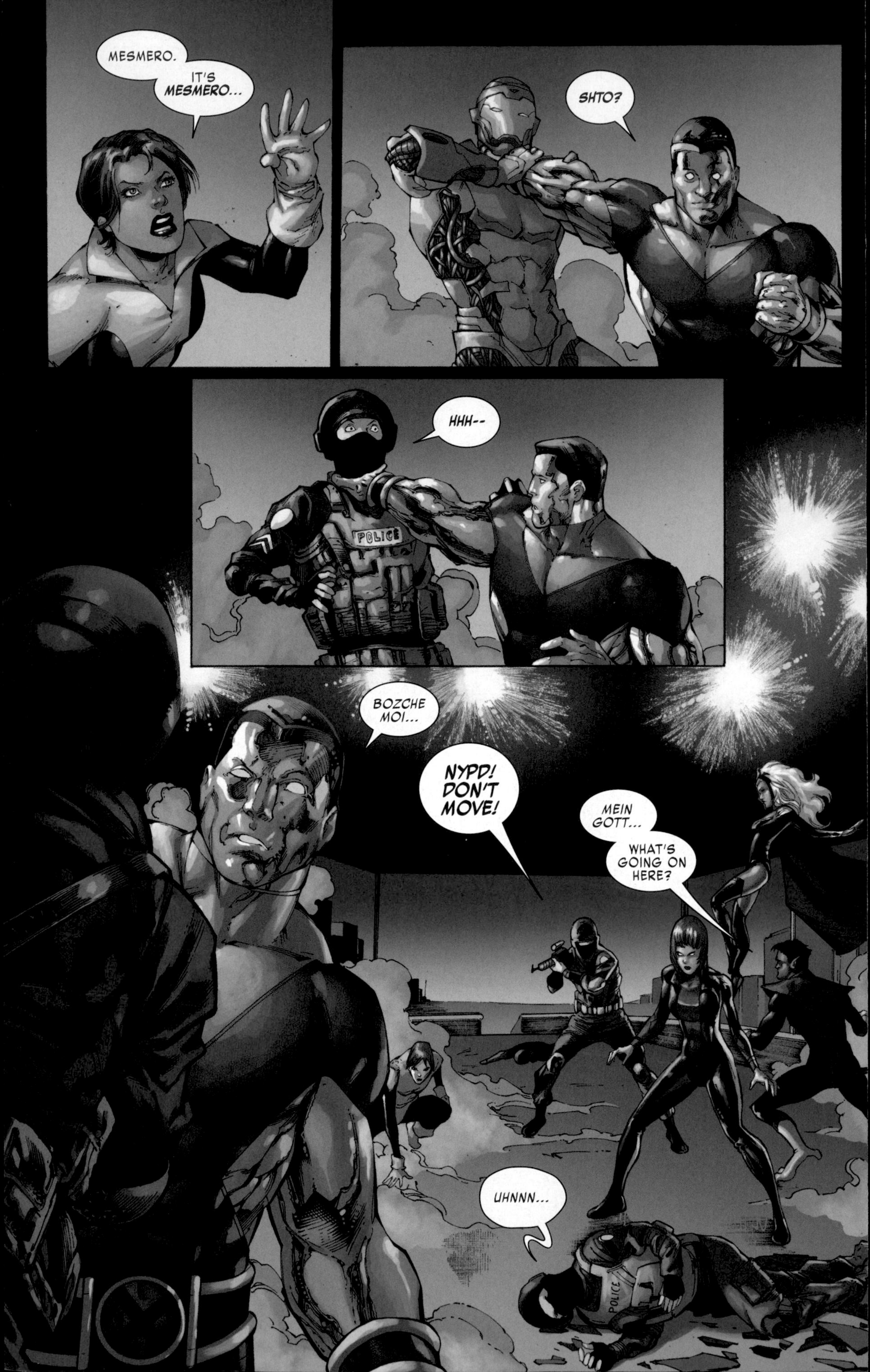
MESMERO.
IT'S MESMERO...
SHTO?
HHH--
BOZCHE MOI...
NYPD! DON'T MOVE!
MEIN GOTT...
WHAT'S GOING ON HERE?
UHNNN...

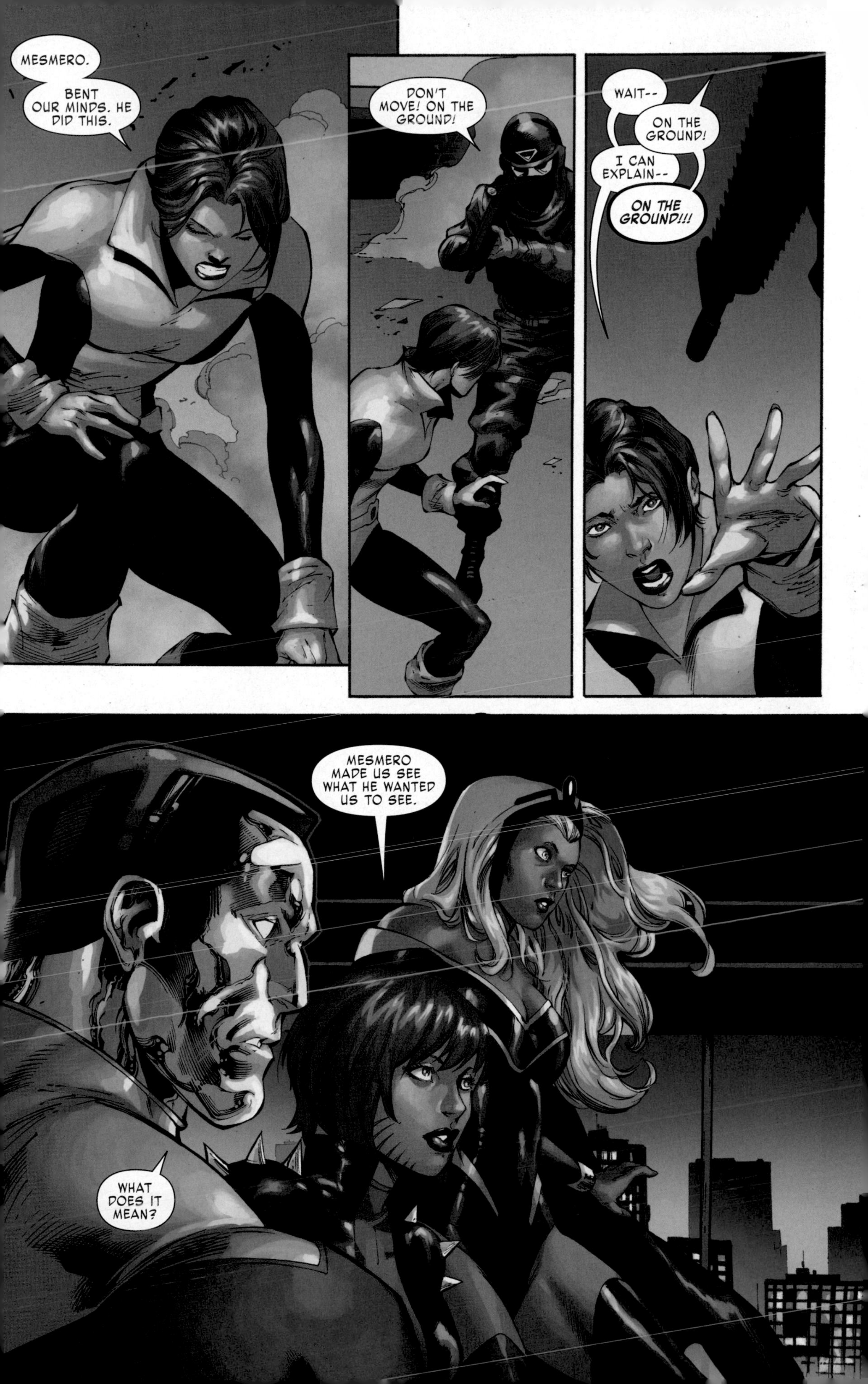
MESMERO.
BENT OUR MINDS. HE DID THIS.
DON'T MOVE! ON THE GROUND!
WAIT--
ON THE GROUND!
I CAN EXPLAIN--
ON THE GROUND!!!
MESMERO MADE US SEE WHAT HE WANTED US TO SEE.
WHAT DOES IT MEAN?

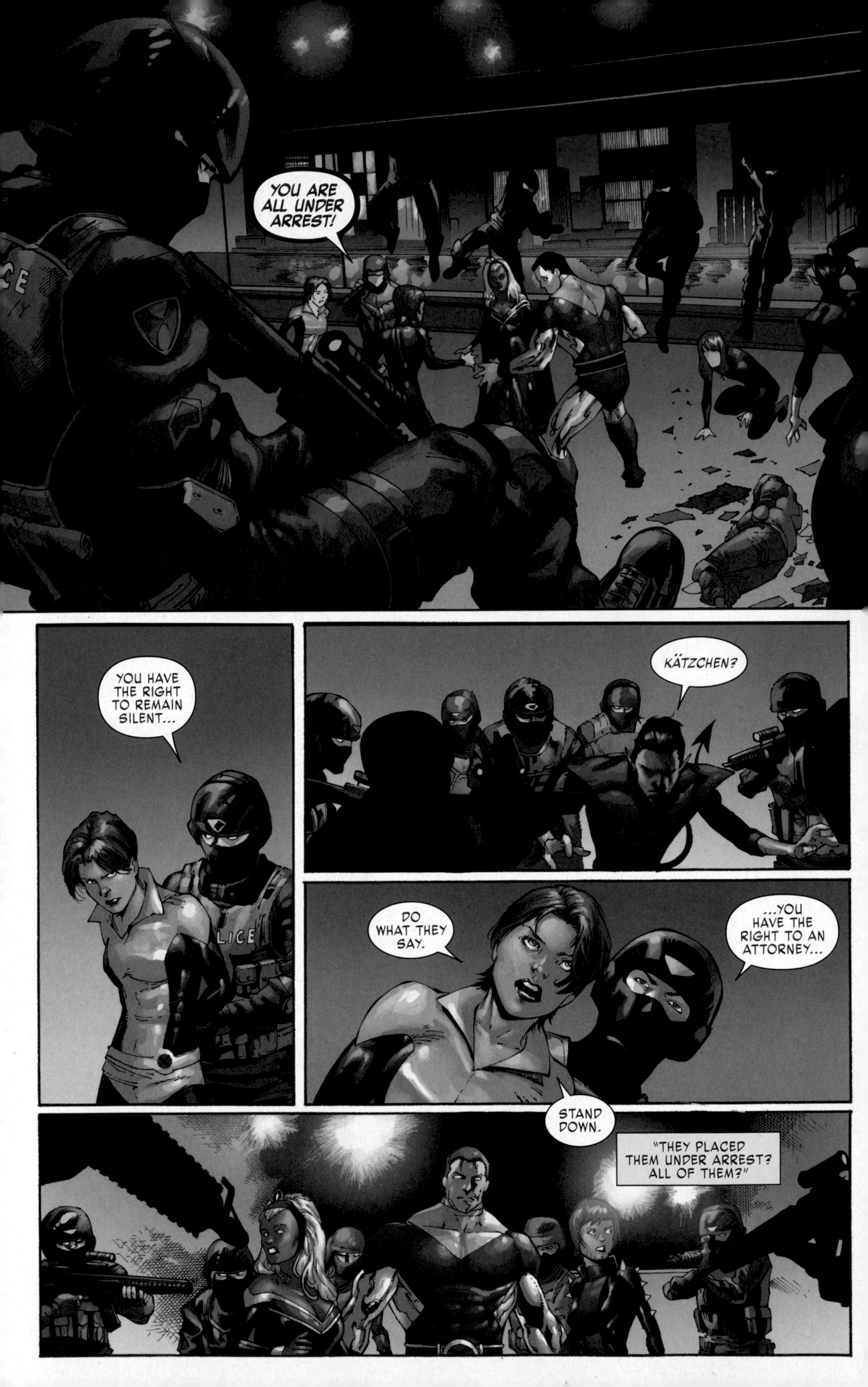
YOU ARE ALL UNDER ARREST!
LICE
YOU HAVE THE RIGHT TO REMAIN SILENT...
KÄTZCHEN?
DO WHAT THEY SAY.
...YOU HAVE THE RIGHT TO AN ATTORNEY...
STAND DOWN.
"THEY PLACED THEM UNDER ARREST? ALL OF THEM?"

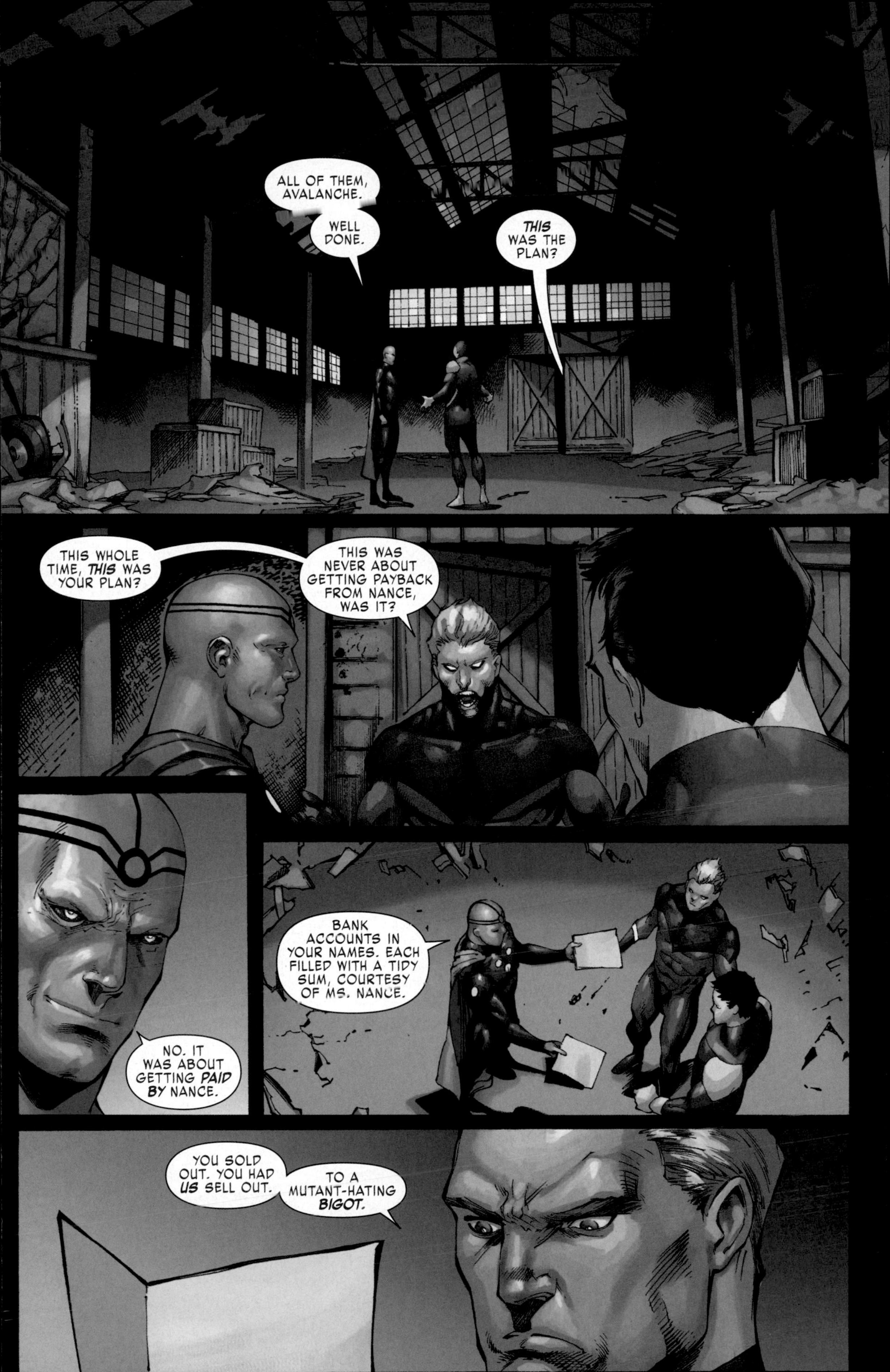
ALL OF THEM, AVALANCHE.
WELL DONE.
THIS WAS THE PLAN?
THIS WHOLE TIME, THIS WAS YOUR PLAN?
THIS WAS NEVER ABOUT GETTING PAYBACK FROM NANCE, WAS IT?
NO. IT WAS ABOUT GETTING PAID BY NANCE.
BANK ACCOUNTS IN YOUR NAMES. EACH FILLED WITH A TIDY SUM, COURTESY OF MS. NANCE.
YOU SOLD OUT. YOU HAD US SELL OUT.
TO A MUTANT-HATING BIGOT.

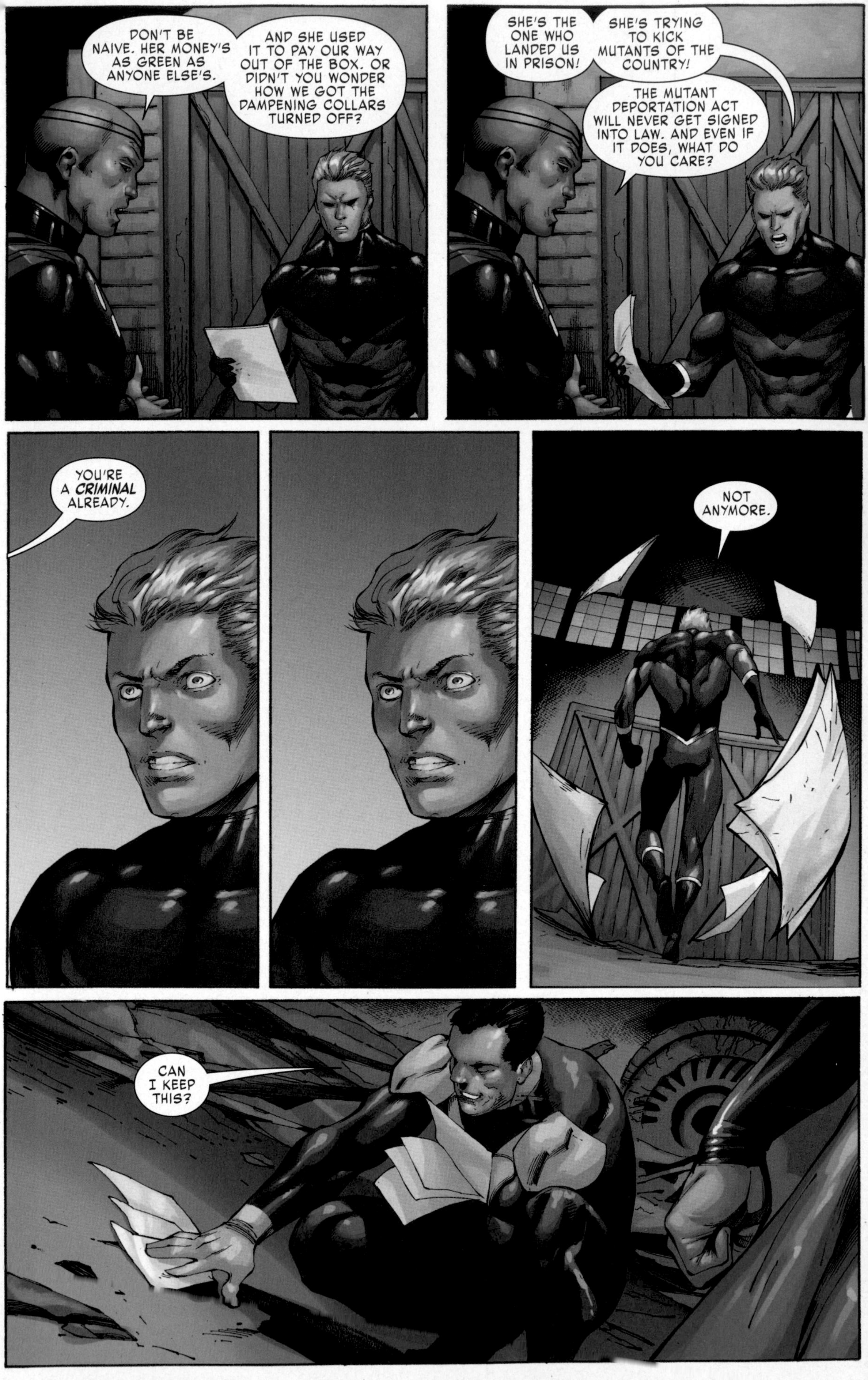
DON'T BE NAIVE. HER MONEY'S AS GREEN AS ANYONE ELSE'S.
AND SHE USED IT TO PAY OUR WAY OUT OF THE BOX. OR DIDN'T YOU WONDER HOW WE GOT THE DAMPENING COLLARS TURNED OFF?
SHE'S THE ONE WHO LANDED US IN PRISON!
SHE'S TRYING TO KICK MUTANTS OF THE COUNTRY!
THE MUTANT DEPORTATION ACT WILL NEVER GET SIGNED INTO LAW. AND EVEN IF IT DOES, WHAT DO YOU CARE?
YOU'RE A **CRIMINAL** ALREADY.
NOT ANYMORE.
CAN I KEEP THIS?

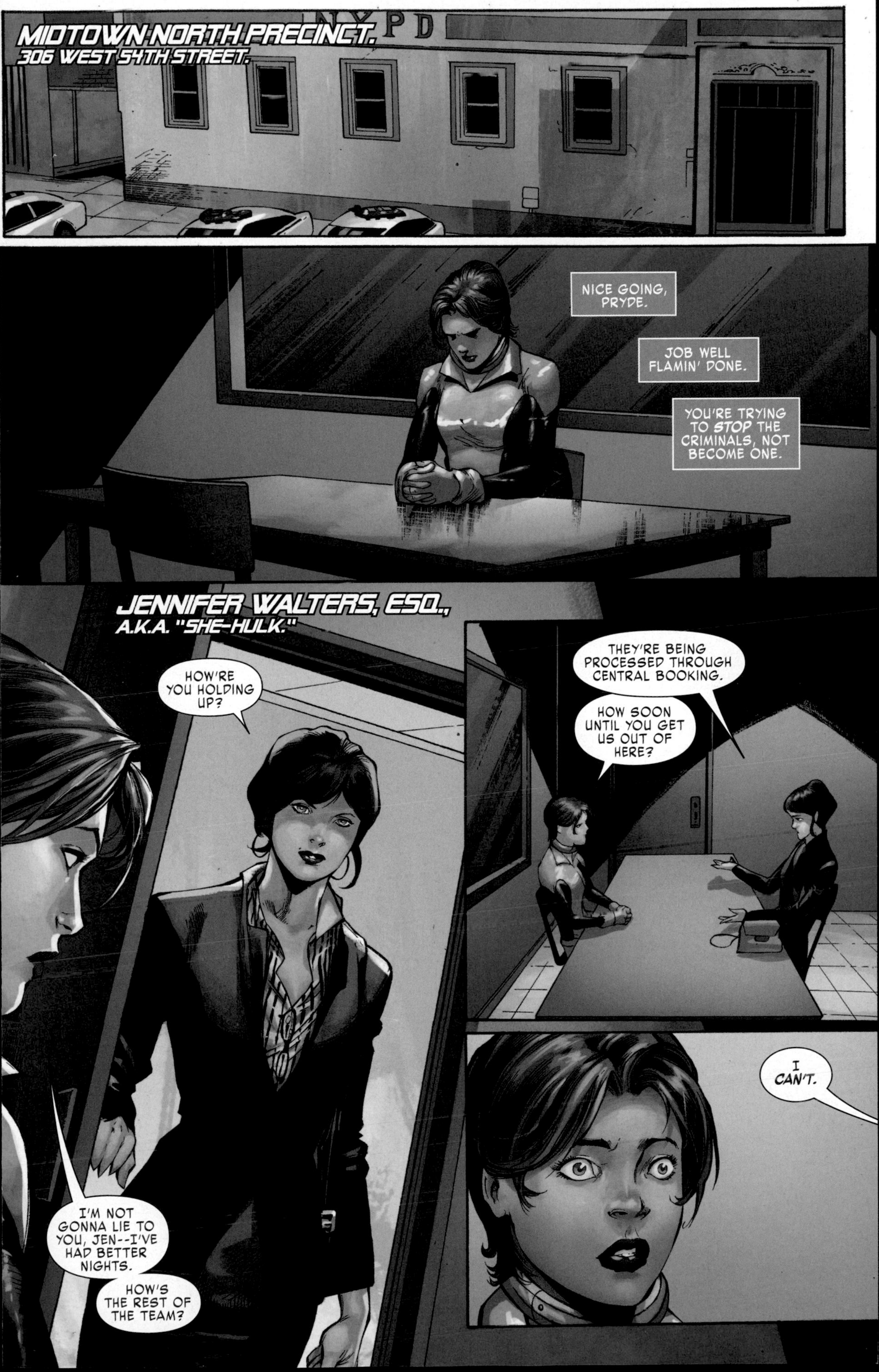
NYPD
MIDTOWN NORTH PRECINCT.
306 WEST 54TH STREET.
NICE GOING, PRYDE.
JOB WELL FLAMIN' DONE.
YOU'RE TRYING TO STOP THE CRIMINALS, NOT BECOME ONE.
JENNIFER WALTERS, ESQ., A.K.A. "SHE-HULK."
HOW'RE YOU HOLDING UP?
I'M NOT GONNA LIE TO YOU, JEN--I'VE HAD BETTER NIGHTS.
HOW'S THE REST OF THE TEAM?
THEY'RE BEING PROCESSED THROUGH CENTRAL BOOKING.
HOW SOON UNTIL YOU GET US OUT OF HERE?
I CAN'T.

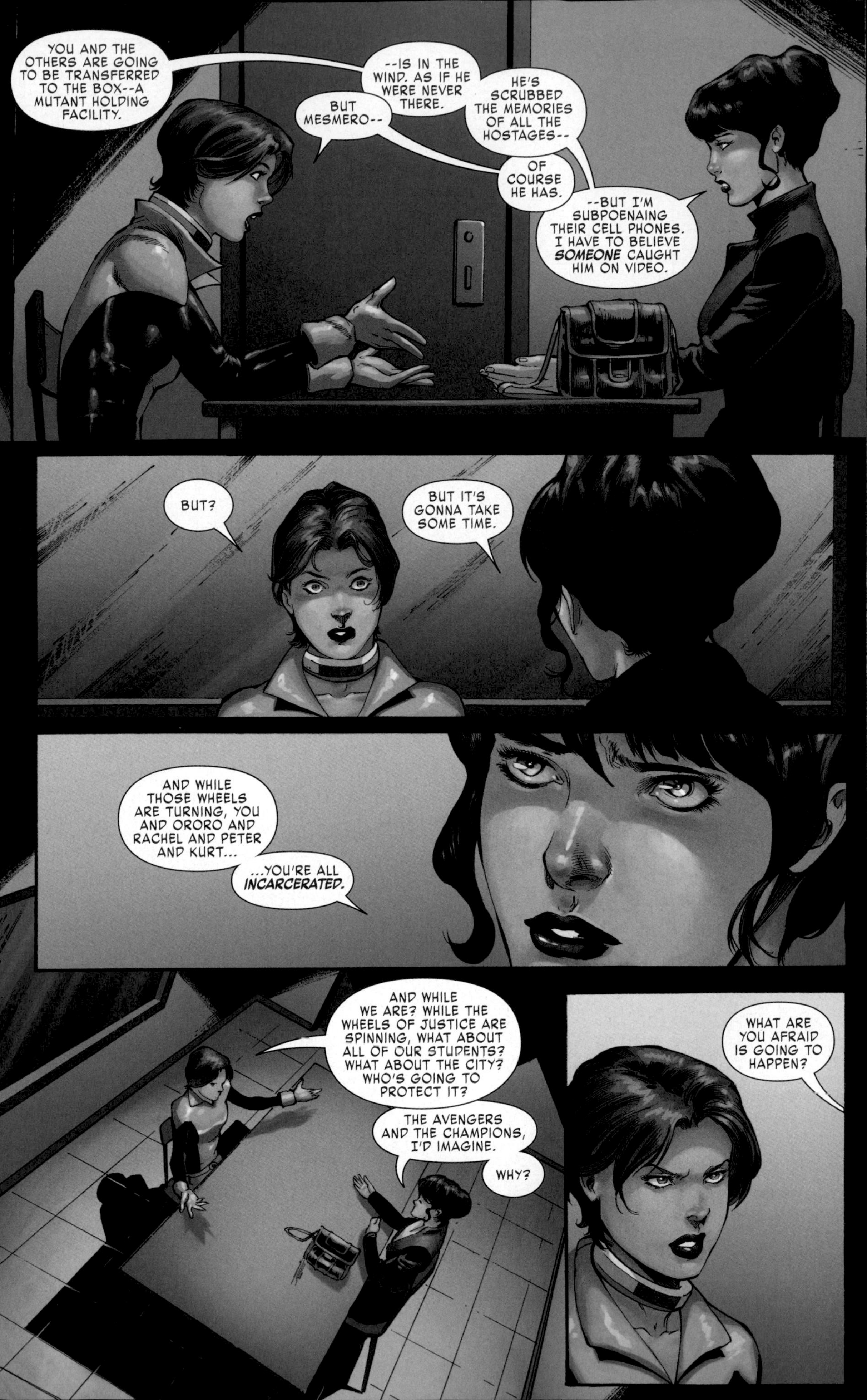

YOU AND THE OTHERS ARE GOING TO BE TRANSFERRED TO THE BOX--A MUTANT HOLDING FACILITY.
BUT MESMERO--
--IS IN THE WIND. AS IF HE WERE NEVER THERE.
HE'S SCRUBBED THE MEMORIES OF ALL THE HOSTAGES--
OF COURSE HE HAS.
--BUT I'M SUBPOENAING THEIR CELL PHONES. I HAVE TO BELIEVE *SOMEONE* CAUGHT HIM ON VIDEO.
BUT?
BUT IT'S GONNA TAKE SOME TIME.
AND WHILE THOSE WHEELS ARE TURNING, YOU AND ORORO AND RACHEL AND PETER AND KURT...
...YOU'RE ALL *INCARCERATED.*
AND WHILE WE ARE? WHILE THE WHEELS OF JUSTICE ARE SPINNING, WHAT ABOUT ALL OF OUR STUDENTS? WHAT ABOUT THE CITY? WHO'S GOING TO PROTECT IT?
THE AVENGERS AND THE CHAMPIONS, I'D IMAGINE.
WHY?
WHAT ARE YOU AFRAID IS GOING TO HAPPEN?

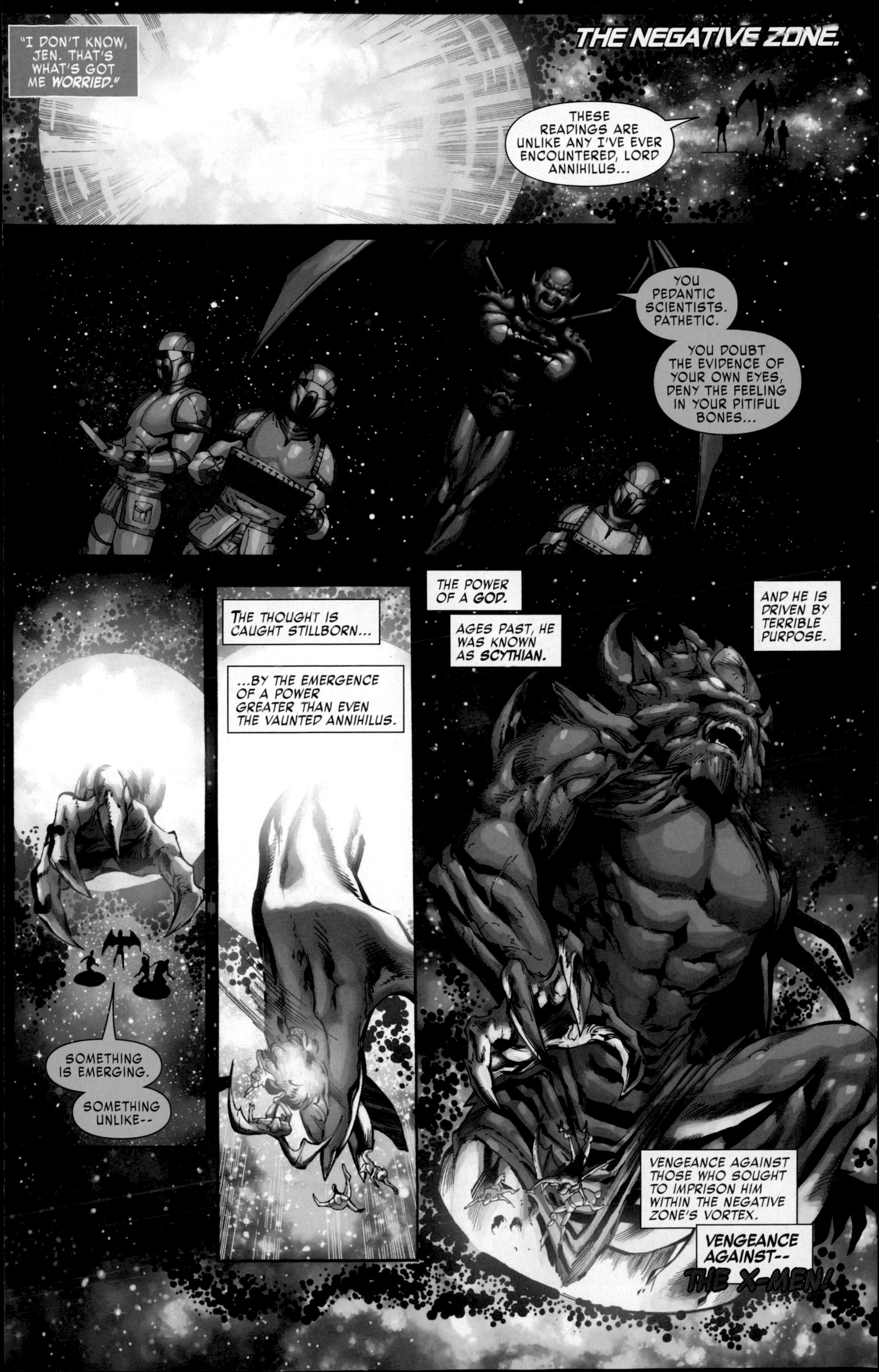
"I DON'T KNOW, JEN. THAT'S WHAT'S GOT ME WORRIED."
THE NEGATIVE ZONE.
THESE READINGS ARE UNLIKE ANY I'VE EVER ENCOUNTERED, LORD ANNIHILUS...
YOU PEDANTIC SCIENTISTS. PATHETIC.
YOU DOUBT THE EVIDENCE OF YOUR OWN EYES, DENY THE FEELING IN YOUR PITIFUL BONES...
SOMETHING IS EMERGING.
SOMETHING UNLIKE--
THE THOUGHT IS CAUGHT STILLBORN...
...BY THE EMERGENCE OF A POWER GREATER THAN EVEN THE VAUNTED ANNIHILUS.
THE POWER OF A GOD.
AGES PAST, HE WAS KNOWN AS SCYTHIAN.
AND HE IS DRIVEN BY TERRIBLE PURPOSE.
VENGEANCE AGAINST THOSE WHO SOUGHT TO IMPRISON HIM WITHIN THE NEGATIVE ZONE'S VORTEX.
VENGEANCE AGAINST--
THE X-MEN!

#21 VARIANT BY **DAN MORA** & **NOLAN WOODARD**

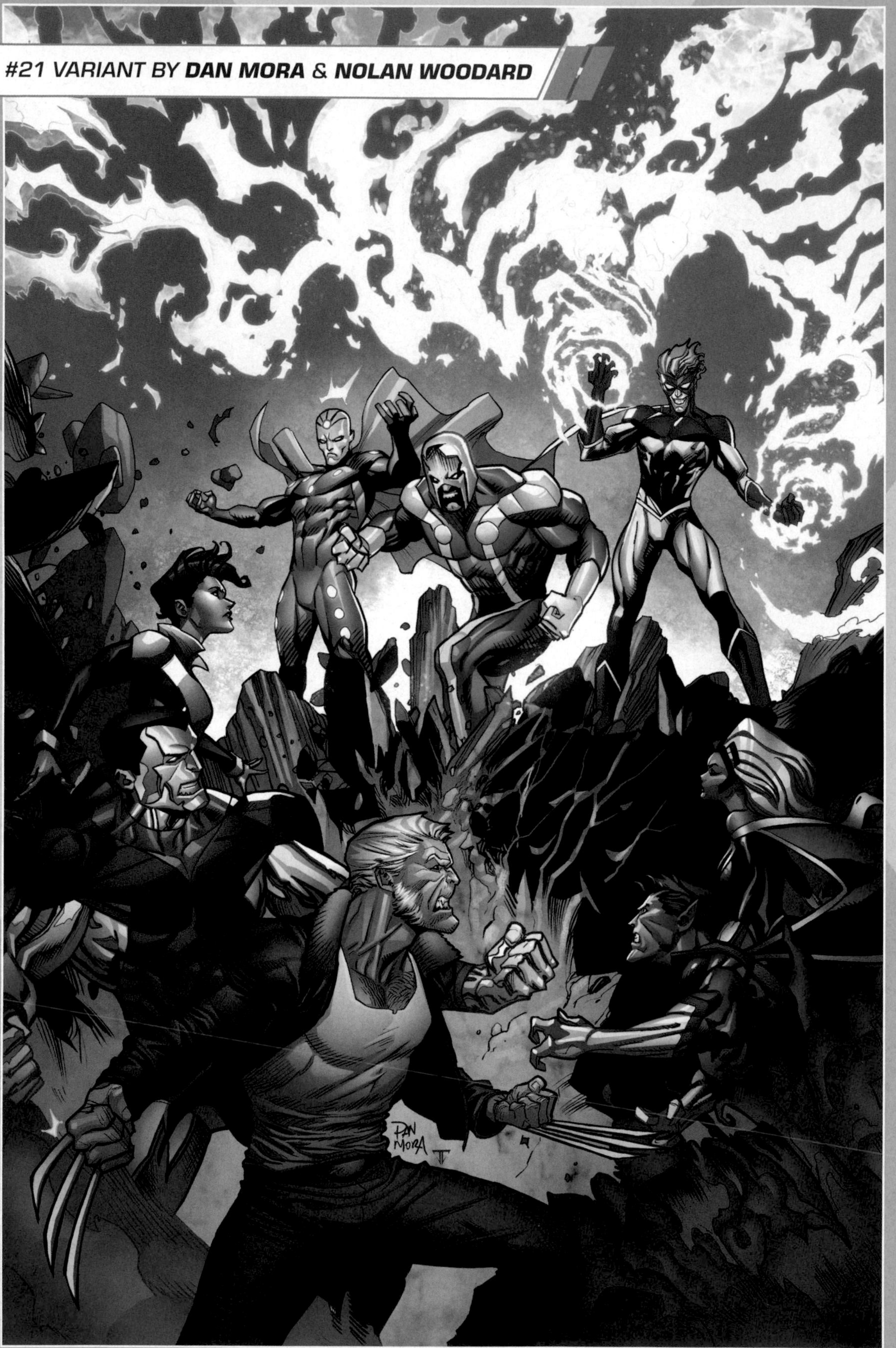
DAN MORA

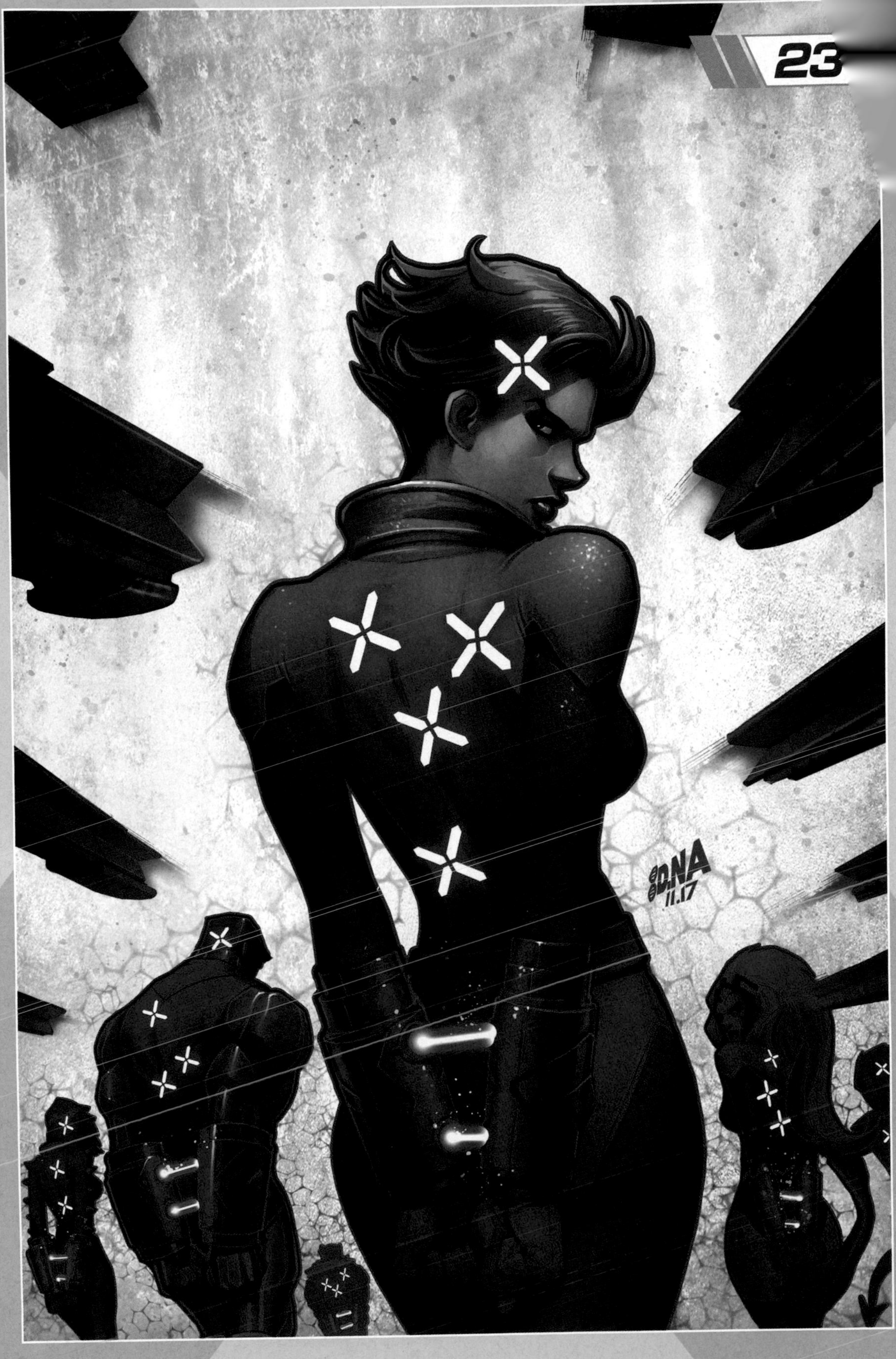
23
D.NA
11.17

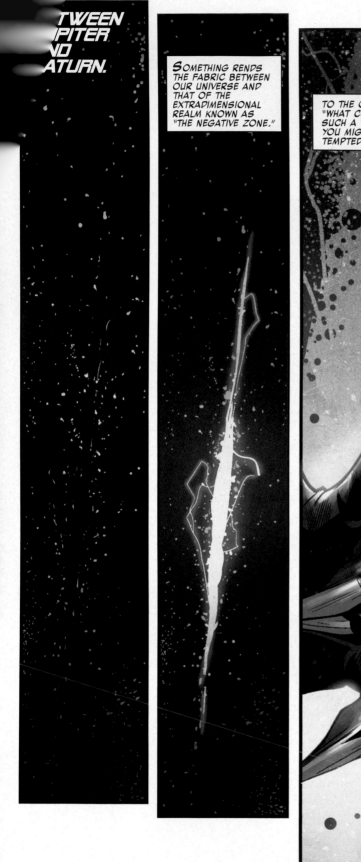

BETWEEN JUPITER AND SATURN.

SOMETHING RENDS THE FABRIC BETWEEN OUR UNIVERSE AND THAT OF THE EXTRADIMENSIONAL REALM KNOWN AS "THE NEGATIVE ZONE."

TO THE QUESTION, "WHAT COULD DO SUCH A THING?" YOU MIGHT BE TEMPTED TO REPLY...

"A GOD."

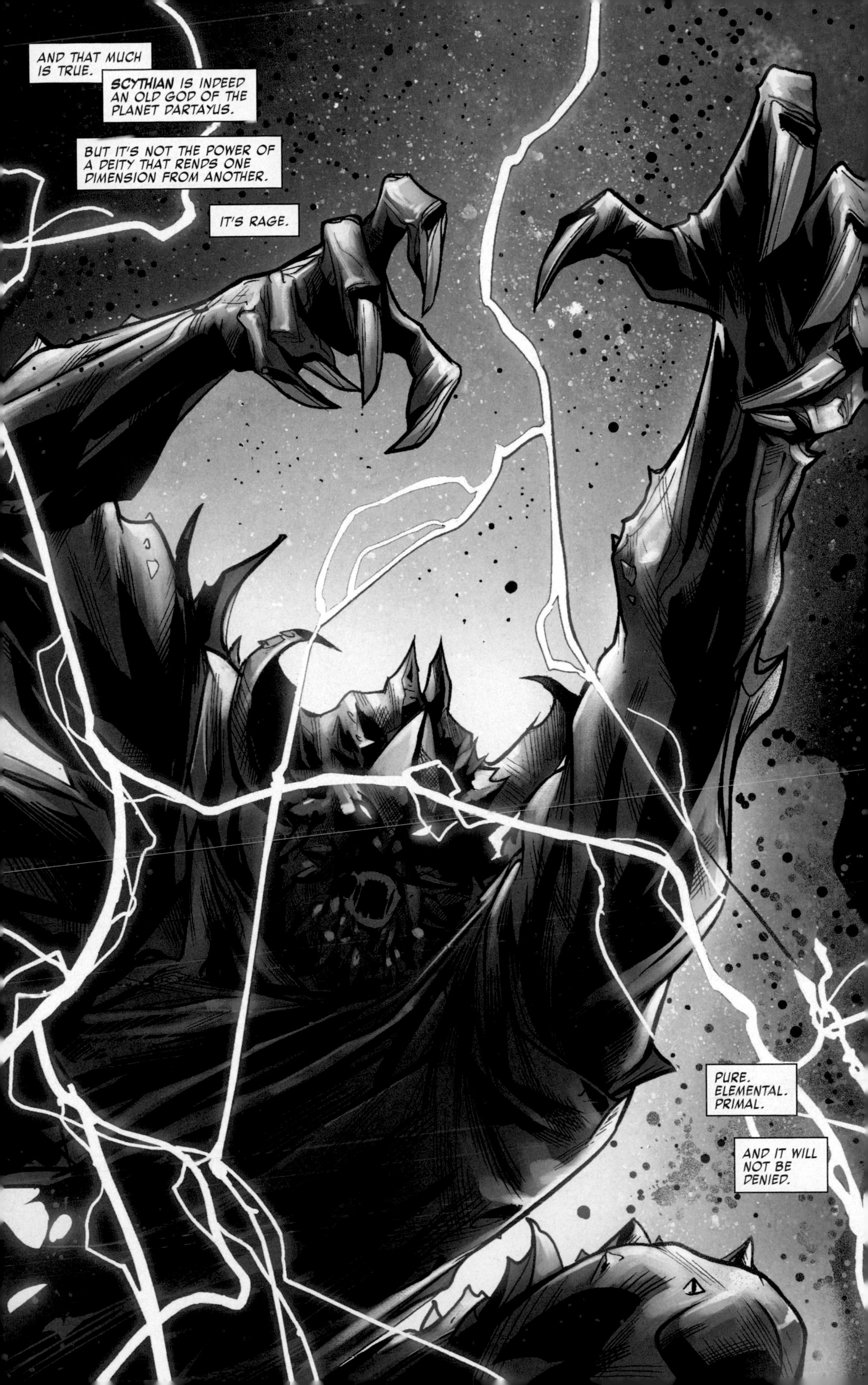
AND THAT MUCH IS TRUE.
SCYTHIAN IS INDEED AN OLD GOD OF THE PLANET DARTAYUS.
BUT IT'S NOT THE POWER OF A DEITY THAT RENDS ONE DIMENSION FROM ANOTHER.
IT'S RAGE.
PURE. ELEMENTAL. PRIMAL.
AND IT WILL NOT BE DENIED.

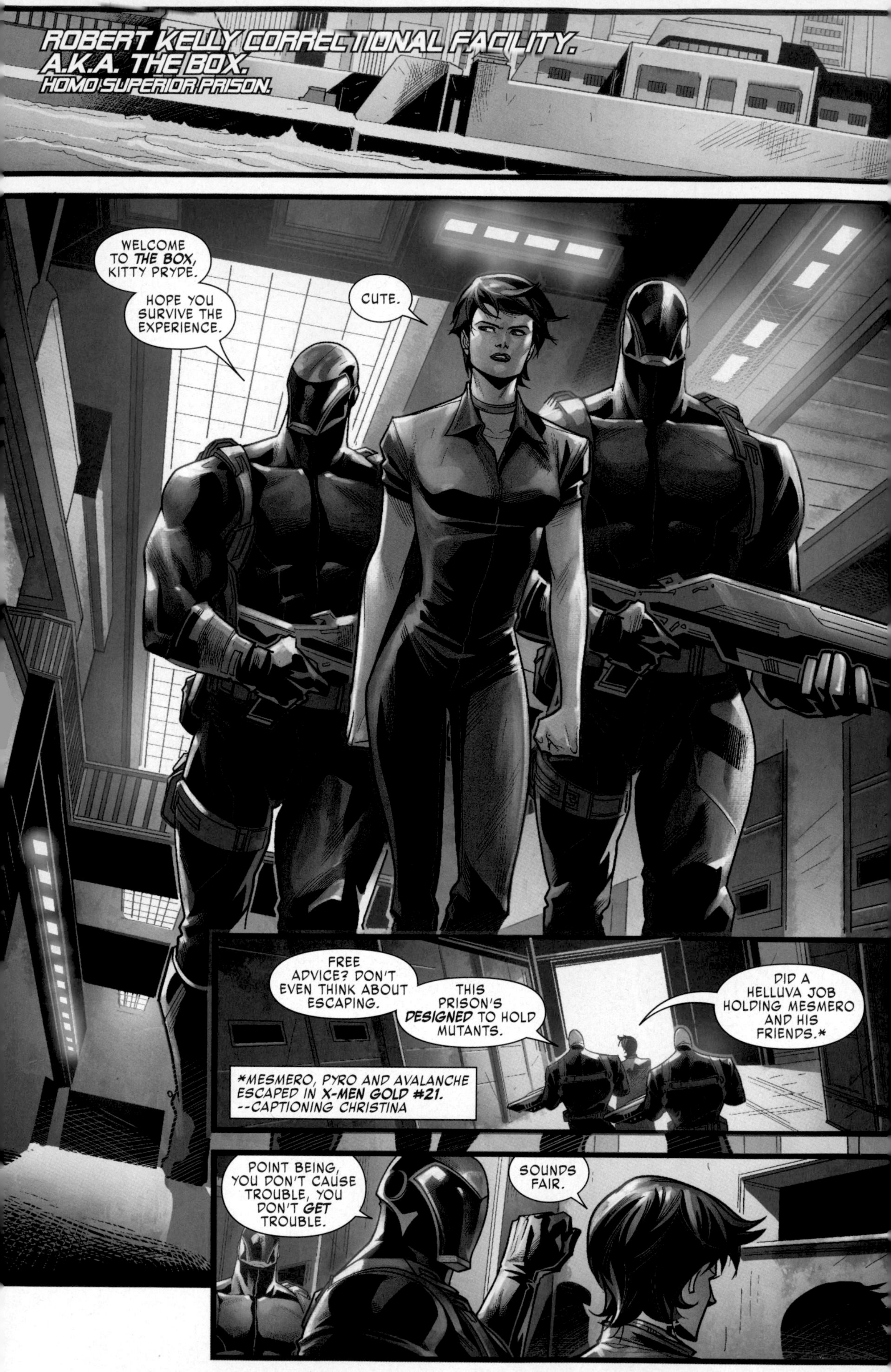
ROBERT KELLY CORRECTIONAL FACILITY.
A.K.A. THE BOX.
HOMO SUPERIOR PRISON.
WELCOME TO THE BOX, KITTY PRYDE.
HOPE YOU SURVIVE THE EXPERIENCE.
CUTE.
FREE ADVICE? DON'T EVEN THINK ABOUT ESCAPING.
THIS PRISON'S DESIGNED TO HOLD MUTANTS.
DID A HELLUVA JOB HOLDING MESMERO AND HIS FRIENDS.*
*MESMERO, PYRO AND AVALANCHE ESCAPED IN X-MEN GOLD #21. --CAPTIONING CHRISTINA
POINT BEING, YOU DON'T CAUSE TROUBLE, YOU DON'T GET TROUBLE.
SOUNDS FAIR.

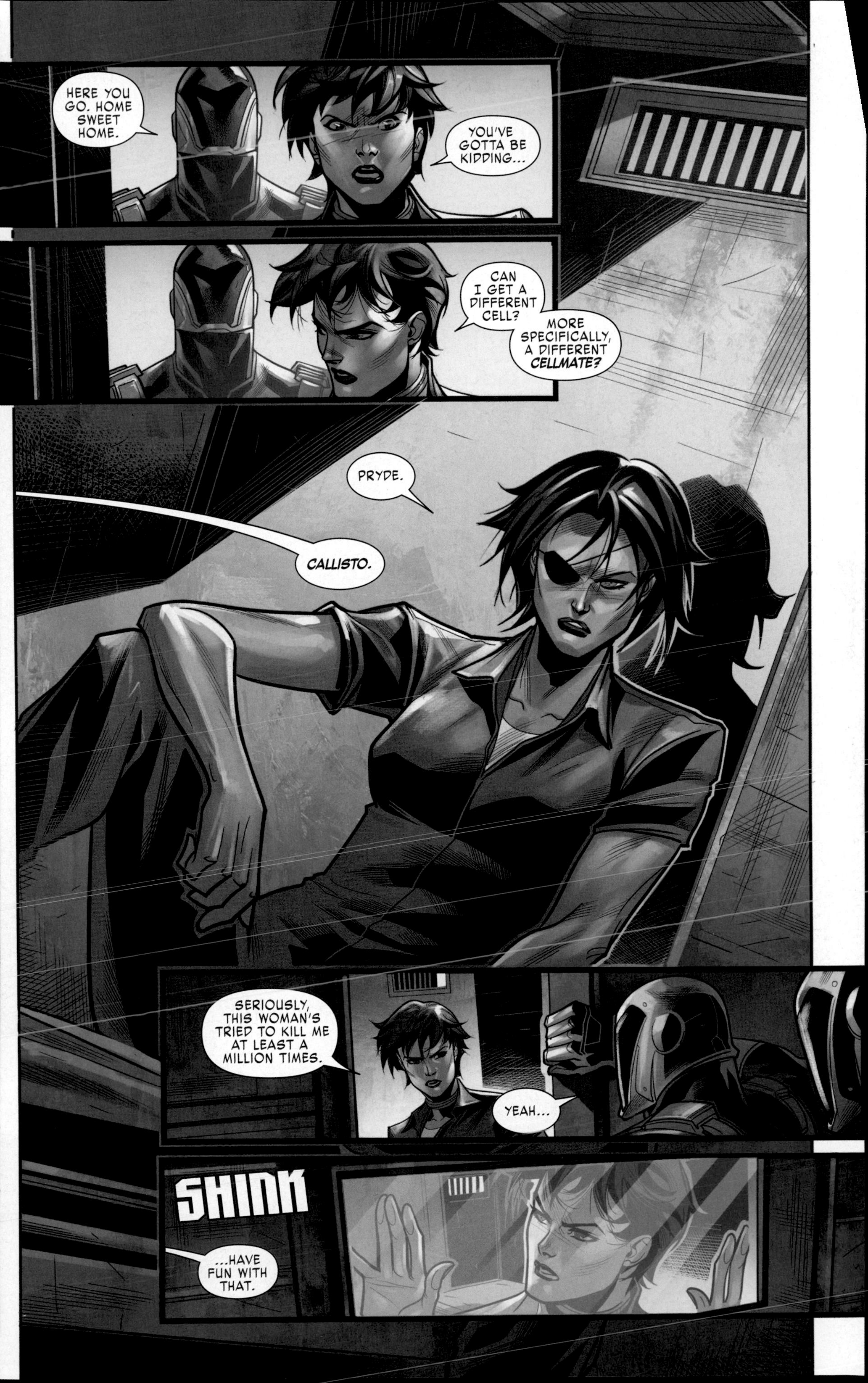
HERE YOU GO. HOME SWEET HOME.
YOU'VE GOTTA BE KIDDING...
CAN I GET A DIFFERENT CELL?
MORE SPECIFICALLY, A DIFFERENT CELLMATE?
PRYDE.
CALLISTO.
SERIOUSLY, THIS WOMAN'S TRIED TO KILL ME AT LEAST A MILLION TIMES.
YEAH...
SHINK
...HAVE FUN WITH THAT.

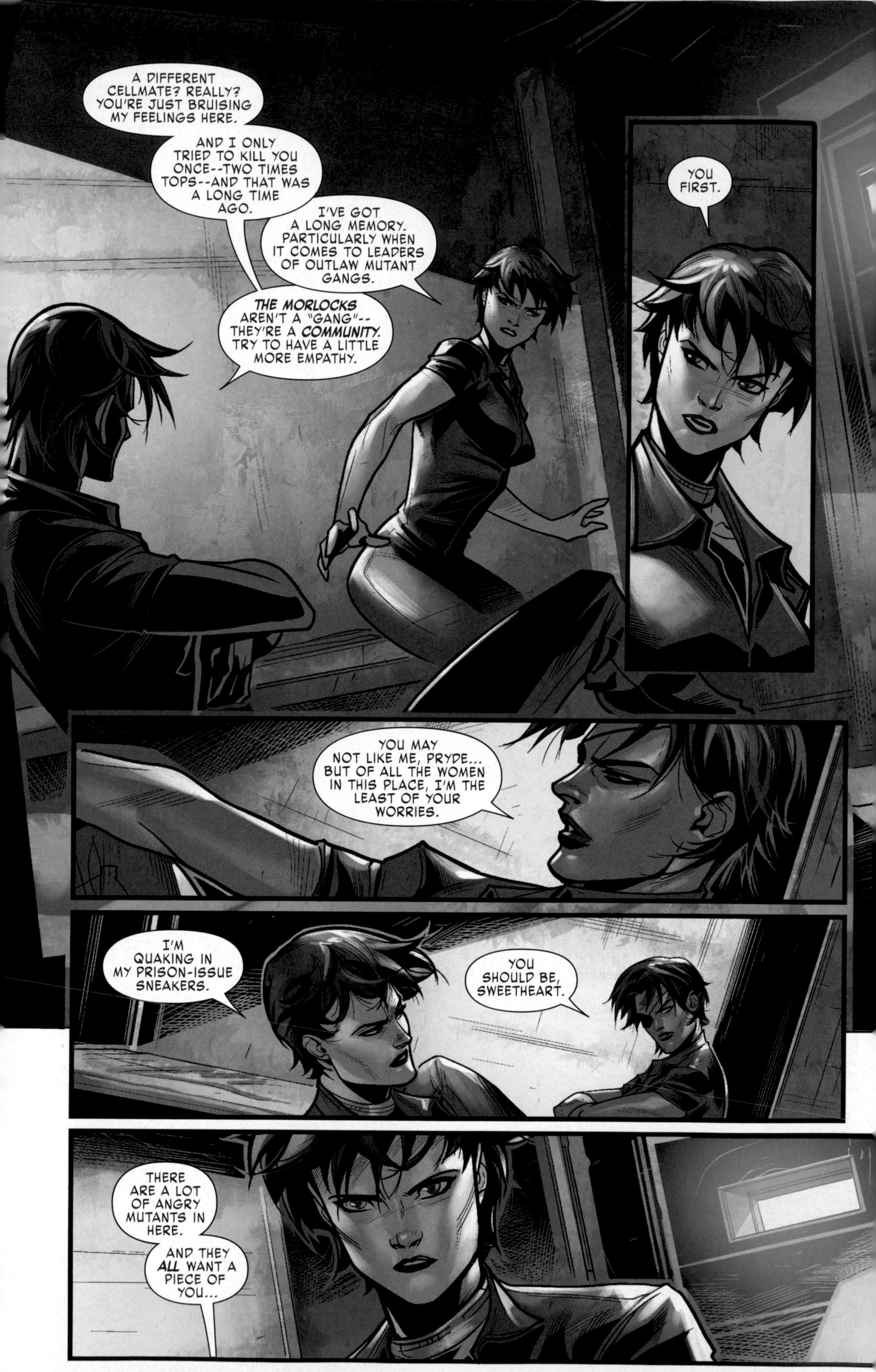
A DIFFERENT CELLMATE? REALLY? YOU'RE JUST BRUISING MY FEELINGS HERE.
AND I ONLY TRIED TO KILL YOU ONCE--TWO TIMES TOPS--AND THAT WAS A LONG TIME AGO.
I'VE GOT A LONG MEMORY. PARTICULARLY WHEN IT COMES TO LEADERS OF OUTLAW MUTANT GANGS.
THE MORLOCKS AREN'T A "GANG"--THEY'RE A COMMUNITY. TRY TO HAVE A LITTLE MORE EMPATHY.
YOU FIRST.
YOU MAY NOT LIKE ME, PRYDE... BUT OF ALL THE WOMEN IN THIS PLACE, I'M THE LEAST OF YOUR WORRIES.
I'M QUAKING IN MY PRISON-ISSUE SNEAKERS.
YOU SHOULD BE, SWEETHEART.
THERE ARE A LOT OF ANGRY MUTANTS IN HERE.
AND THEY ALL WANT A PIECE OF YOU...

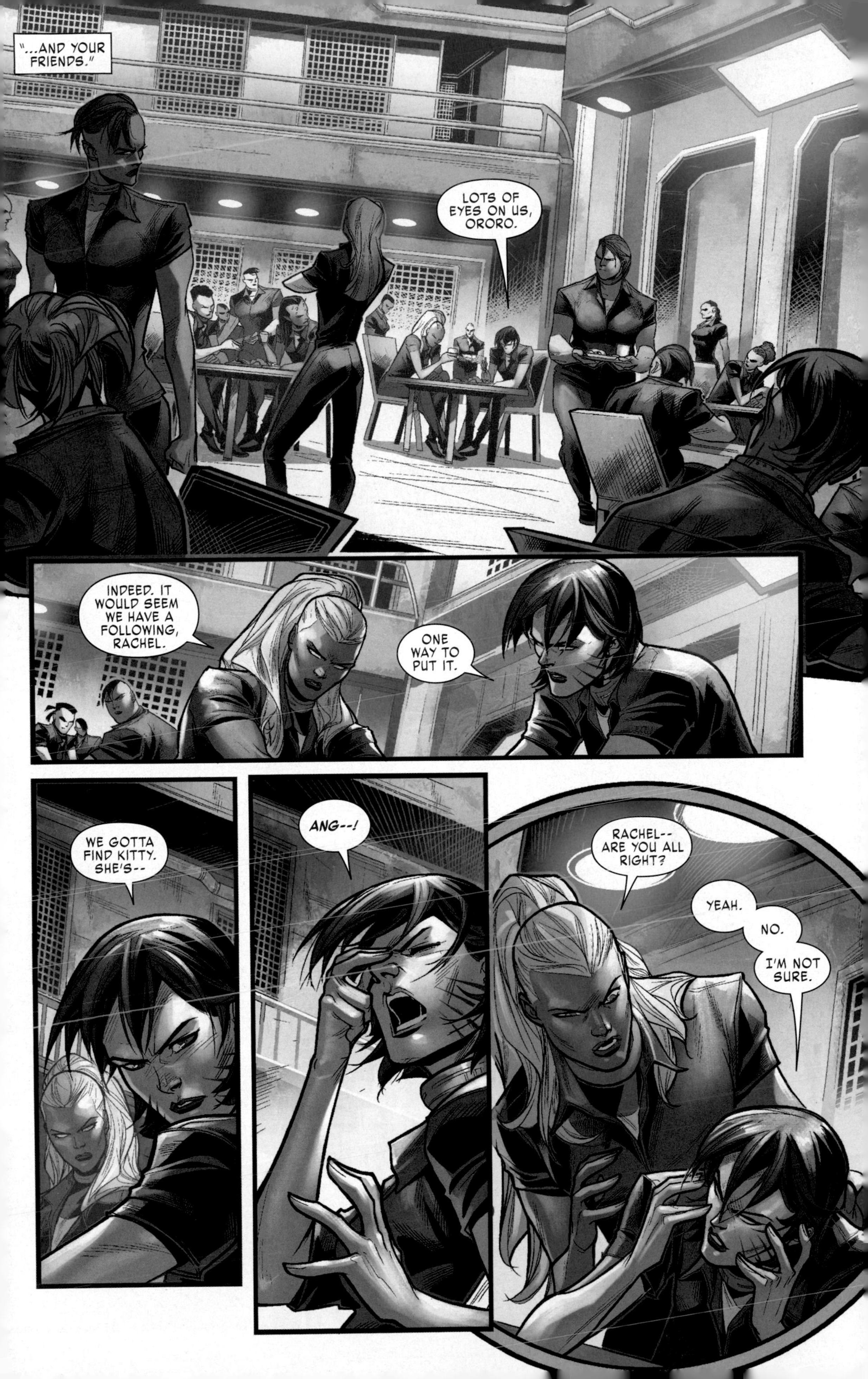
"...AND YOUR FRIENDS."
LOTS OF EYES ON US, ORORO.
INDEED. IT WOULD SEEM WE HAVE A FOLLOWING, RACHEL.
ONE WAY TO PUT IT.
WE GOTTA FIND KITTY. SHE'S--
ANG--!
RACHEL-- ARE YOU ALL RIGHT?
YEAH.
NO.
I'M NOT SURE.

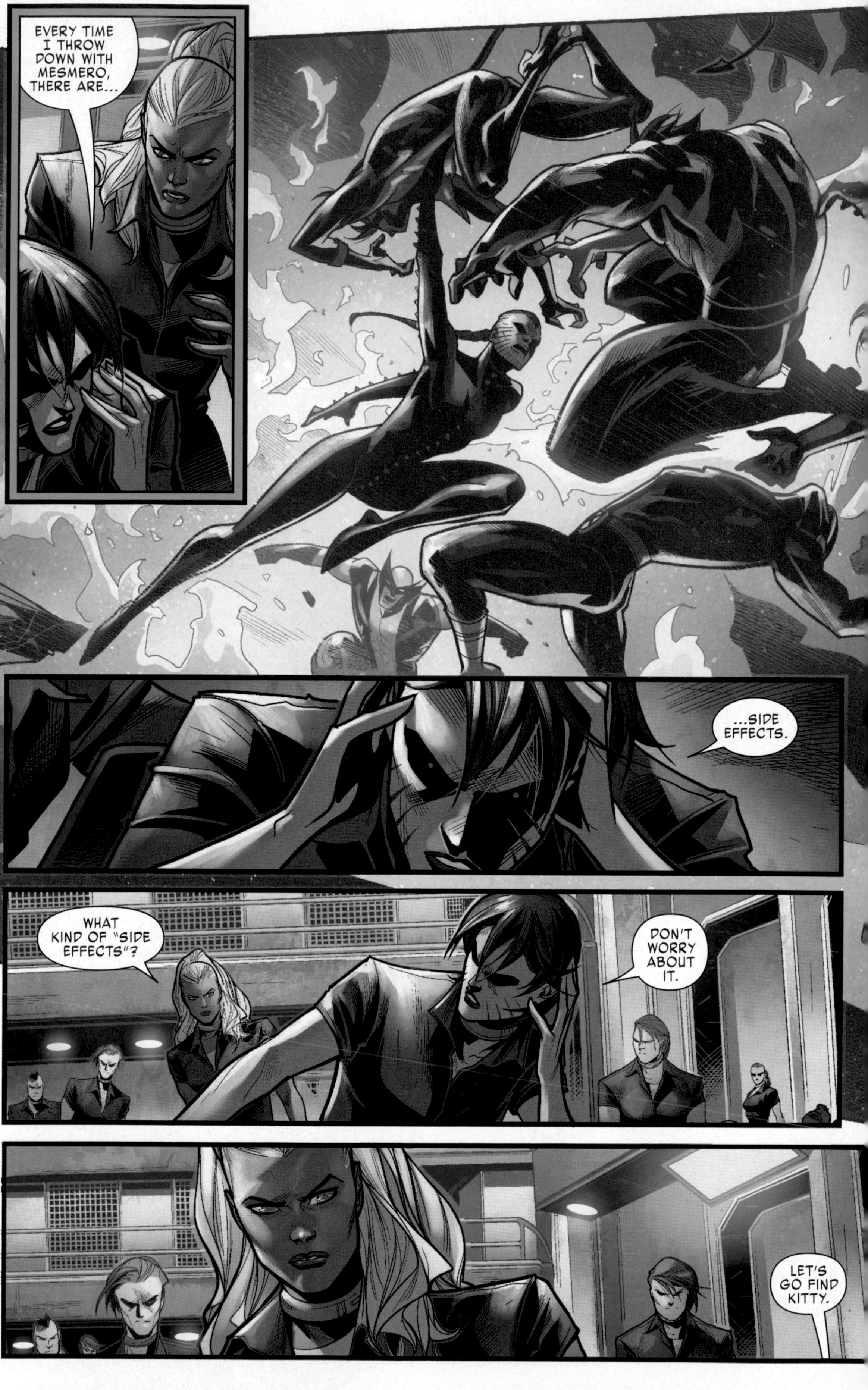
EVERY TIME I THROW DOWN WITH MESMERO, THERE ARE...
...SIDE EFFECTS.
WHAT KIND OF "SIDE EFFECTS"?
DON'T WORRY ABOUT IT.
LET'S GO FIND KITTY.

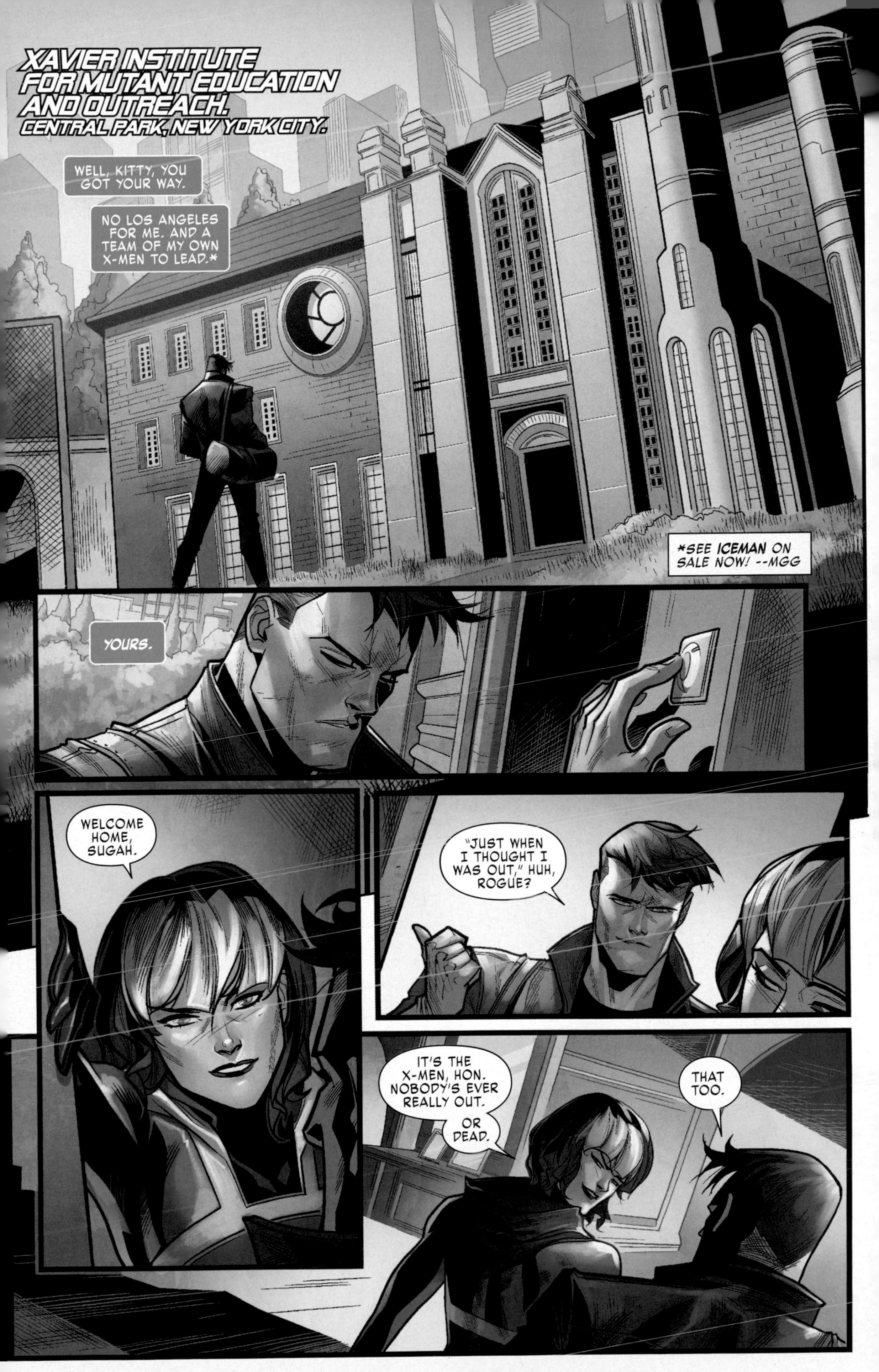
XAVIER INSTITUTE FOR MUTANT EDUCATION AND OUTREACH.
CENTRAL PARK, NEW YORK CITY.
WELL, KITTY, YOU GOT YOUR WAY.
NO LOS ANGELES FOR ME. AND A TEAM OF MY OWN X-MEN TO LEAD.*
*SEE ICEMAN ON SALE NOW! --MGG
YOURS.
WELCOME HOME, SUGAH.
"JUST WHEN I THOUGHT I WAS OUT," HUH, ROGUE?
IT'S THE X-MEN, HON. NOBODY'S EVER REALLY OUT.
OR DEAD.
THAT TOO.

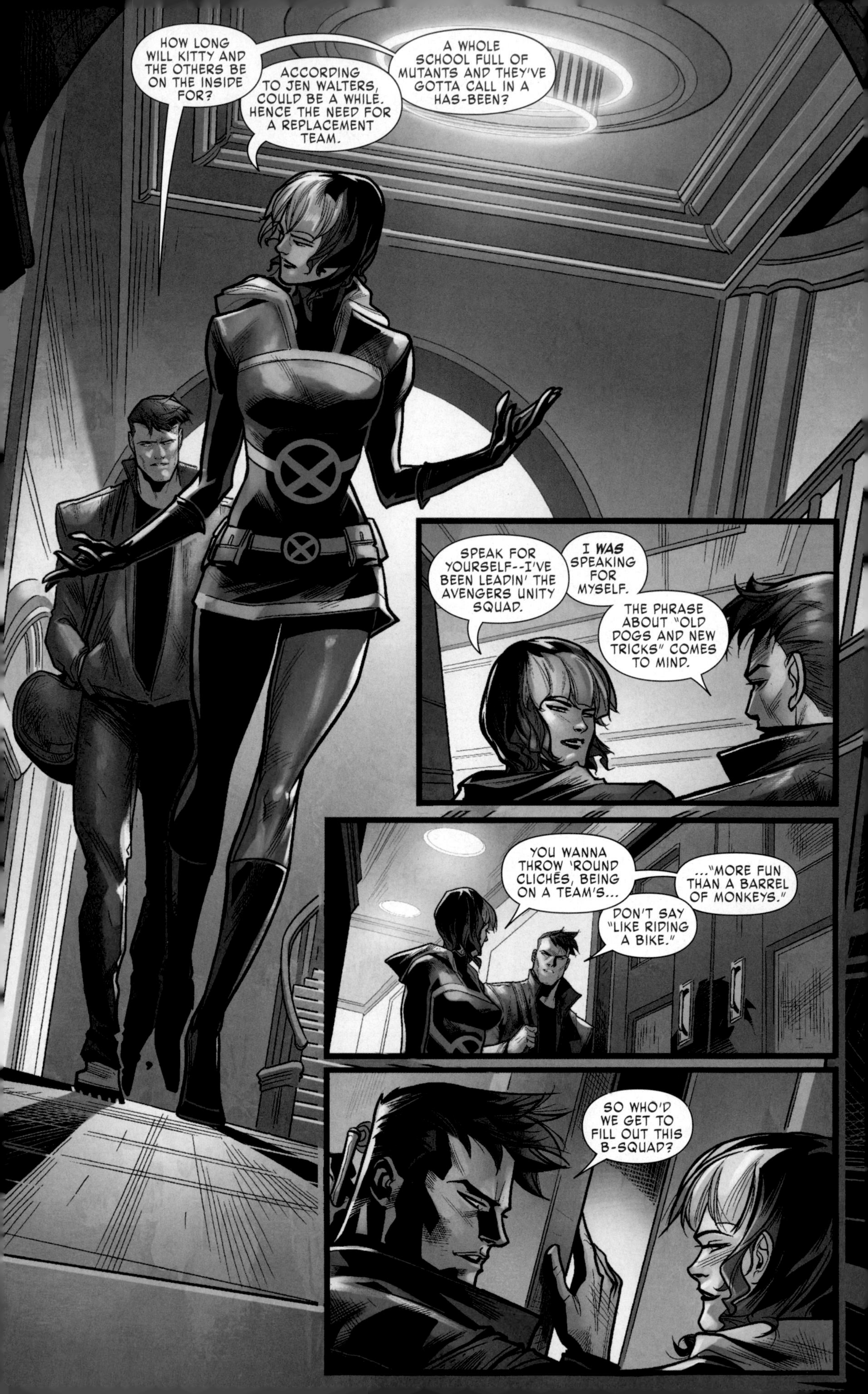
HOW LONG WILL KITTY AND THE OTHERS BE ON THE INSIDE FOR?
ACCORDING TO JEN WALTERS, COULD BE A WHILE. HENCE THE NEED FOR A REPLACEMENT TEAM.
A WHOLE SCHOOL FULL OF MUTANTS AND THEY'VE GOTTA CALL IN A HAS-BEEN?
SPEAK FOR YOURSELF--I'VE BEEN LEADIN' THE AVENGERS UNITY SQUAD.
I *WAS* SPEAKING FOR MYSELF.
THE PHRASE ABOUT "OLD DOGS AND NEW TRICKS" COMES TO MIND.
YOU WANNA THROW 'ROUND CLICHÉS, BEING ON A TEAM'S...
..."MORE FUN THAN A BARREL OF MONKEYS."
DON'T SAY "LIKE RIDING A BIKE."
SO WHO'D WE GET TO FILL OUT THIS B-SQUAD?

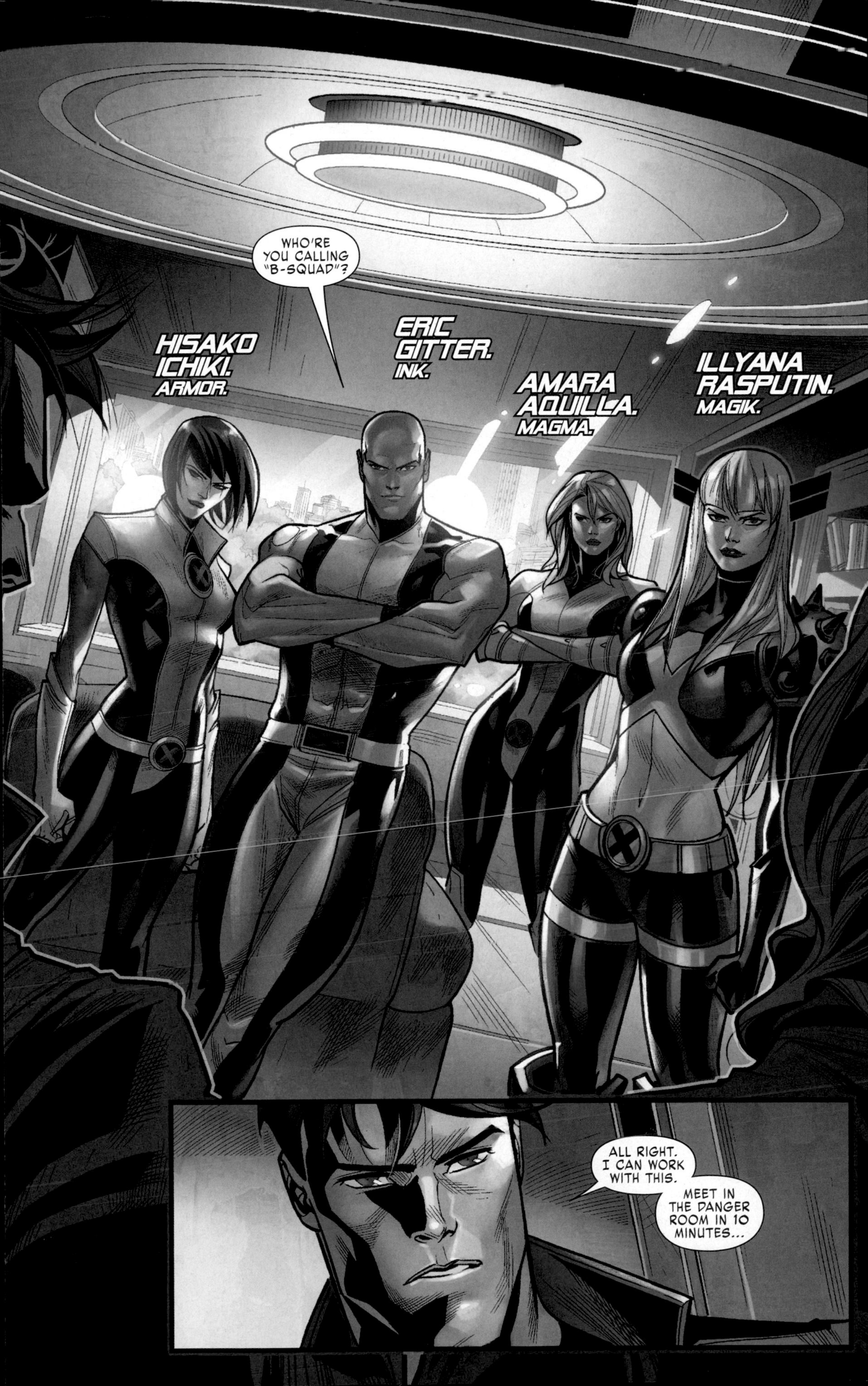

WHO'RE YOU CALLING "B-SQUAD"?
HISAKO ICHIKI. ARMOR.
ERIC GITTER. INK.
AMARA AQUILLA. MAGMA.
ILLYANA RASPUTIN. MAGIK.
ALL RIGHT. I CAN WORK WITH THIS.
MEET IN THE DANGER ROOM IN 10 MINUTES...

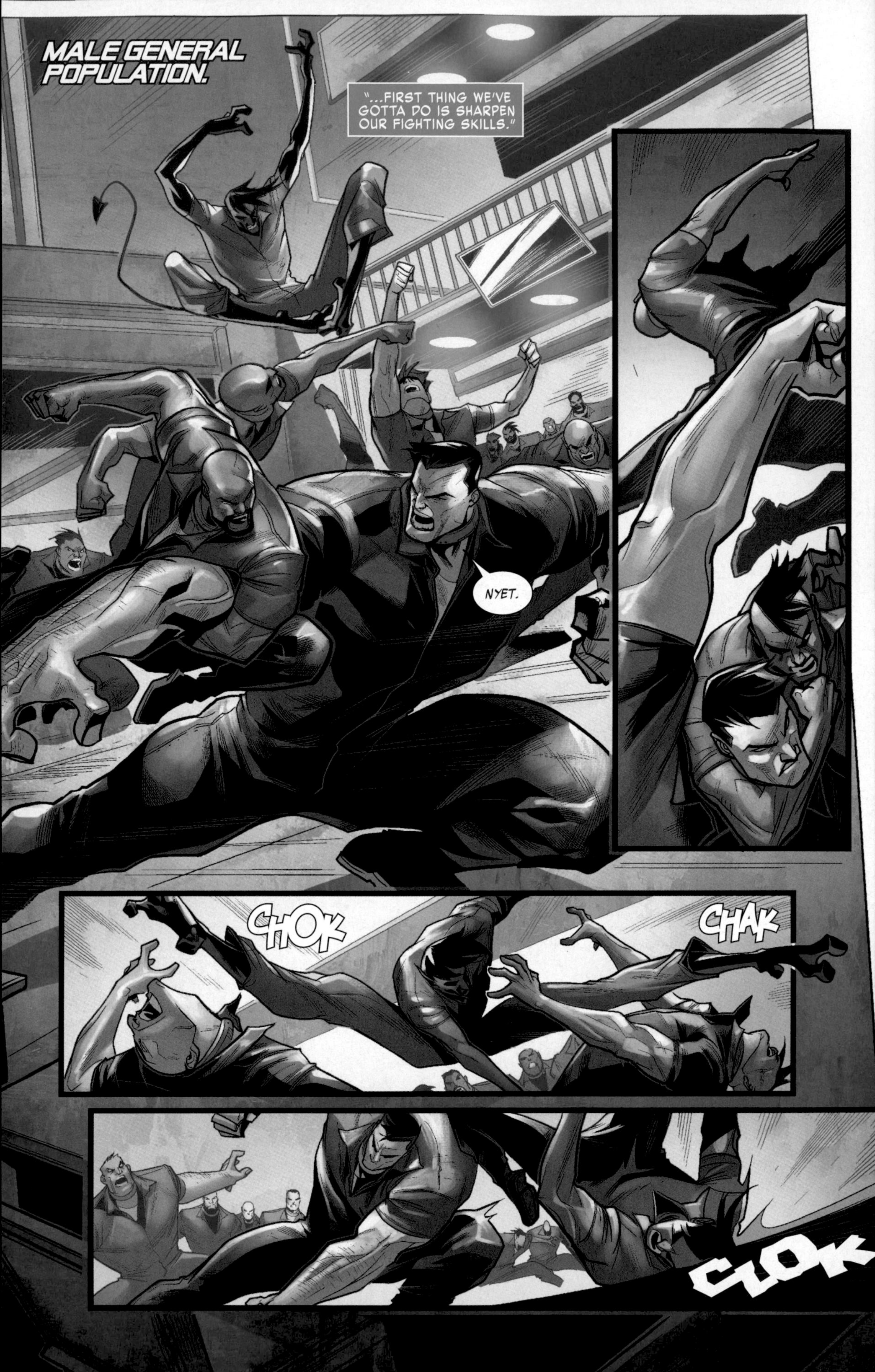
MALE GENERAL POPULATION.
"...FIRST THING WE'VE GOTTA DO IS SHARPEN OUR FIGHTING SKILLS."
NYET.
CHOK
CHAK
CLOK

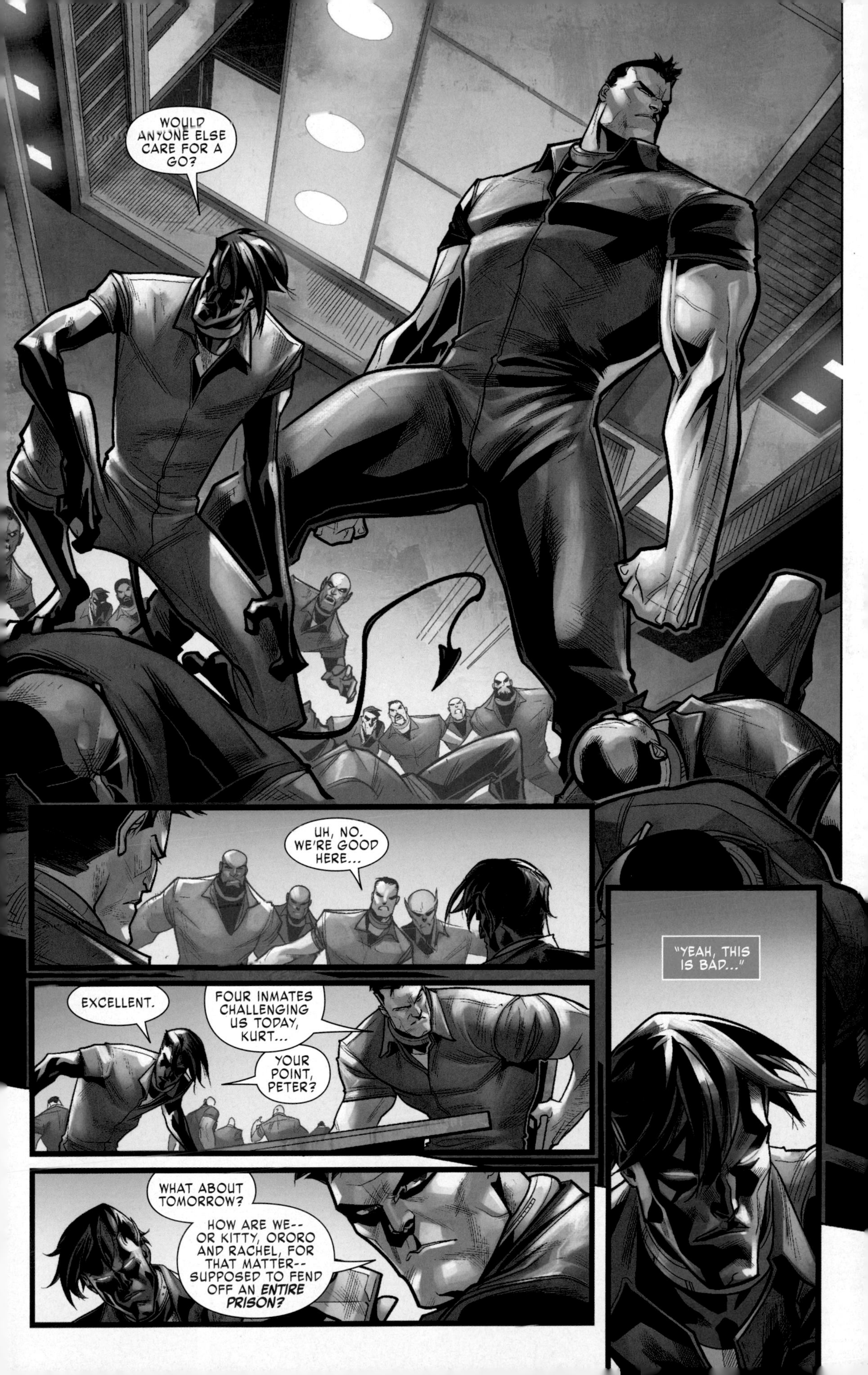
WOULD ANYONE ELSE CARE FOR A GO?
UH, NO. WE'RE GOOD HERE...
EXCELLENT.
FOUR INMATES CHALLENGING US TODAY, KURT...
YOUR POINT, PETER?
WHAT ABOUT TOMORROW?
HOW ARE WE-- OR KITTY, ORORO AND RACHEL, FOR THAT MATTER-- SUPPOSED TO FEND OFF AN *ENTIRE PRISON?*
"YEAH, THIS IS BAD..."

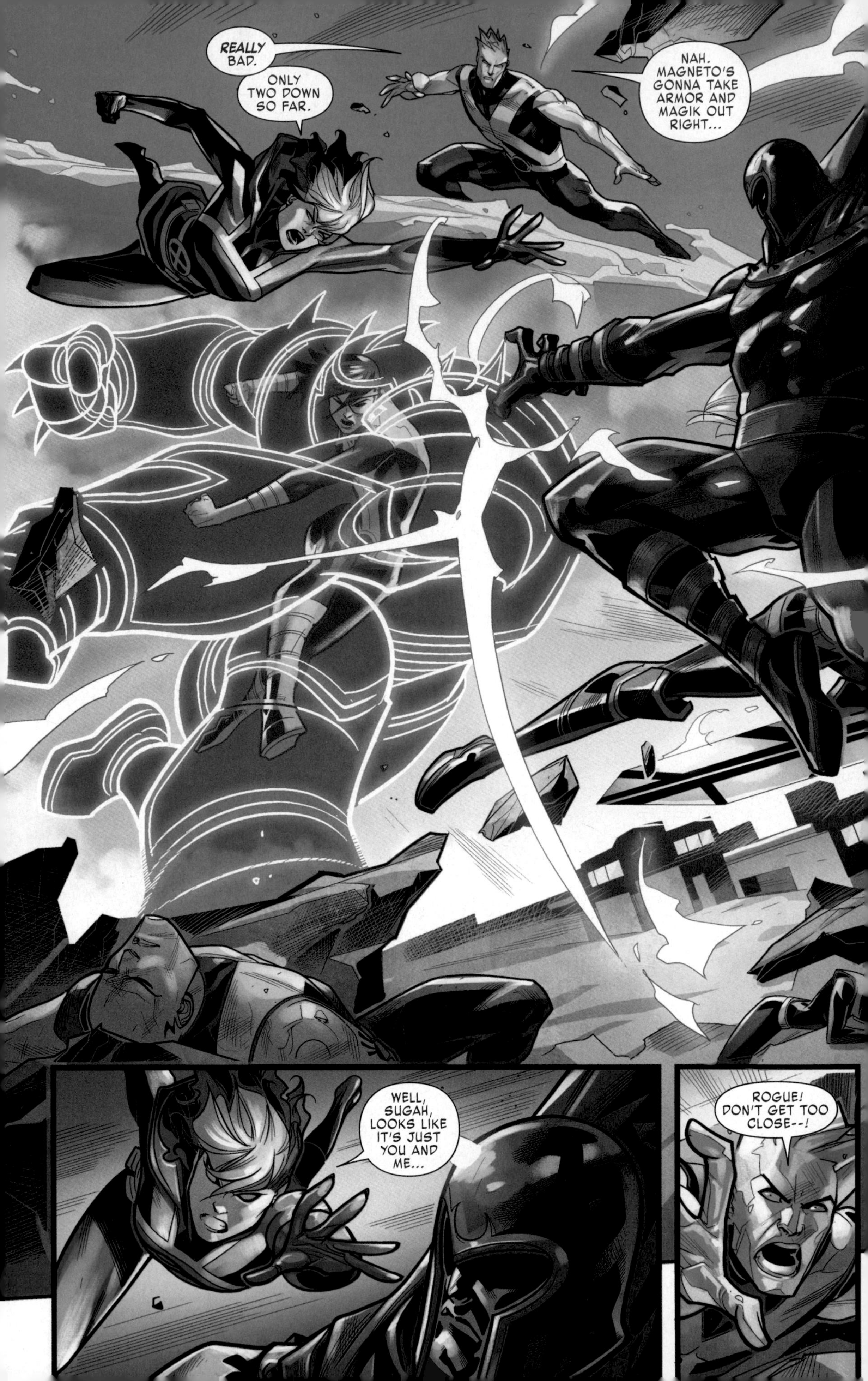
REALLY BAD.
ONLY TWO DOWN SO FAR.
NAH. MAGNETO'S GONNA TAKE ARMOR AND MAGIK OUT RIGHT...
WELL, SUGAH, LOOKS LIKE IT'S JUST YOU AND ME...
ROGUE! DON'T GET TOO CLOSE--!

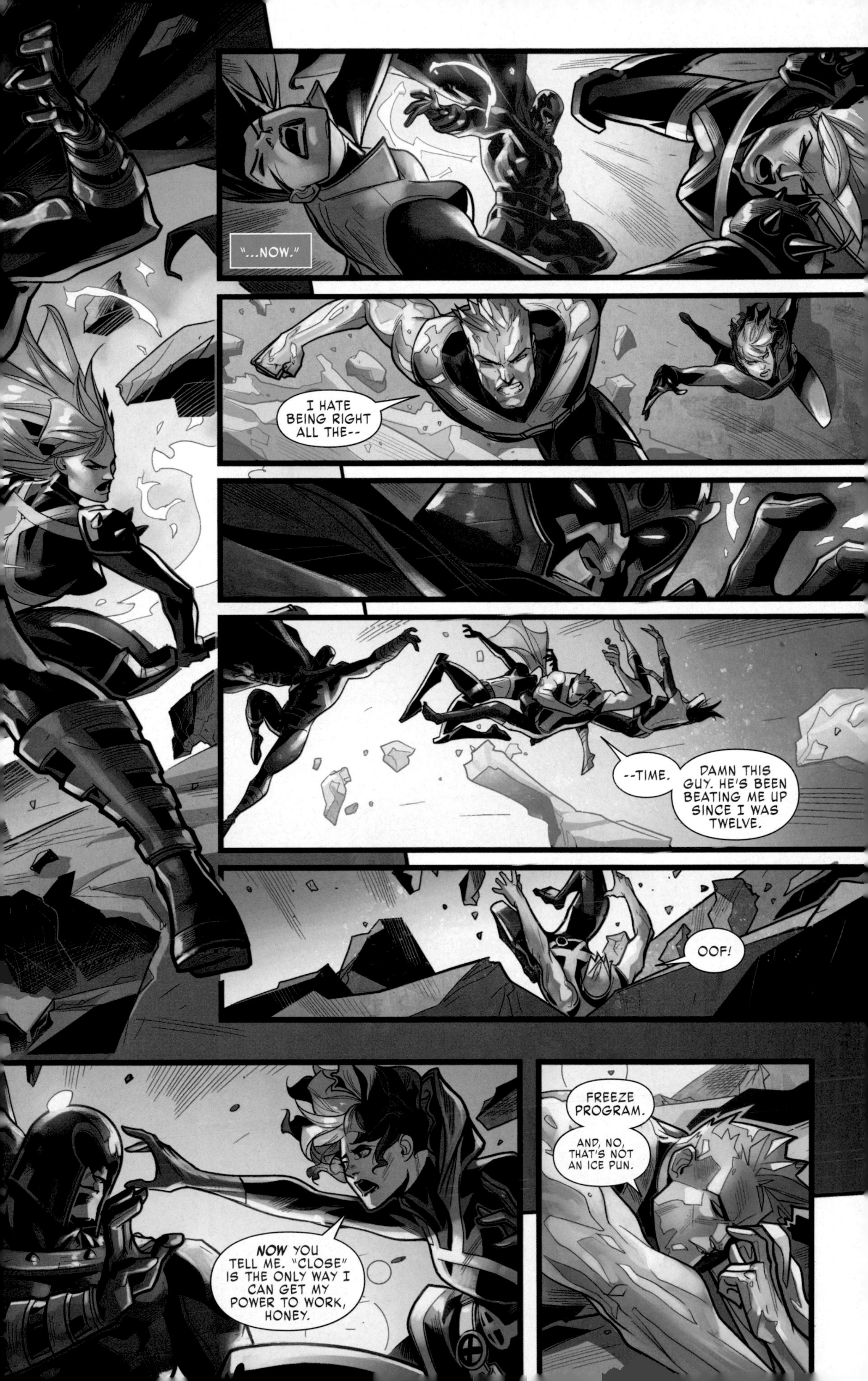
"...NOW."
I HATE BEING RIGHT ALL THE--
--TIME.
DAMN THIS GUY. HE'S BEEN BEATING ME UP SINCE I WAS TWELVE.
OOF!
NOW YOU TELL ME. "CLOSE" IS THE ONLY WAY I CAN GET MY POWER TO WORK, HONEY.
FREEZE PROGRAM.
AND, NO, THAT'S NOT AN ICE PUN.

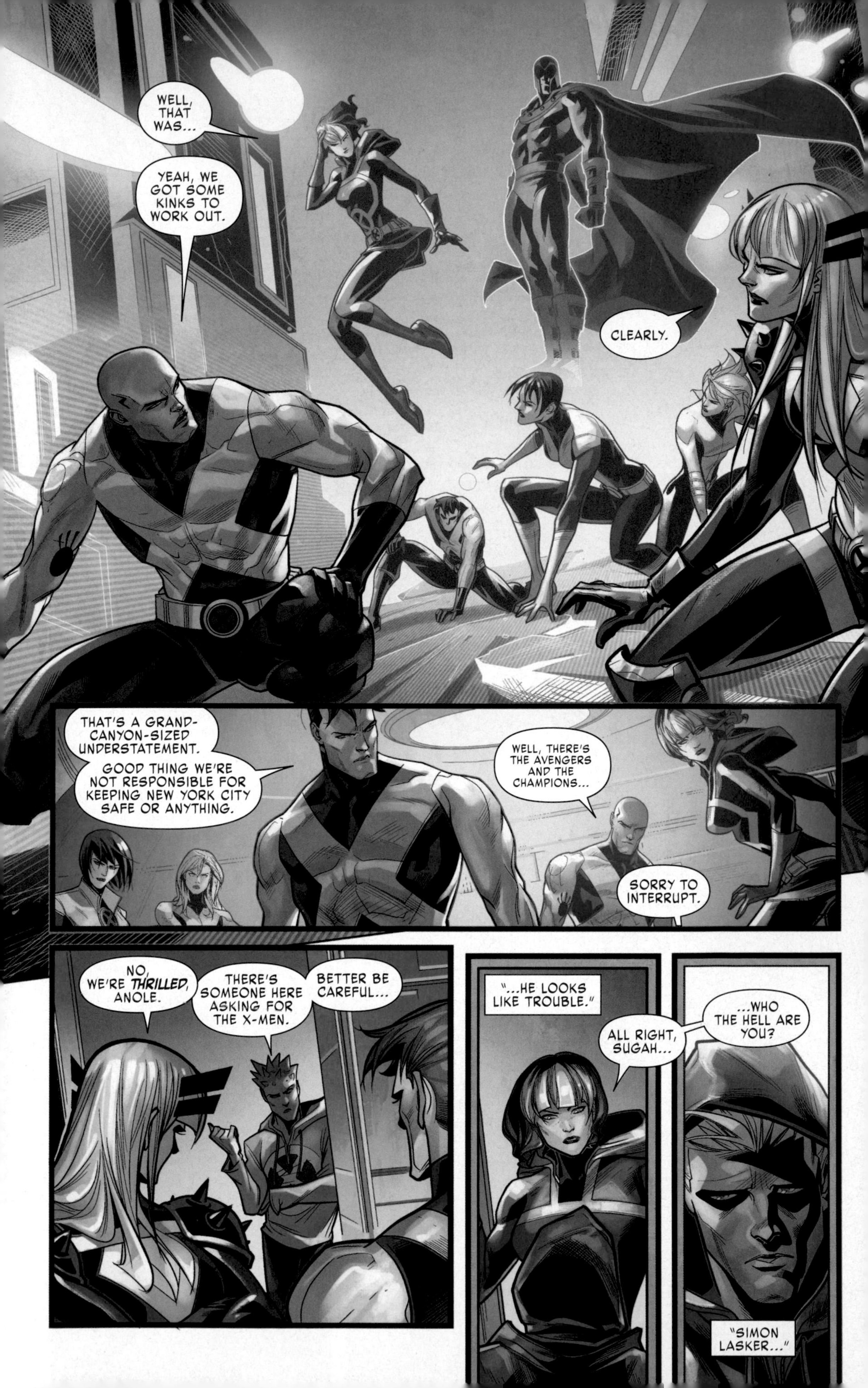

WELL, THAT WAS...
YEAH, WE GOT SOME KINKS TO WORK OUT.
CLEARLY.
THAT'S A GRAND-CANYON-SIZED UNDERSTATEMENT.
GOOD THING WE'RE NOT RESPONSIBLE FOR KEEPING NEW YORK CITY SAFE OR ANYTHING.
WELL, THERE'S THE AVENGERS AND THE CHAMPIONS...
SORRY TO INTERRUPT.
NO, WE'RE *THRILLED*, ANOLE.
THERE'S SOMEONE HERE ASKING FOR THE X-MEN.
BETTER BE CAREFUL...
"...HE LOOKS LIKE TROUBLE."
ALL RIGHT, SUGAH...
...WHO THE HELL ARE YOU?
"SIMON LASKER..."

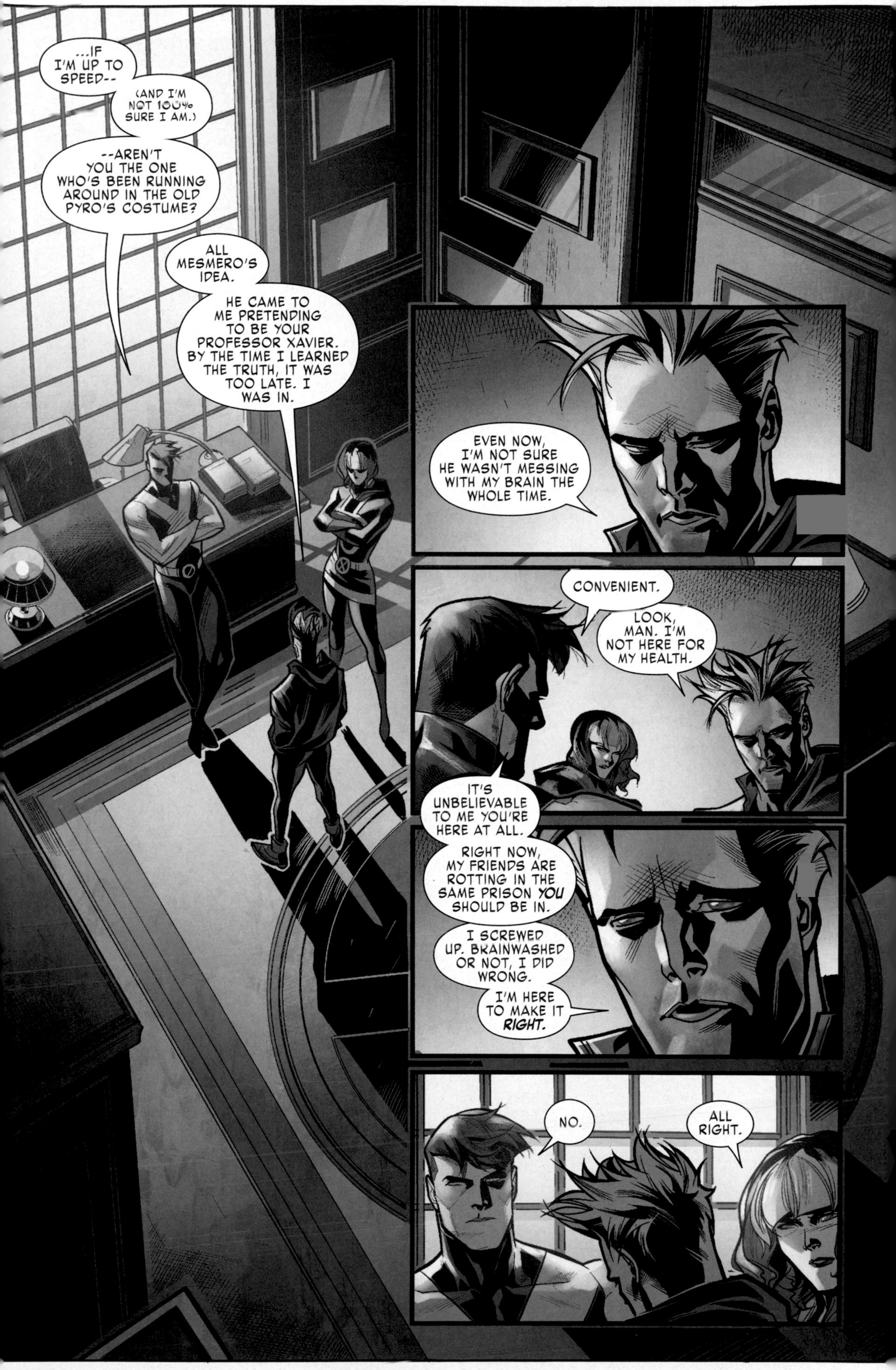
...IF I'M UP TO SPEED--
(AND I'M NOT 100% SURE I AM.)
--AREN'T YOU THE ONE WHO'S BEEN RUNNING AROUND IN THE OLD PYRO'S COSTUME?
ALL MESMERO'S IDEA.
HE CAME TO ME PRETENDING TO BE YOUR PROFESSOR XAVIER. BY THE TIME I LEARNED THE TRUTH, IT WAS TOO LATE. I WAS IN.
EVEN NOW, I'M NOT SURE HE WASN'T MESSING WITH MY BRAIN THE WHOLE TIME.
CONVENIENT.
LOOK, MAN. I'M NOT HERE FOR MY HEALTH.
IT'S UNBELIEVABLE TO ME YOU'RE HERE AT ALL.
RIGHT NOW, MY FRIENDS ARE ROTTING IN THE SAME PRISON YOU SHOULD BE IN.
I SCREWED UP. BRAINWASHED OR NOT, I DID WRONG.
I'M HERE TO MAKE IT RIGHT.
NO.
ALL RIGHT.

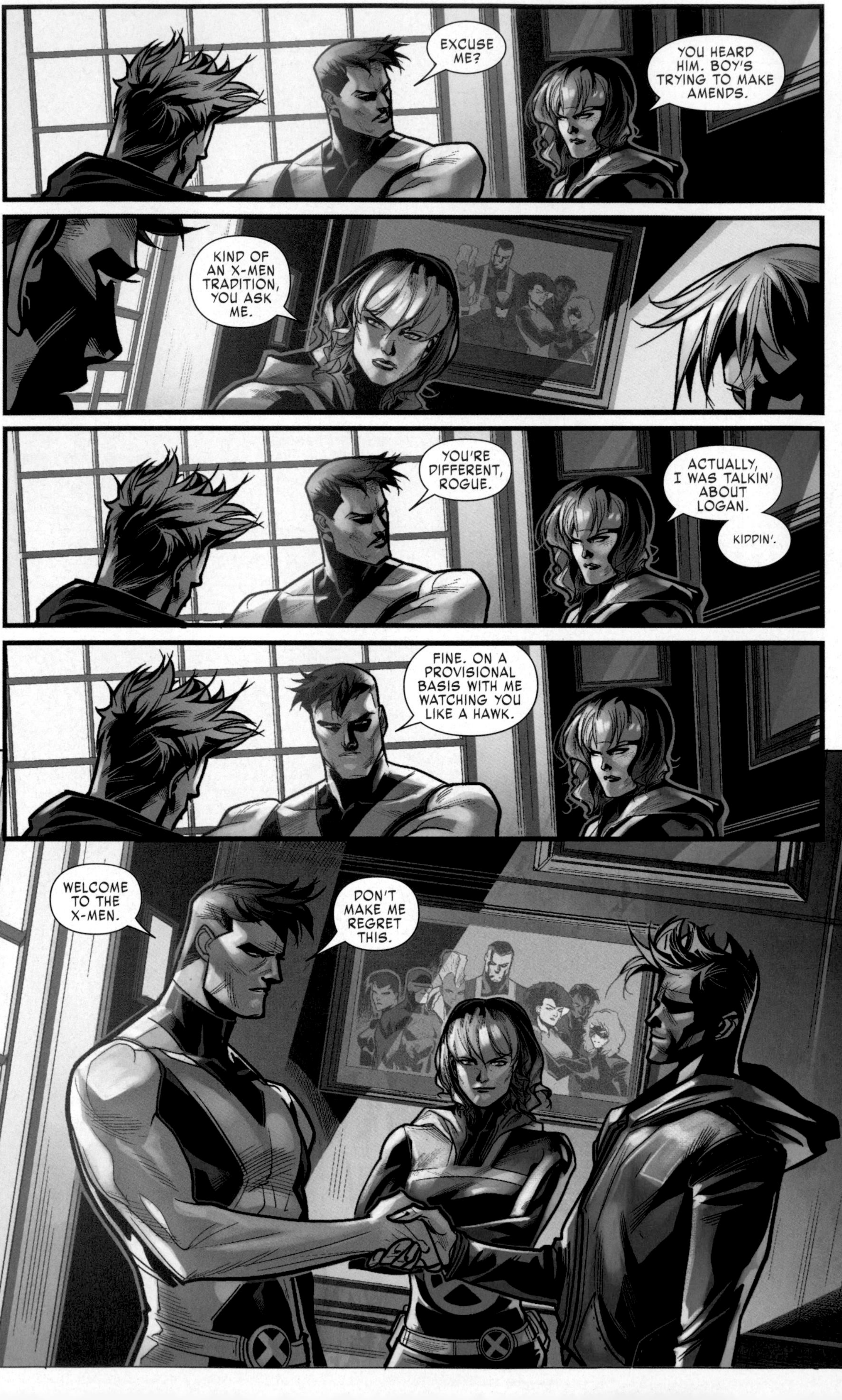
EXCUSE ME?
YOU HEARD HIM. BOY'S TRYING TO MAKE AMENDS.
KIND OF AN X-MEN TRADITION, YOU ASK ME.
YOU'RE DIFFERENT, ROGUE.
ACTUALLY, I WAS TALKIN' ABOUT LOGAN.
KIDDIN'.
FINE. ON A PROVISIONAL BASIS WITH ME WATCHING YOU LIKE A HAWK.
WELCOME TO THE X-MEN.
DON'T MAKE ME REGRET THIS.

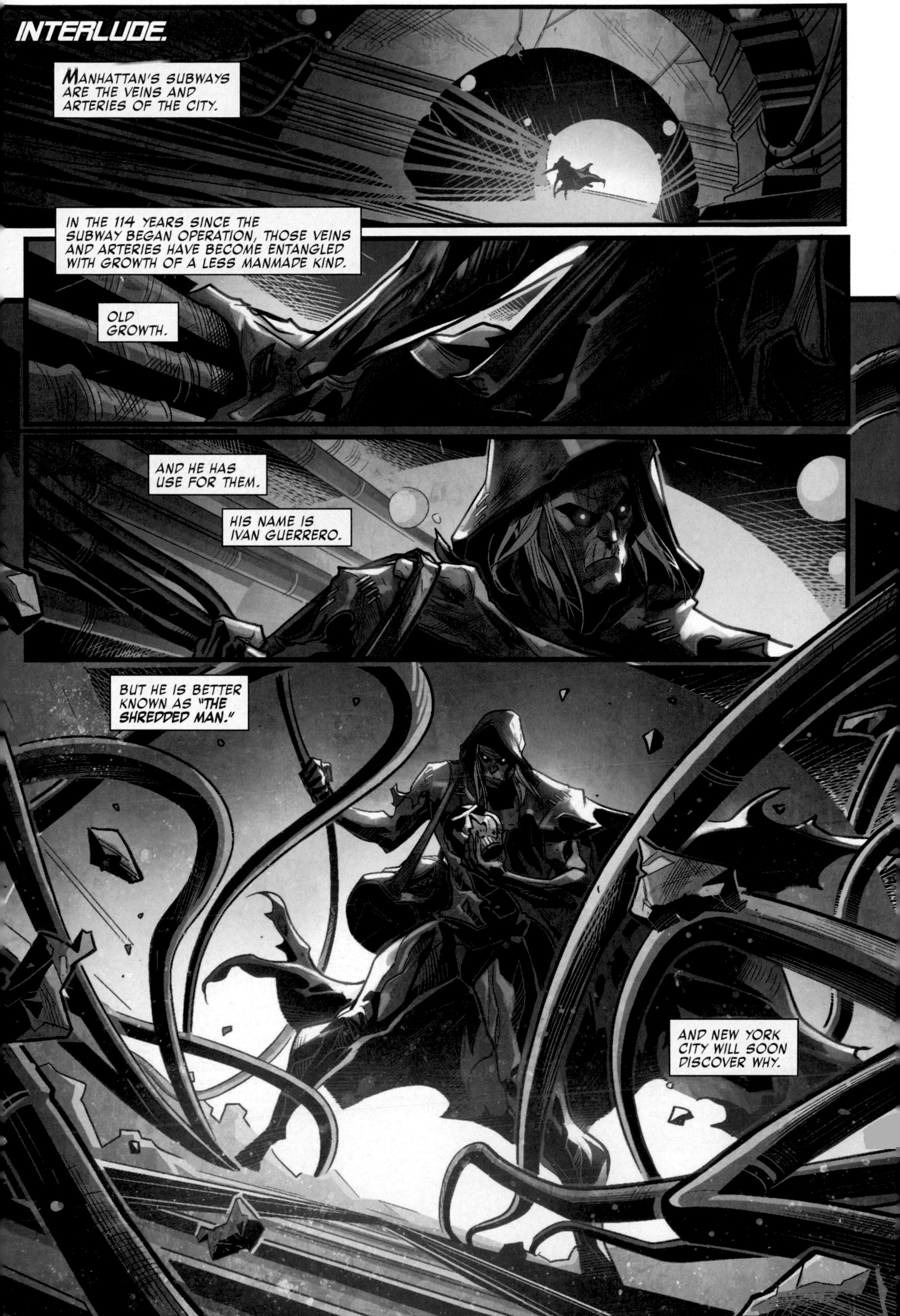
INTERLUDE.
MANHATTAN'S SUBWAYS ARE THE VEINS AND ARTERIES OF THE CITY.
IN THE 114 YEARS SINCE THE SUBWAY BEGAN OPERATION, THOSE VEINS AND ARTERIES HAVE BECOME ENTANGLED WITH GROWTH OF A LESS MANMADE KIND.
OLD GROWTH.
AND HE HAS USE FOR THEM.
HIS NAME IS IVAN GUERRERO.
BUT HE IS BETTER KNOWN AS "THE SHREDDED MAN."
AND NEW YORK CITY WILL SOON DISCOVER WHY.
END OF INTERLUDE.

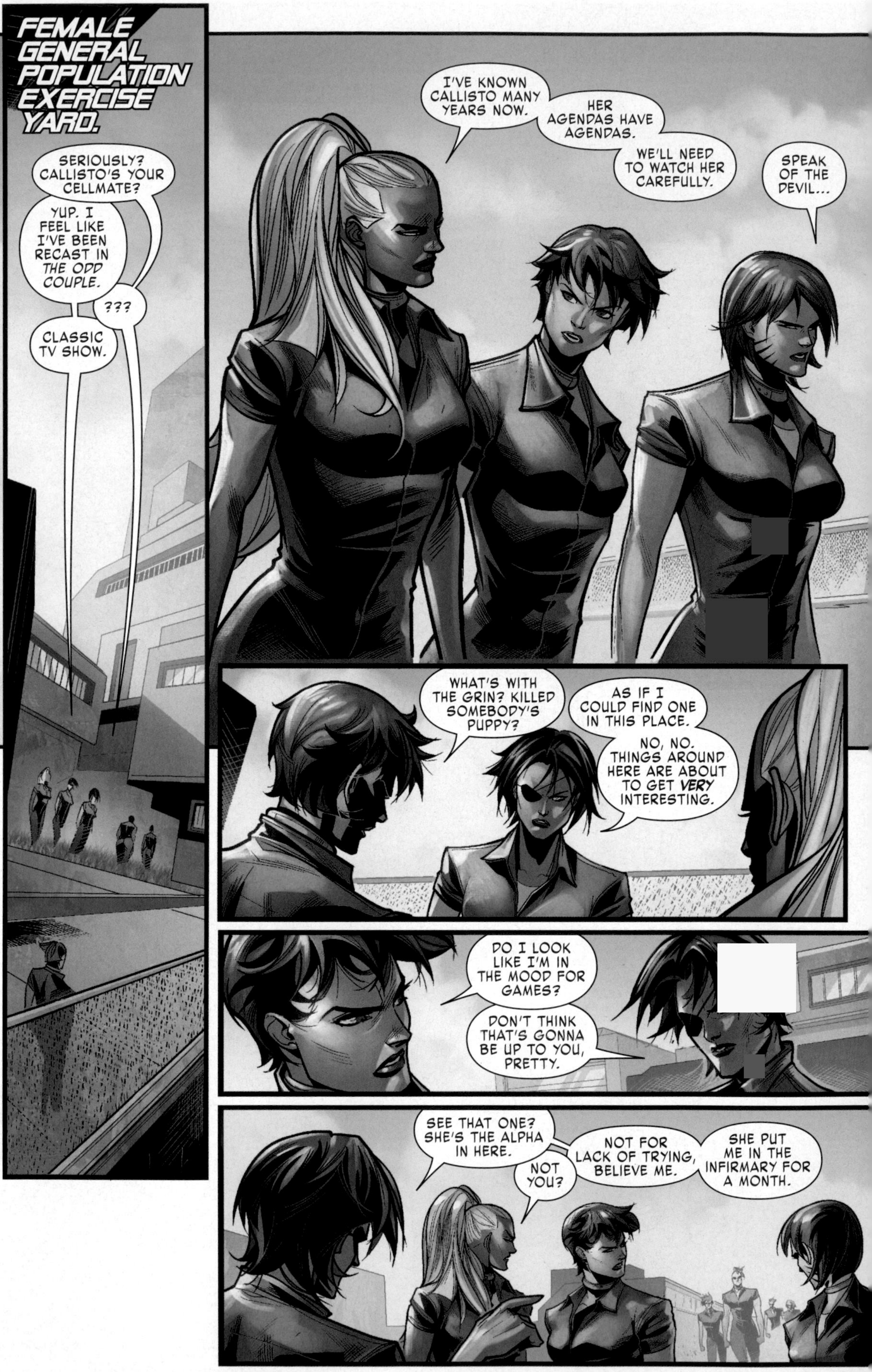
FEMALE GENERAL POPULATION EXERCISE YARD.
SERIOUSLY? CALLISTO'S YOUR CELLMATE?
YUP. I FEEL LIKE I'VE BEEN RECAST IN THE ODD COUPLE.
???
CLASSIC TV SHOW.
I'VE KNOWN CALLISTO MANY YEARS NOW.
HER AGENDAS HAVE AGENDAS.
WE'LL NEED TO WATCH HER CAREFULLY.
SPEAK OF THE DEVIL...
WHAT'S WITH THE GRIN? KILLED SOMEBODY'S PUPPY?
AS IF I COULD FIND ONE IN THIS PLACE.
NO, NO. THINGS AROUND HERE ARE ABOUT TO GET VERY INTERESTING.
DO I LOOK LIKE I'M IN THE MOOD FOR GAMES?
DON'T THINK THAT'S GONNA BE UP TO YOU, PRETTY.
SEE THAT ONE? SHE'S THE ALPHA IN HERE.
NOT YOU?
NOT FOR LACK OF TRYING, BELIEVE ME.
SHE PUT ME IN THE INFIRMARY FOR A MONTH.

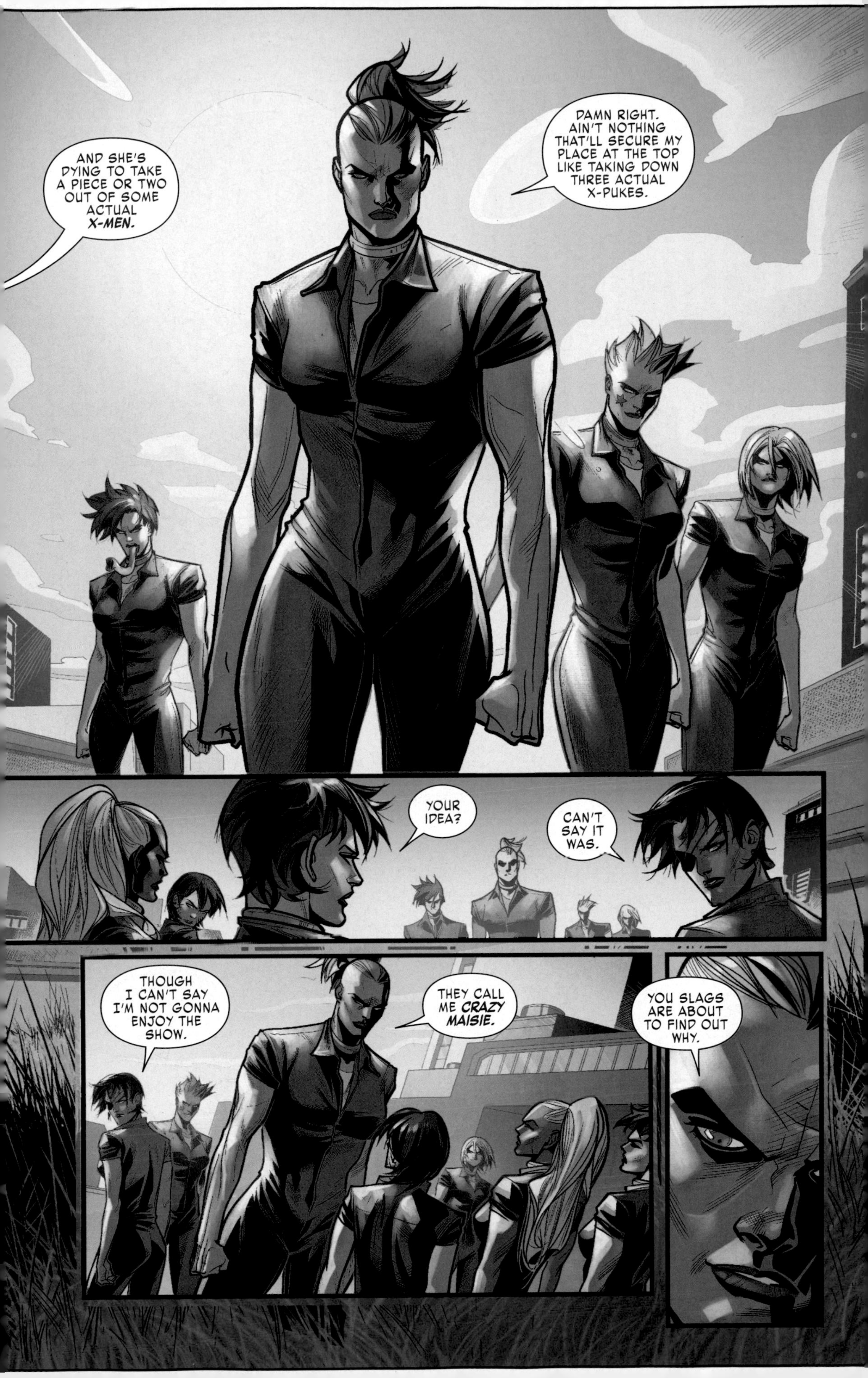
AND SHE'S DYING TO TAKE A PIECE OR TWO OUT OF SOME ACTUAL X-MEN.
DAMN RIGHT. AIN'T NOTHING THAT'LL SECURE MY PLACE AT THE TOP LIKE TAKING DOWN THREE ACTUAL X-PUKES.
YOUR IDEA?
CAN'T SAY IT WAS.
THOUGH I CAN'T SAY I'M NOT GONNA ENJOY THE SHOW.
THEY CALL ME CRAZY MAISIE.
YOU SLAGS ARE ABOUT TO FIND OUT WHY.

24

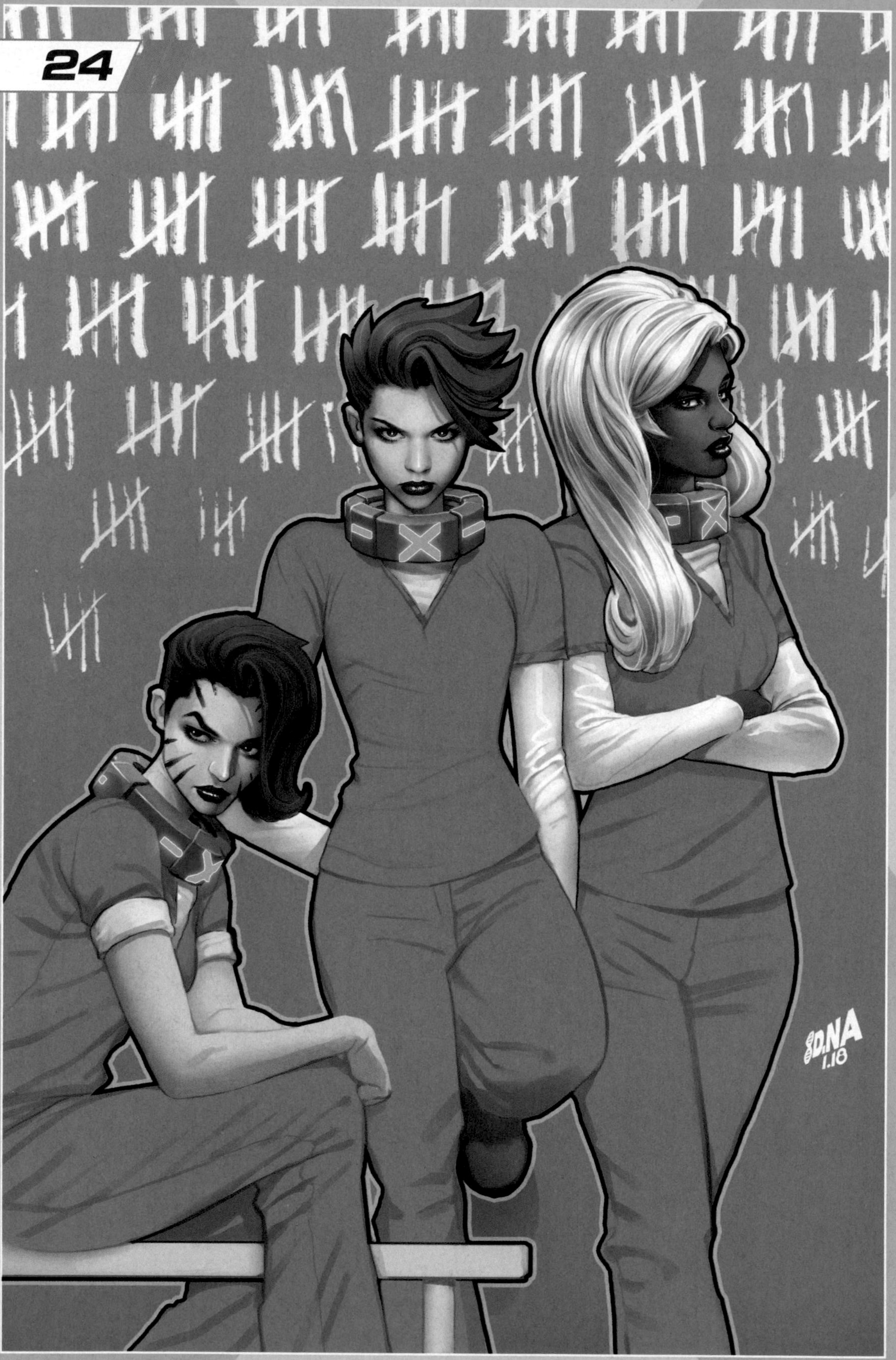
D.NA
1.18

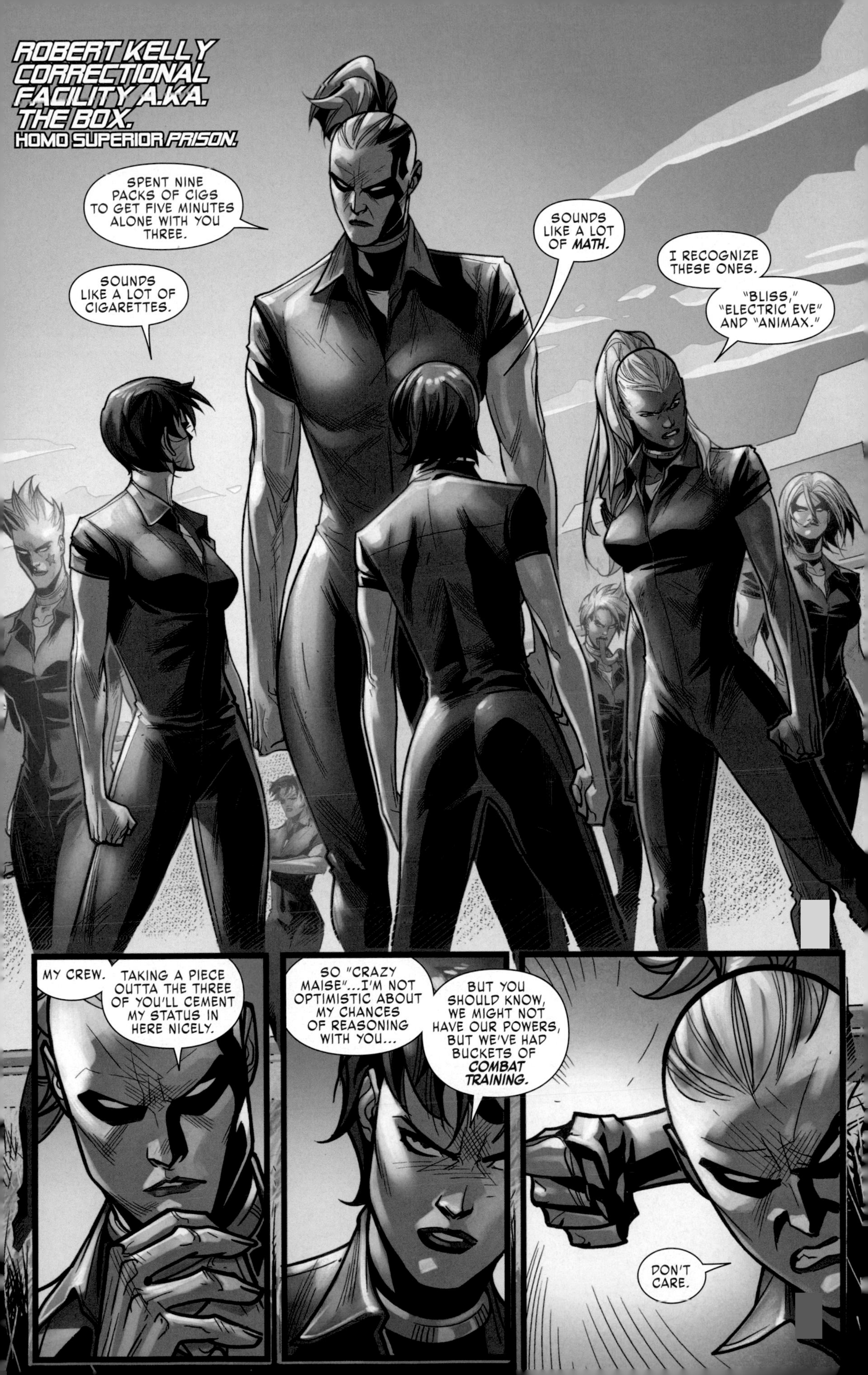
ROBERT KELLY CORRECTIONAL FACILITY A.K.A. THE BOX.
HOMO SUPERIOR PRISON.
SPENT NINE PACKS OF CIGS TO GET FIVE MINUTES ALONE WITH YOU THREE.
SOUNDS LIKE A LOT OF CIGARETTES.
SOUNDS LIKE A LOT OF MATH.
I RECOGNIZE THESE ONES.
"BLISS," "ELECTRIC EVE" AND "ANIMAX."
MY CREW.
TAKING A PIECE OUTTA THE THREE OF YOU'LL CEMENT MY STATUS IN HERE NICELY.
SO "CRAZY MAISE"...I'M NOT OPTIMISTIC ABOUT MY CHANCES OF REASONING WITH YOU...
BUT YOU SHOULD KNOW, WE MIGHT NOT HAVE OUR POWERS, BUT WE'VE HAD BUCKETS OF COMBAT TRAINING.
DON'T CARE.

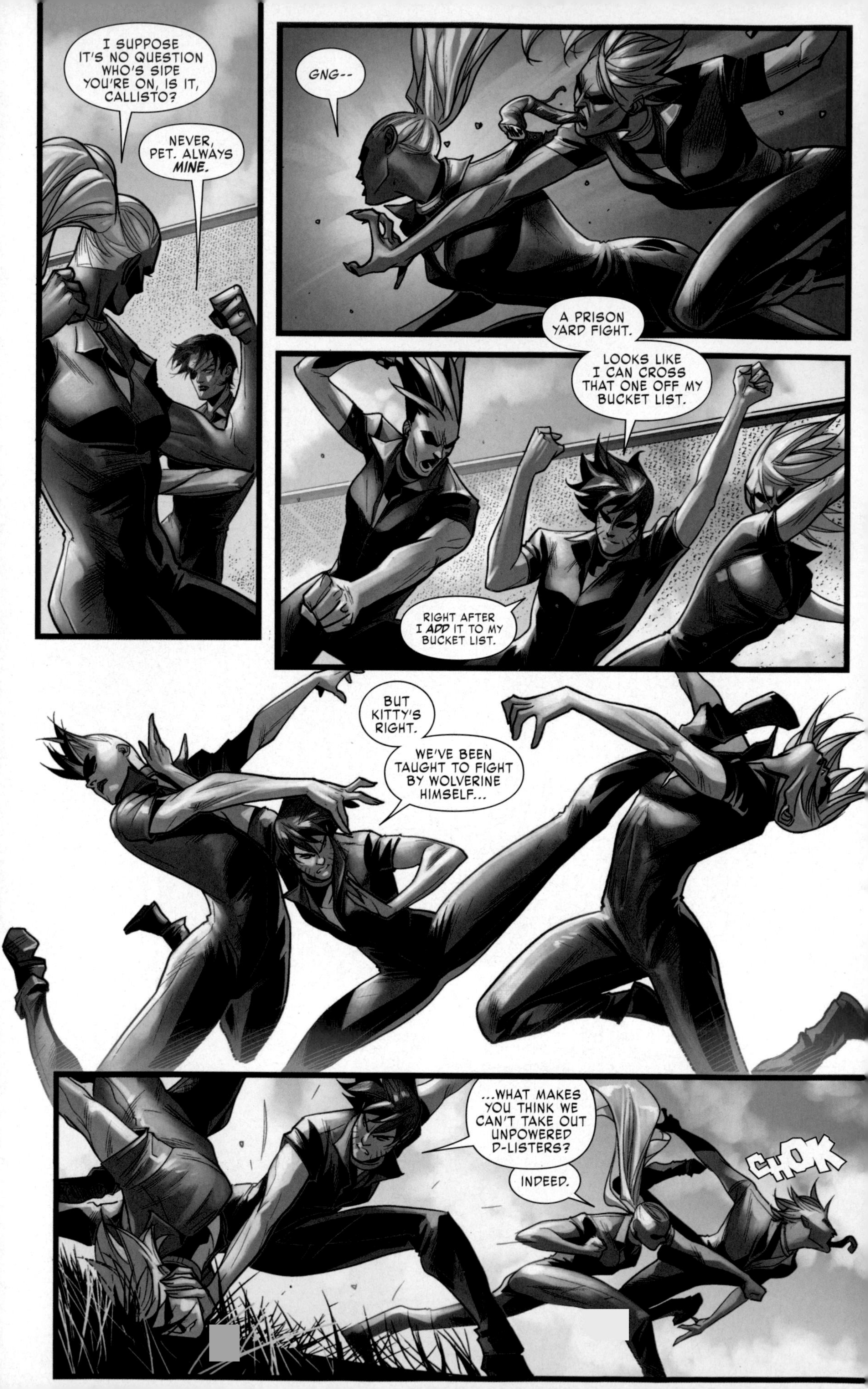
I SUPPOSE IT'S NO QUESTION WHO'S SIDE YOU'RE ON, IS IT, CALLISTO?
NEVER, PET. ALWAYS MINE.
GNG--
A PRISON YARD FIGHT.
LOOKS LIKE I CAN CROSS THAT ONE OFF MY BUCKET LIST.
RIGHT AFTER I ADD IT TO MY BUCKET LIST.
BUT KITTY'S RIGHT.
WE'VE BEEN TAUGHT TO FIGHT BY WOLVERINE HIMSELF...
...WHAT MAKES YOU THINK WE CAN'T TAKE OUT UNPOWERED D-LISTERS?
INDEED.
CHOK

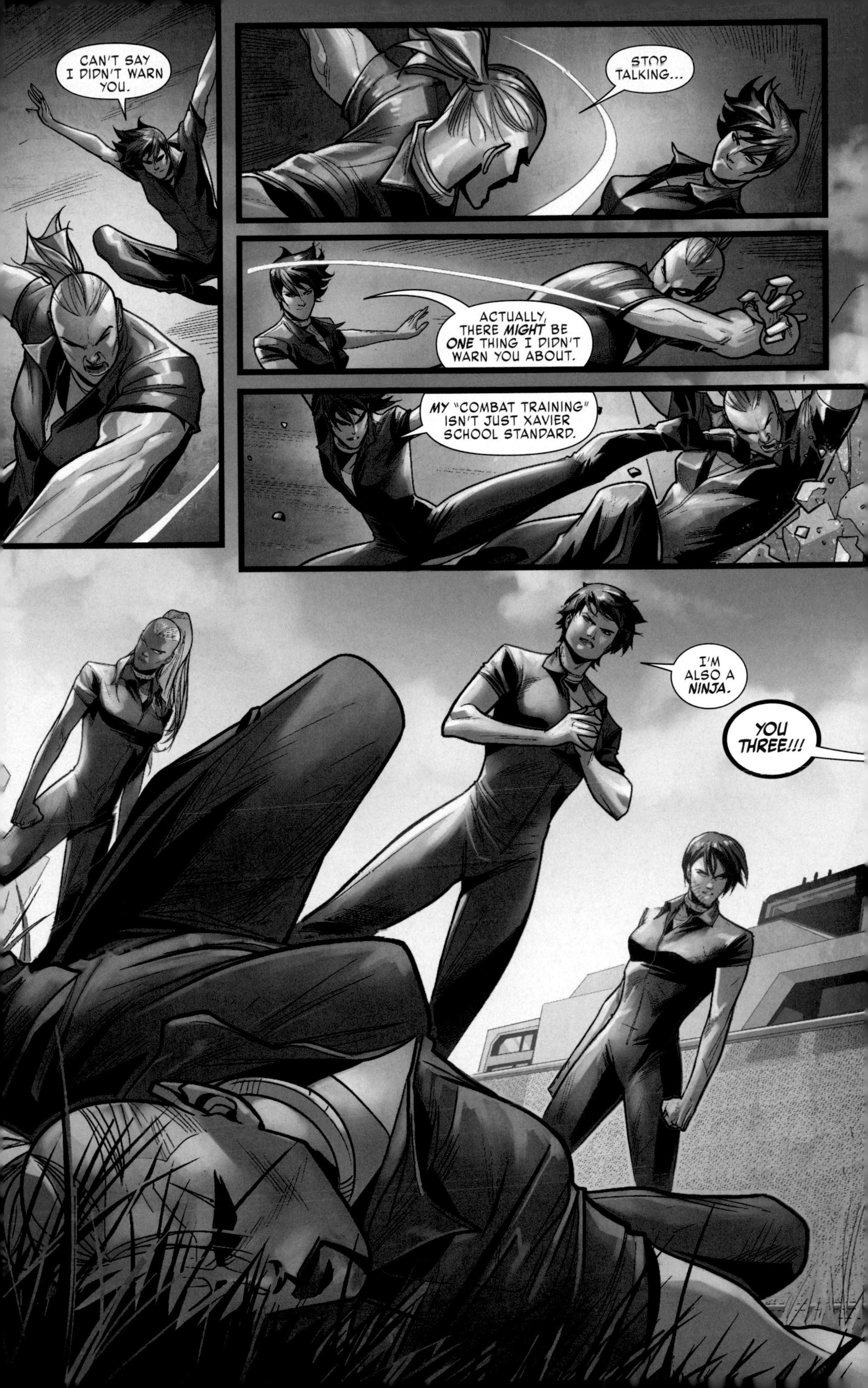
CAN'T SAY I DIDN'T WARN YOU.
STOP TALKING...
ACTUALLY, THERE MIGHT BE ONE THING I DIDN'T WARN YOU ABOUT.
MY "COMBAT TRAINING" ISN'T JUST XAVIER SCHOOL STANDARD.
I'M ALSO A NINJA.
YOU THREE!!!

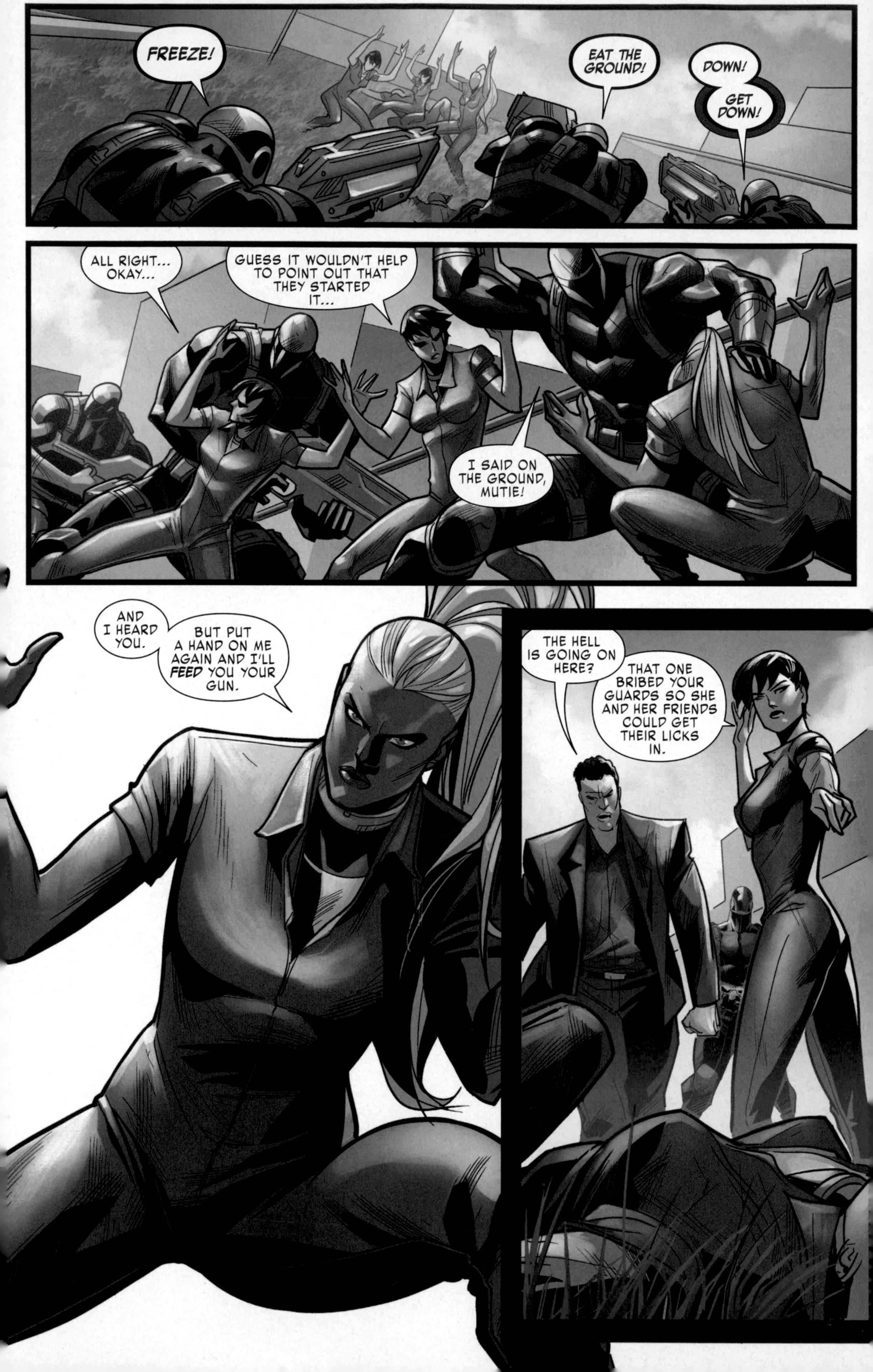
FREEZE!
EAT THE GROUND!
DOWN!
GET DOWN!
ALL RIGHT... OKAY...
GUESS IT WOULDN'T HELP TO POINT OUT THAT THEY STARTED IT...
I SAID ON THE GROUND, MUTIE!
AND I HEARD YOU.
BUT PUT A HAND ON ME AGAIN AND I'LL FEED YOU YOUR GUN.
THE HELL IS GOING ON HERE?
THAT ONE BRIBED YOUR GUARDS SO SHE AND HER FRIENDS COULD GET THEIR LICKS IN.

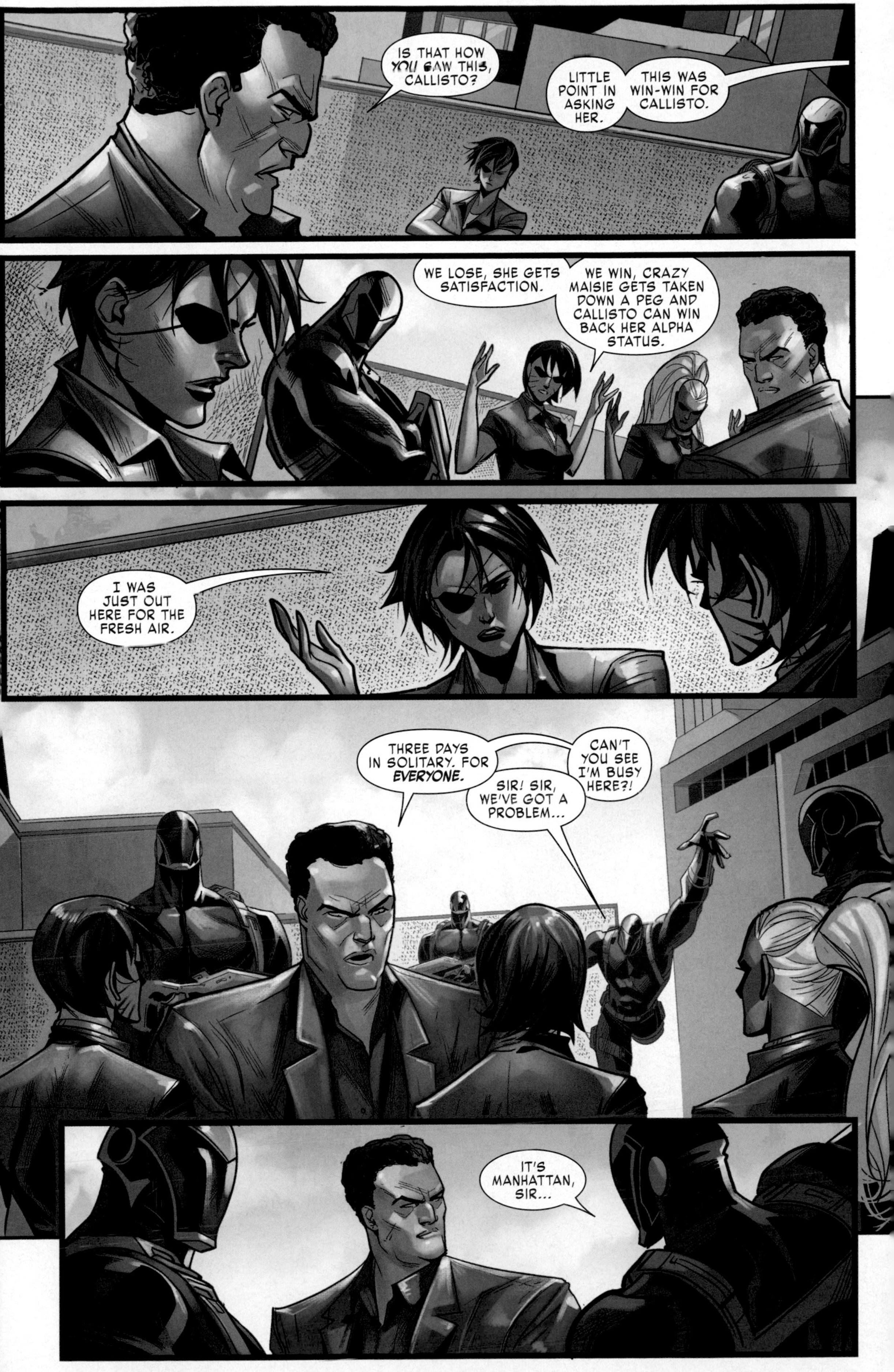
IS THAT HOW YOU SAW THIS, CALLISTO?
LITTLE POINT IN ASKING HER.
THIS WAS WIN-WIN FOR CALLISTO.
WE LOSE, SHE GETS SATISFACTION.
WE WIN, CRAZY MAISIE GETS TAKEN DOWN A PEG AND CALLISTO CAN WIN BACK HER ALPHA STATUS.
I WAS JUST OUT HERE FOR THE FRESH AIR.
THREE DAYS IN SOLITARY. FOR EVERYONE.
SIR! SIR, WE'VE GOT A PROBLEM...
CAN'T YOU SEE I'M BUSY HERE?!
IT'S MANHATTAN, SIR...

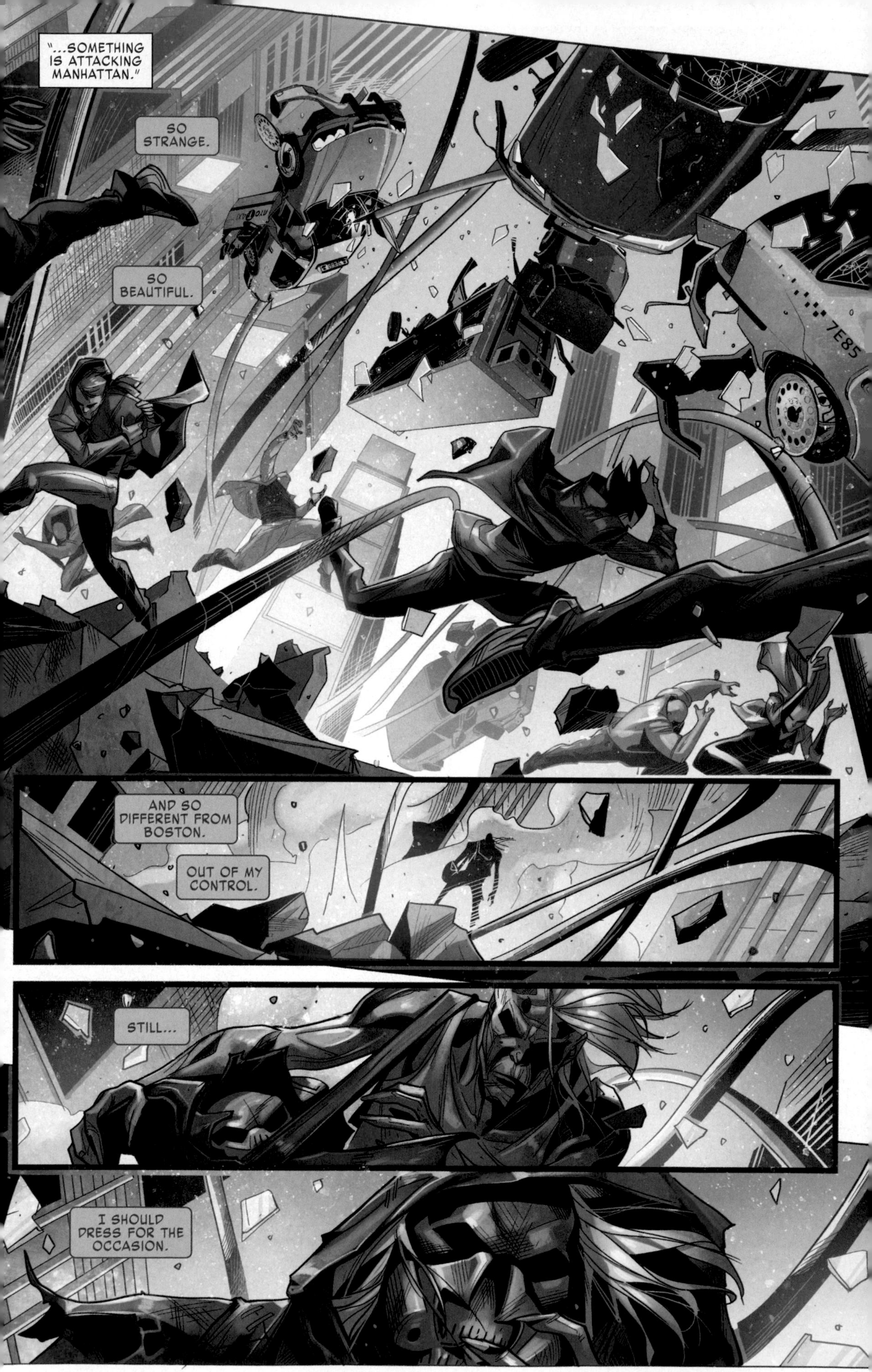
"...SOMETHING IS ATTACKING MANHATTAN."
SO STRANGE.
SO BEAUTIFUL.
7E85
AND SO DIFFERENT FROM BOSTON.
OUT OF MY CONTROL.
STILL...
I SHOULD DRESS FOR THE OCCASION.

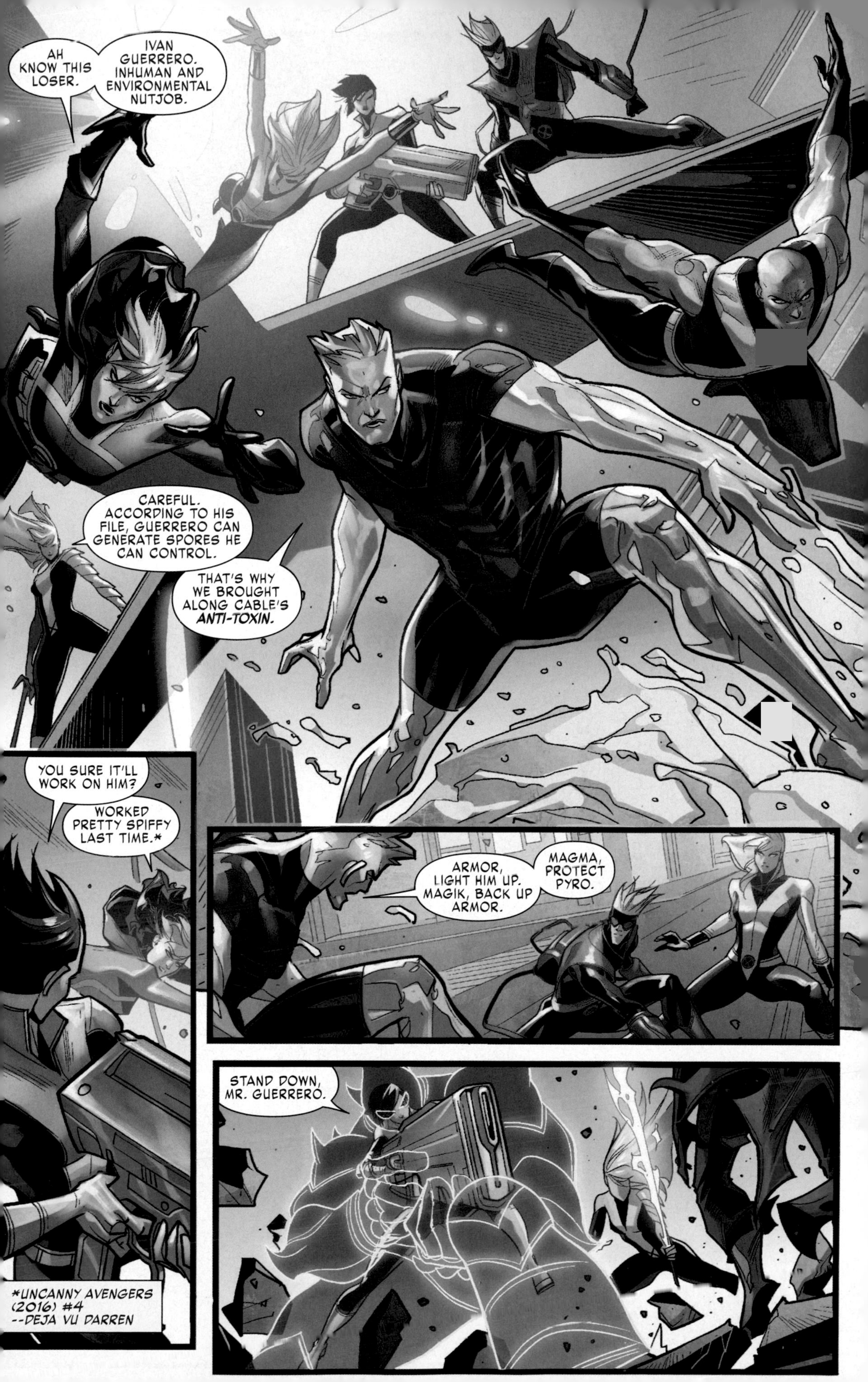
AH KNOW THIS LOSER.
IVAN GUERRERO. INHUMAN AND ENVIRONMENTAL NUTJOB.
CAREFUL. ACCORDING TO HIS FILE, GUERRERO CAN GENERATE SPORES HE CAN CONTROL.
THAT'S WHY WE BROUGHT ALONG CABLE'S ANTI-TOXIN.
YOU SURE IT'LL WORK ON HIM?
WORKED PRETTY SPIFFY LAST TIME.*
*UNCANNY AVENGERS (2016) #4 --DEJA VU DARREN
ARMOR, LIGHT HIM UP. MAGIK, BACK UP ARMOR.
MAGMA, PROTECT PYRO.
STAND DOWN, MR. GUERRERO.

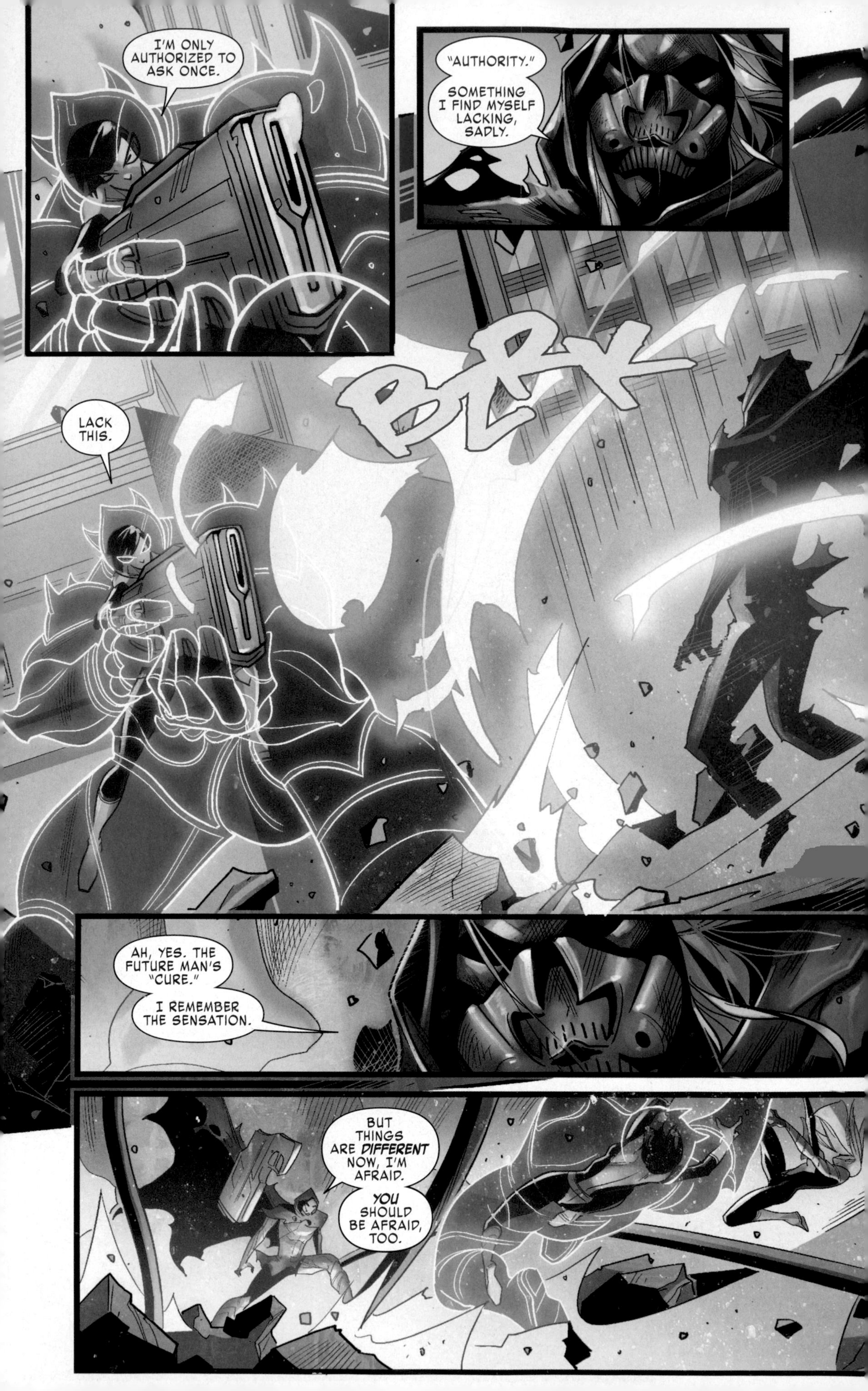
I'M ONLY AUTHORIZED TO ASK ONCE.
"AUTHORITY."
SOMETHING I FIND MYSELF LACKING, SADLY.
LACK THIS.
BZZK
AH, YES. THE FUTURE MAN'S "CURE."
I REMEMBER THE SENSATION.
BUT THINGS ARE *DIFFERENT* NOW, I'M AFRAID.
YOU SHOULD BE AFRAID, TOO.

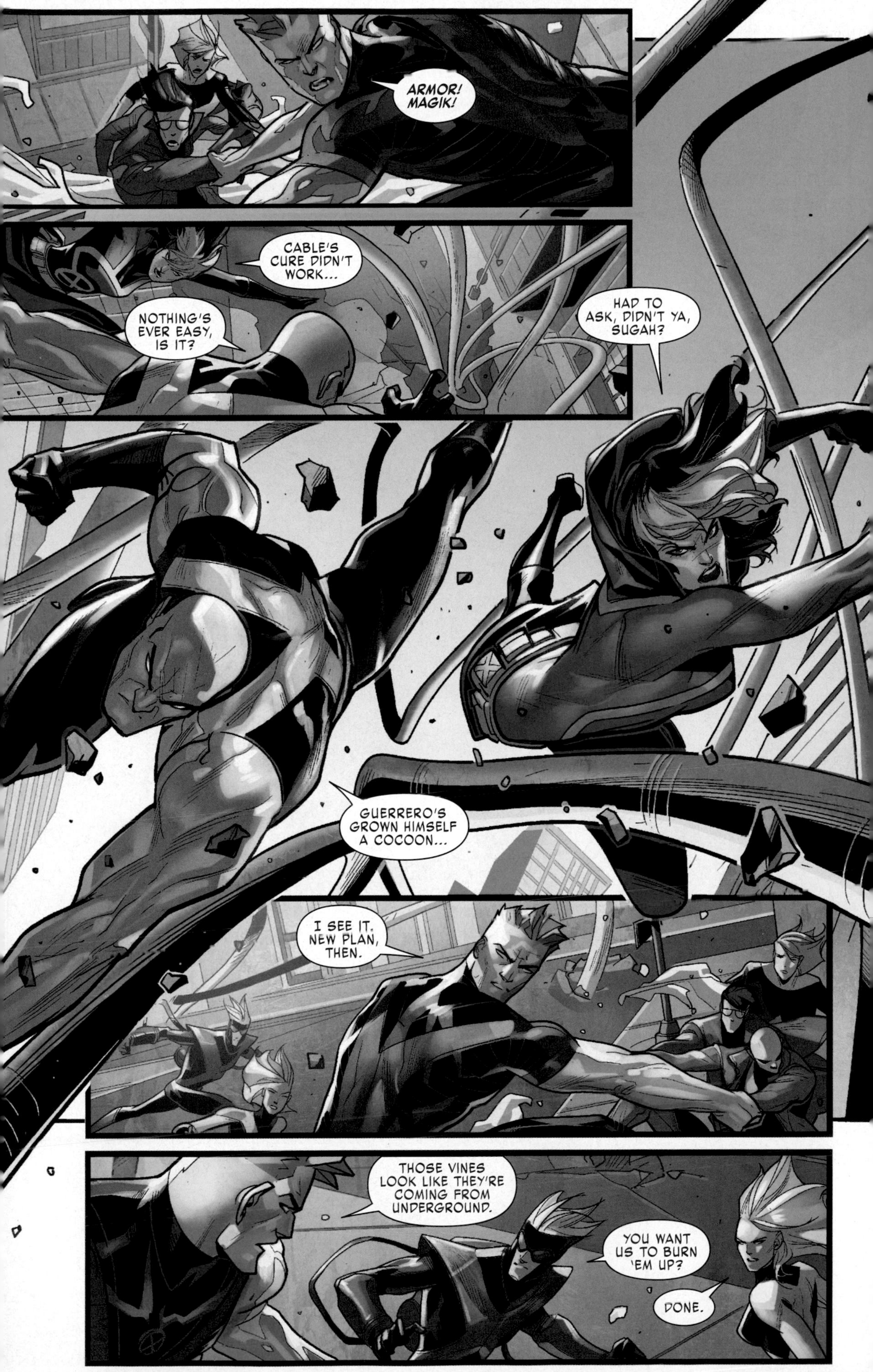
ARMOR! MAGIK!
CABLE'S CURE DIDN'T WORK...
NOTHING'S EVER EASY, IS IT?
HAD TO ASK, DIDN'T YA, SUGAH?
GUERRERO'S GROWN HIMSELF A COCOON...
I SEE IT. NEW PLAN, THEN.
THOSE VINES LOOK LIKE THEY'RE COMING FROM UNDERGROUND.
YOU WANT US TO BURN 'EM UP?
DONE.

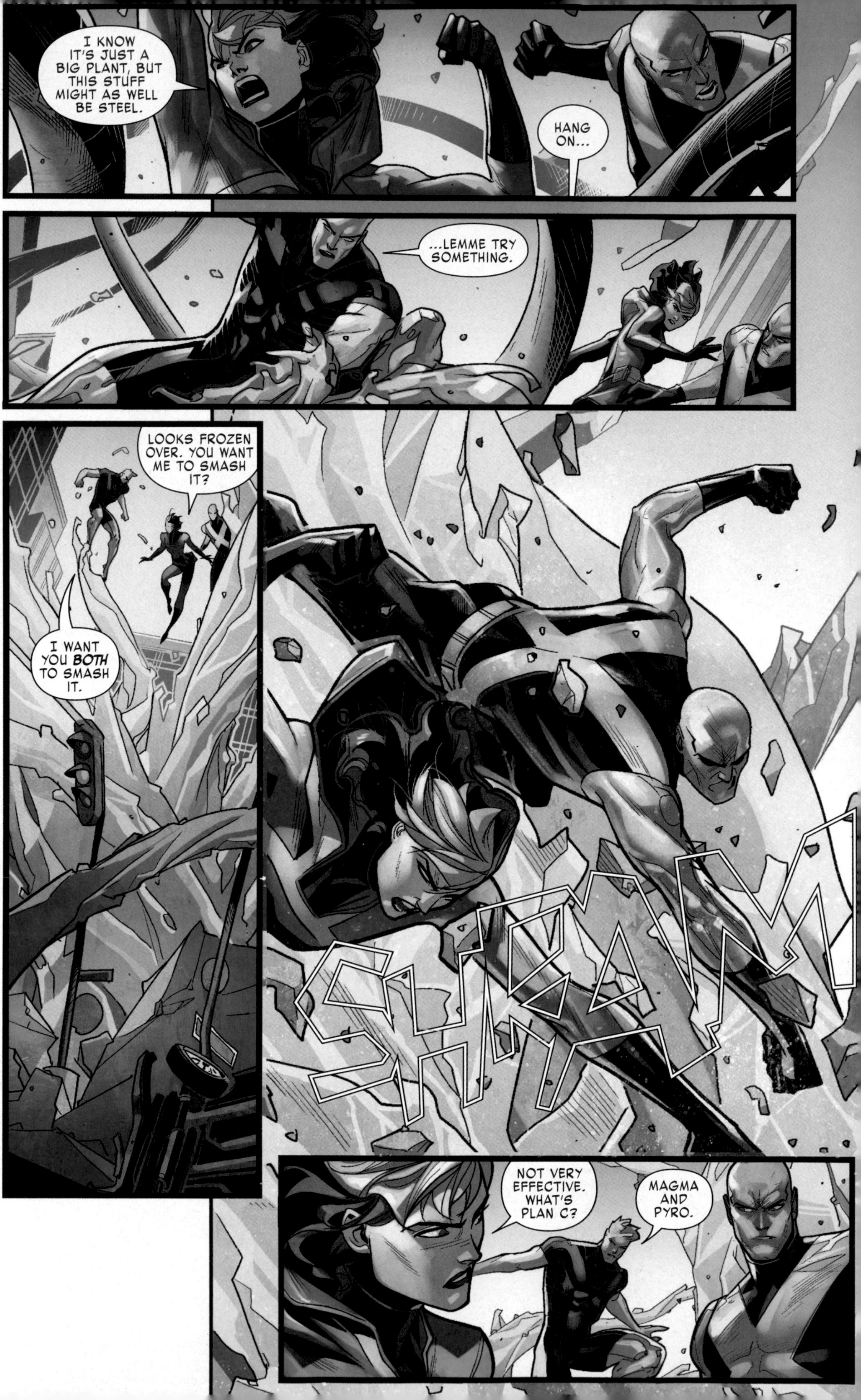
I KNOW IT'S JUST A BIG PLANT, BUT THIS STUFF MIGHT AS WELL BE STEEL.
HANG ON...
...LEMME TRY SOMETHING.
LOOKS FROZEN OVER. YOU WANT ME TO SMASH IT?
I WANT YOU **BOTH** TO SMASH IT.
NOT VERY EFFECTIVE. WHAT'S PLAN C?
MAGMA AND PYRO.

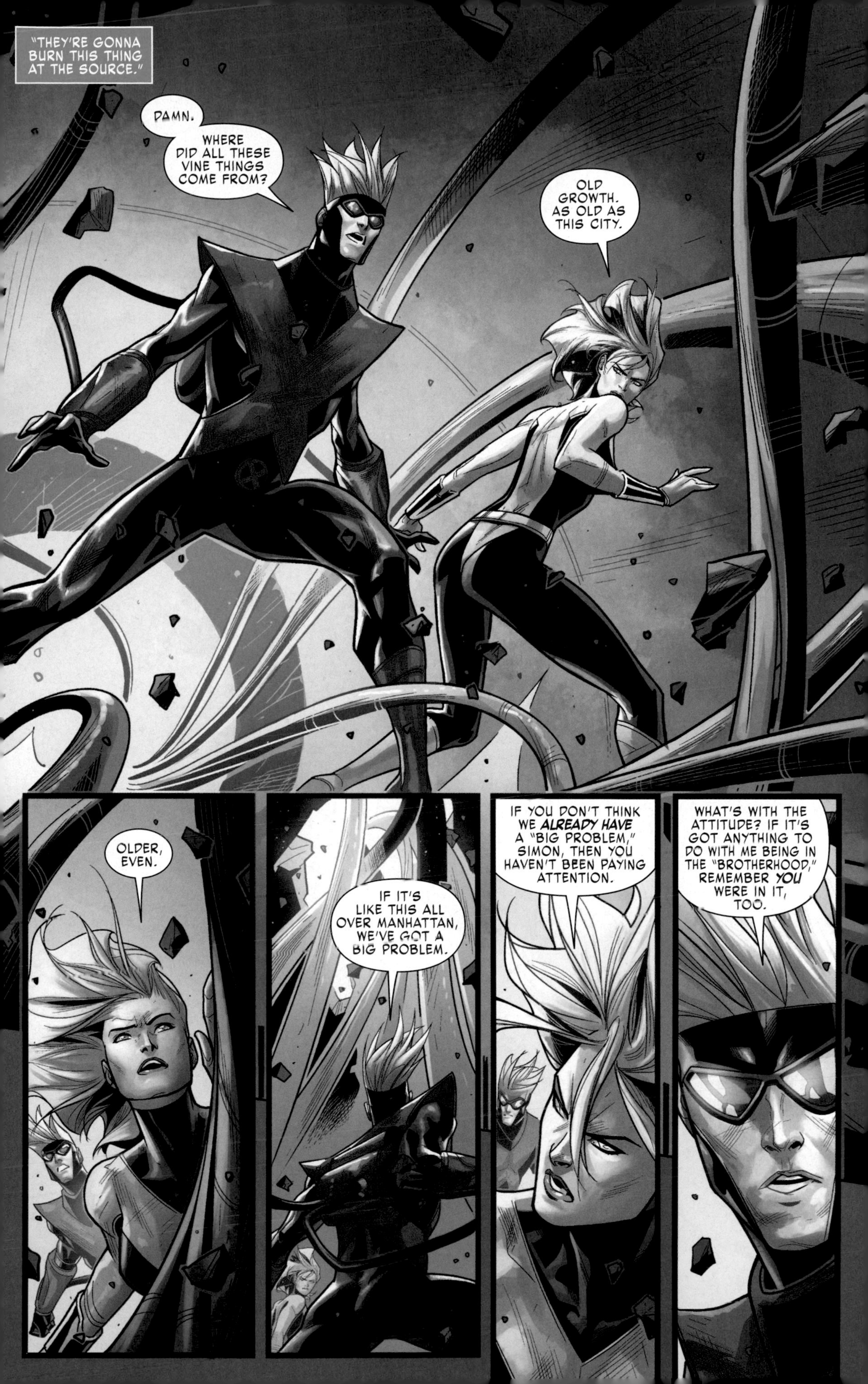
"THEY'RE GONNA BURN THIS THING AT THE SOURCE."
DAMN.
WHERE DID ALL THESE VINE THINGS COME FROM?
OLD GROWTH. AS OLD AS THIS CITY.
OLDER, EVEN.
IF IT'S LIKE THIS ALL OVER MANHATTAN, WE'VE GOT A BIG PROBLEM.
IF YOU DON'T THINK WE *ALREADY HAVE* A "BIG PROBLEM," SIMON, THEN YOU HAVEN'T BEEN PAYING ATTENTION.
WHAT'S WITH THE ATTITUDE? IF IT'S GOT ANYTHING TO DO WITH ME BEING IN THE "BROTHERHOOD," REMEMBER *YOU* WERE IN IT, TOO.

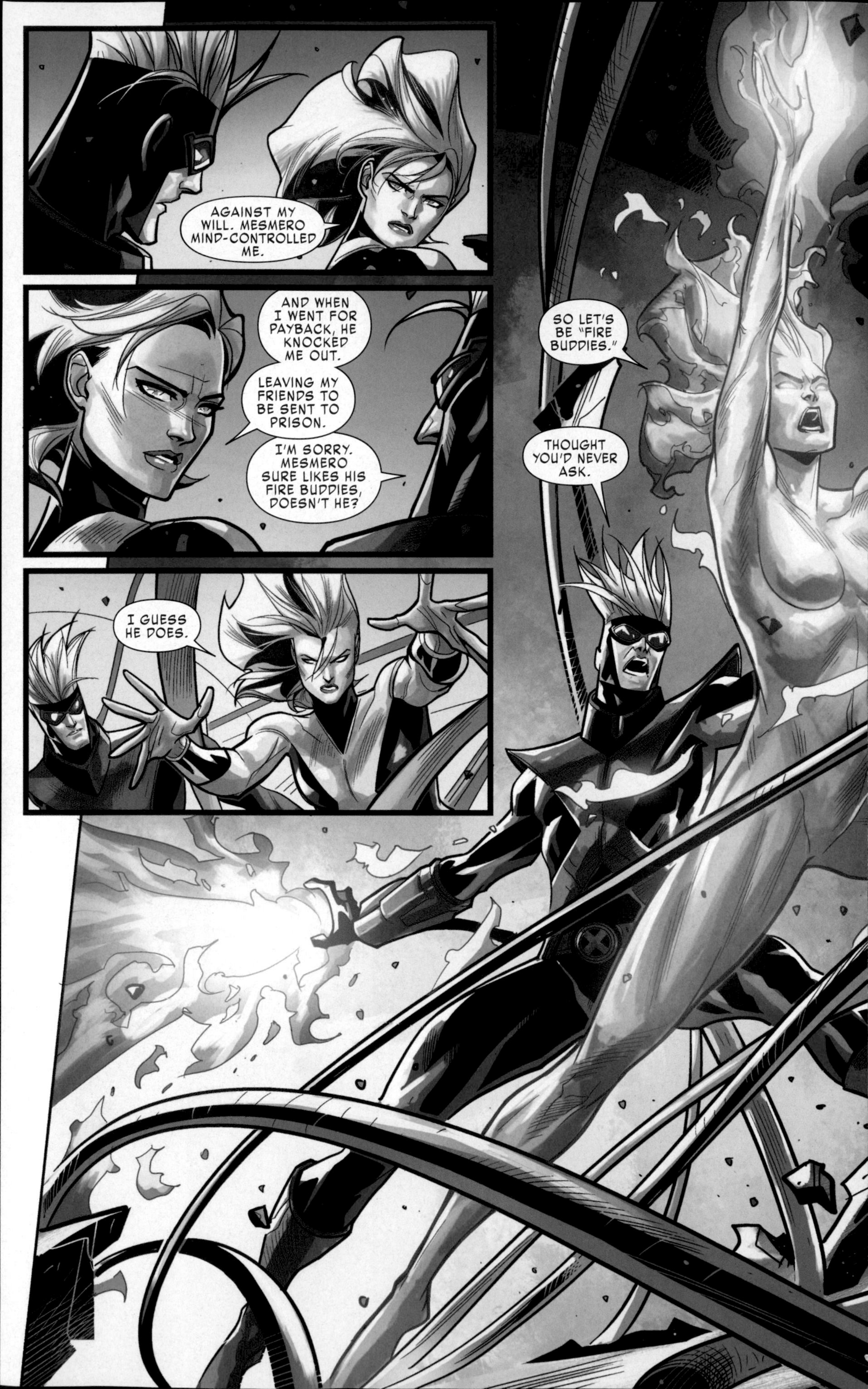

AGAINST MY WILL. MESMERO MIND-CONTROLLED ME.
AND WHEN I WENT FOR PAYBACK, HE KNOCKED ME OUT.
LEAVING MY FRIENDS TO BE SENT TO PRISON.
I'M SORRY. MESMERO SURE LIKES HIS FIRE BUDDIES, DOESN'T HE?
I GUESS HE DOES.
SO LET'S BE "FIRE BUDDIES."
THOUGHT YOU'D NEVER ASK.

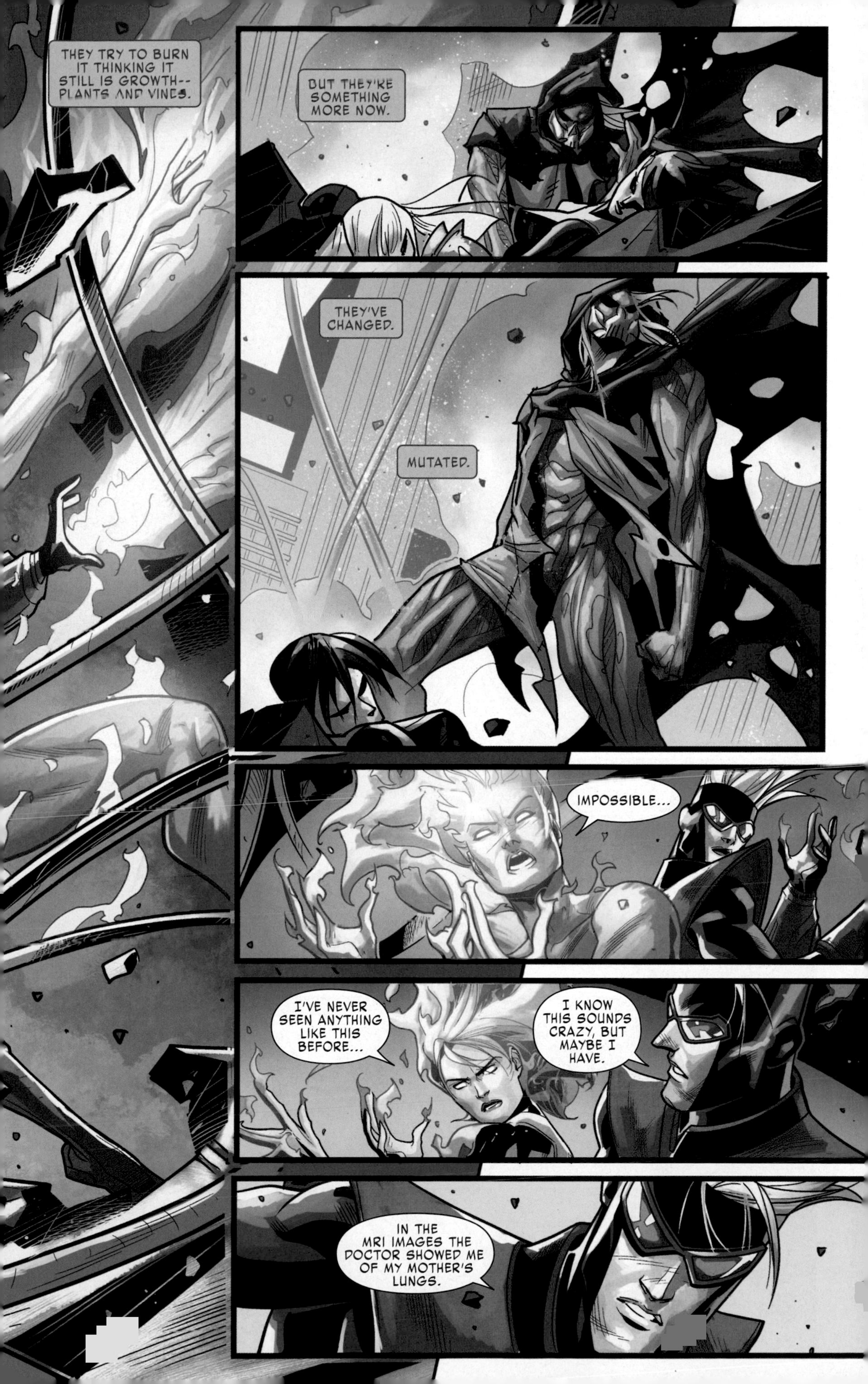
THEY TRY TO BURN IT THINKING IT STILL IS GROWTH--PLANTS AND VINES.
BUT THEY'RE SOMETHING MORE NOW.
THEY'VE CHANGED.
MUTATED.
IMPOSSIBLE...
I'VE NEVER SEEN ANYTHING LIKE THIS BEFORE...
I KNOW THIS SOUNDS CRAZY, BUT MAYBE I HAVE.
IN THE MRI IMAGES THE DOCTOR SHOWED ME OF MY MOTHER'S LUNGS.

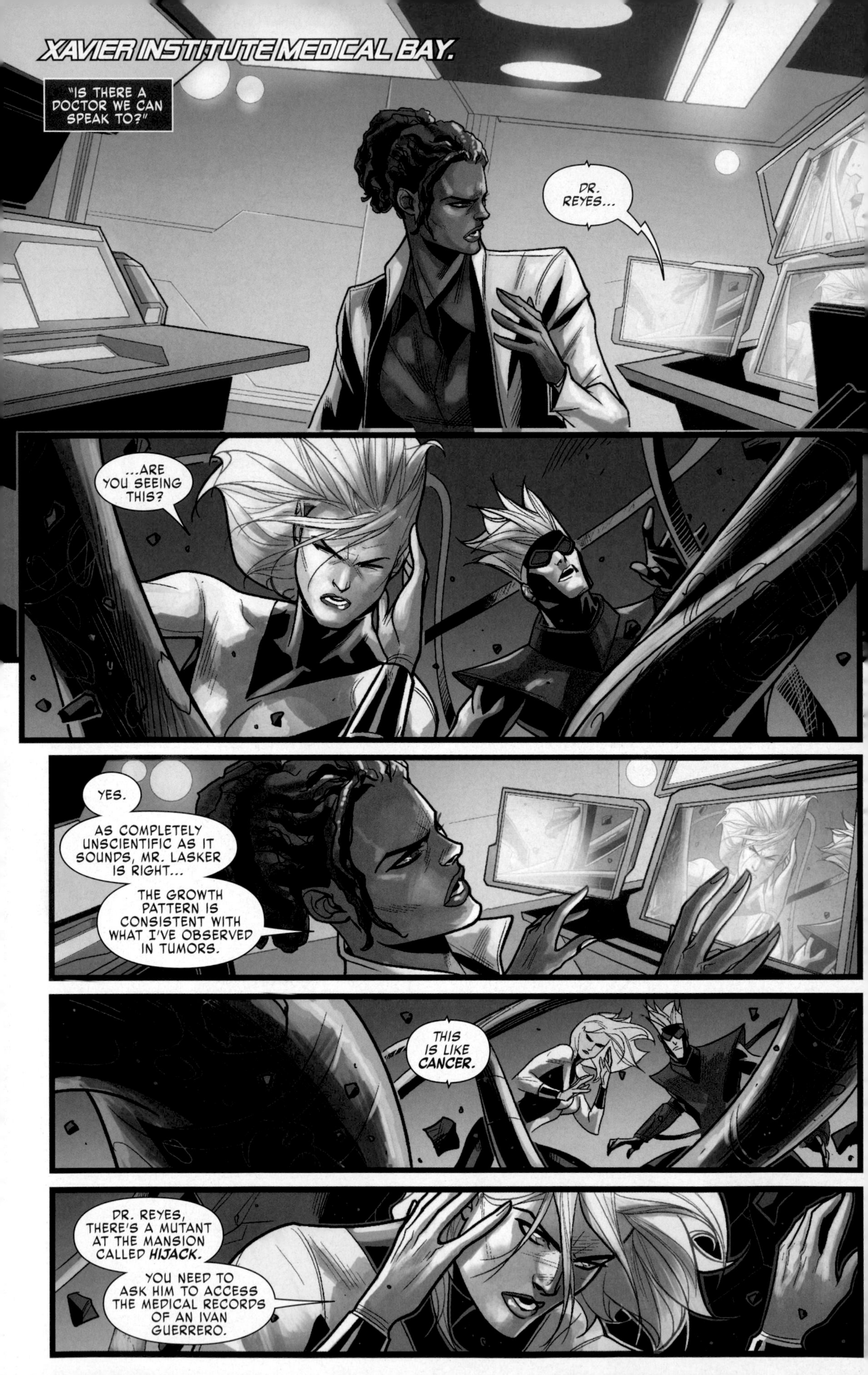
XAVIER INSTITUTE MEDICAL BAY.
"IS THERE A DOCTOR WE CAN SPEAK TO?"
DR. REYES...
...ARE YOU SEEING THIS?
YES.
AS COMPLETELY UNSCIENTIFIC AS IT SOUNDS, MR. LASKER IS RIGHT...
THE GROWTH PATTERN IS CONSISTENT WITH WHAT I'VE OBSERVED IN TUMORS.
THIS IS LIKE CANCER.
DR. REYES, THERE'S A MUTANT AT THE MANSION CALLED HIJACK.
YOU NEED TO ASK HIM TO ACCESS THE MEDICAL RECORDS OF AN IVAN GUERRERO.

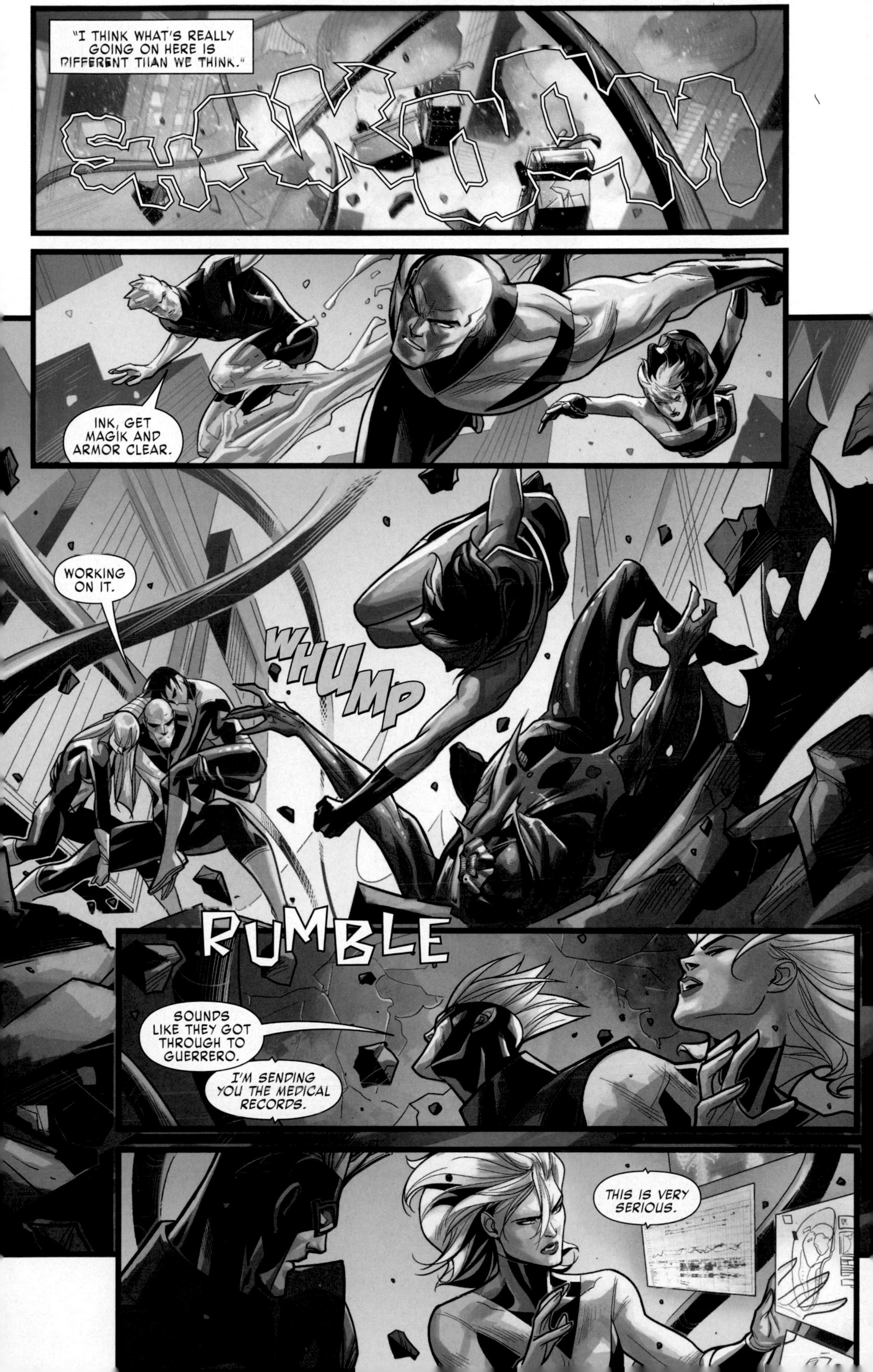
"I THINK WHAT'S REALLY GOING ON HERE IS DIFFERENT THAN WE THINK."
INK, GET MAGIK AND ARMOR CLEAR.
WORKING ON IT.
WHUMP
RUMBLE
SOUNDS LIKE THEY GOT THROUGH TO GUERRERO.
I'M SENDING YOU THE MEDICAL RECORDS.
THIS IS VERY SERIOUS.

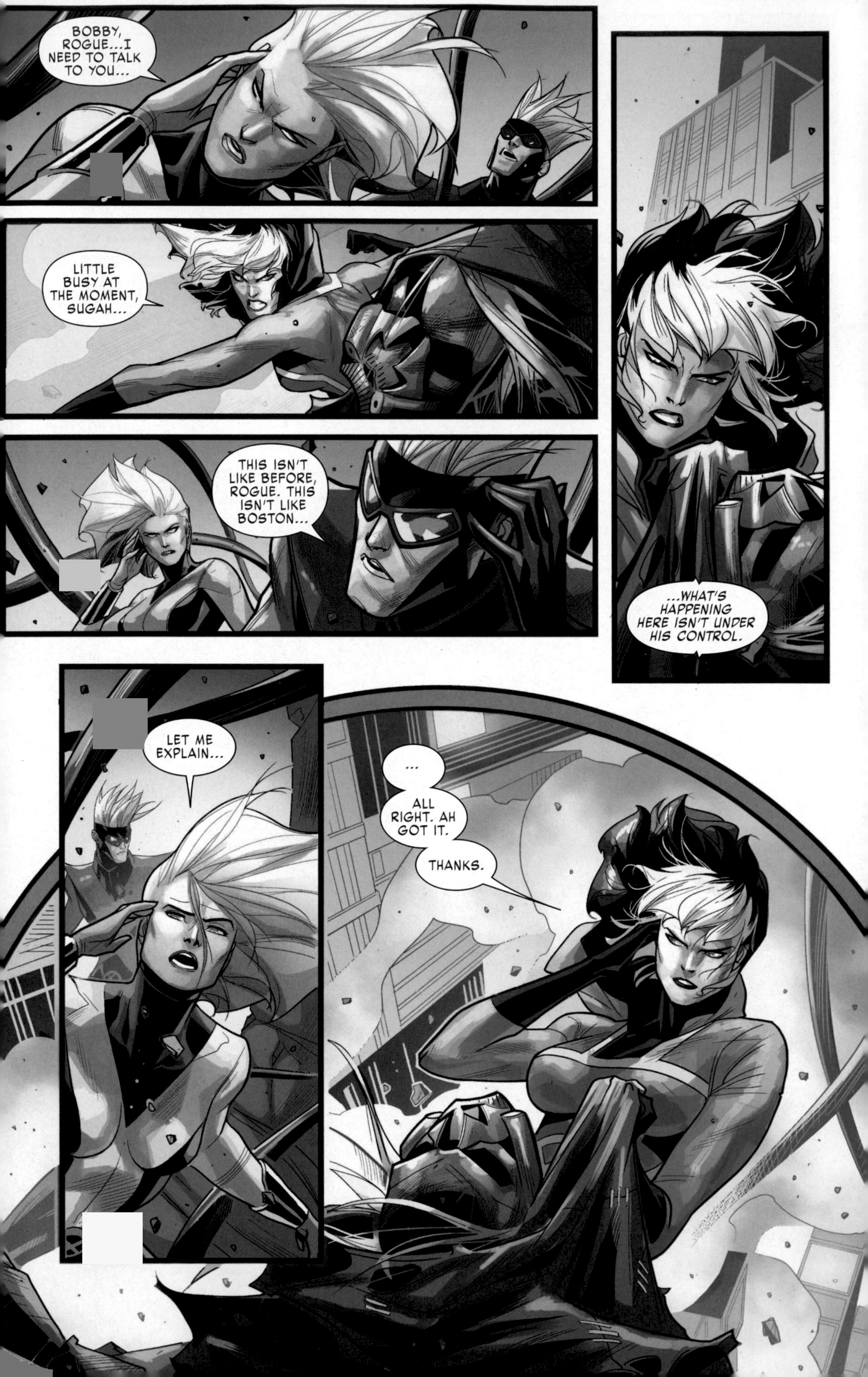

BOBBY, ROGUE...I NEED TO TALK TO YOU...
LITTLE BUSY AT THE MOMENT, SUGAH...
THIS ISN'T LIKE BEFORE, ROGUE. THIS ISN'T LIKE BOSTON...
...WHAT'S HAPPENING HERE ISN'T UNDER HIS CONTROL.
LET ME EXPLAIN...
...
ALL RIGHT. AH GOT IT.
THANKS.

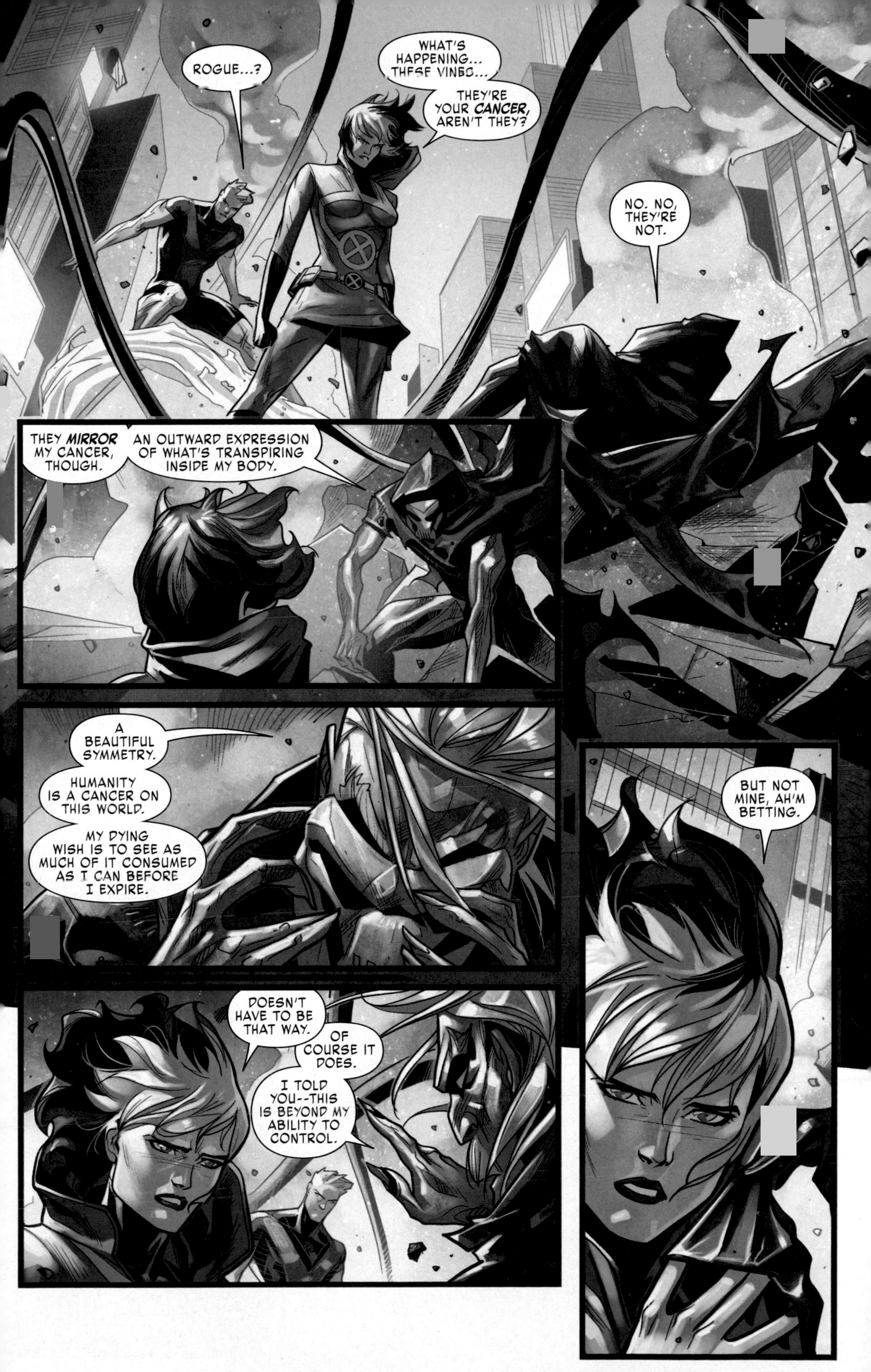
ROGUE...?
WHAT'S HAPPENING... THESE VINES...
THEY'RE YOUR *CANCER*, AREN'T THEY?
NO. NO, THEY'RE NOT.
THEY *MIRROR* MY CANCER, THOUGH.
AN OUTWARD EXPRESSION OF WHAT'S TRANSPIRING INSIDE MY BODY.
A BEAUTIFUL SYMMETRY.
HUMANITY IS A CANCER ON THIS WORLD.
MY DYING WISH IS TO SEE AS MUCH OF IT CONSUMED AS I CAN BEFORE I EXPIRE.
BUT NOT MINE, AH'M BETTING.
DOESN'T HAVE TO BE THAT WAY.
OF COURSE IT DOES.
I TOLD YOU--THIS IS BEYOND MY ABILITY TO CONTROL.

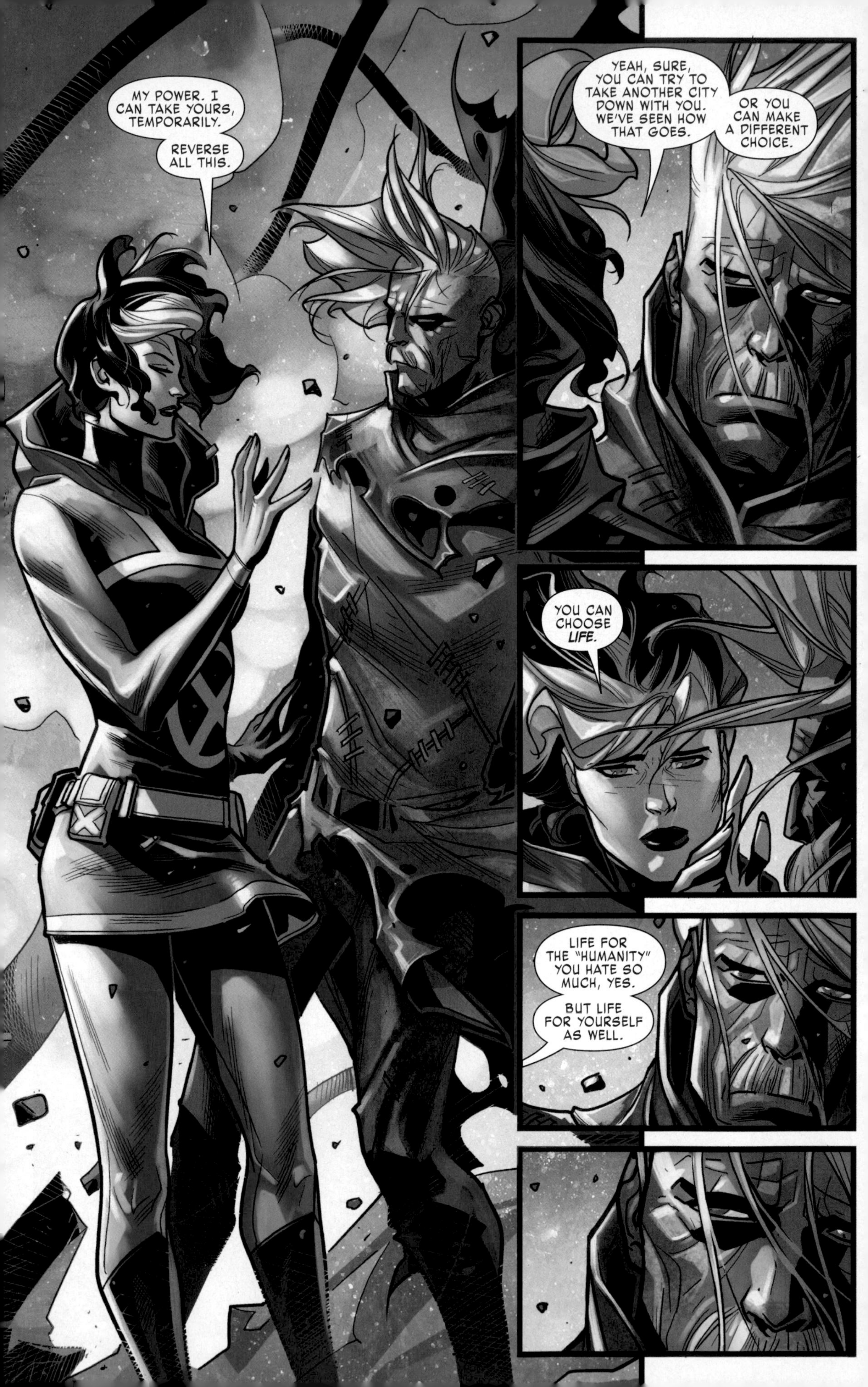
MY POWER. I CAN TAKE YOURS, TEMPORARILY.
REVERSE ALL THIS.
YEAH, SURE, YOU CAN TRY TO TAKE ANOTHER CITY DOWN WITH YOU. WE'VE SEEN HOW THAT GOES.
OR YOU CAN MAKE A DIFFERENT CHOICE.
YOU CAN CHOOSE *LIFE.*
LIFE FOR THE "HUMANITY" YOU HATE SO MUCH, YES.
BUT LIFE FOR YOURSELF AS WELL.

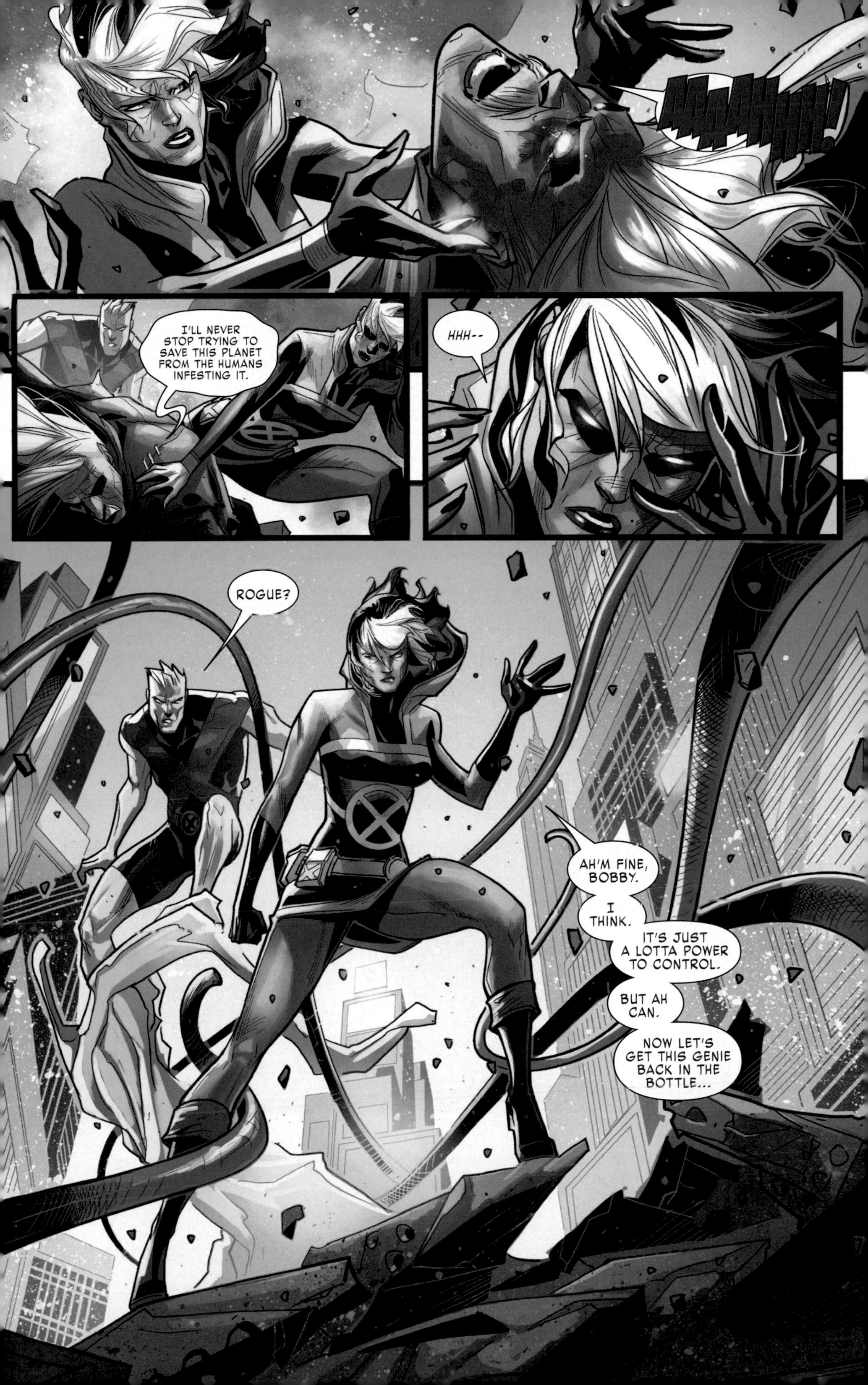
AAAAHHH!
I'LL NEVER STOP TRYING TO SAVE THIS PLANET FROM THE HUMANS INFESTING IT.
HHH--
ROGUE?
AH'M FINE, BOBBY.
I THINK.
IT'S JUST A LOTTA POWER TO CONTROL.
BUT AH CAN.
NOW LET'S GET THIS GENIE BACK IN THE BOTTLE...

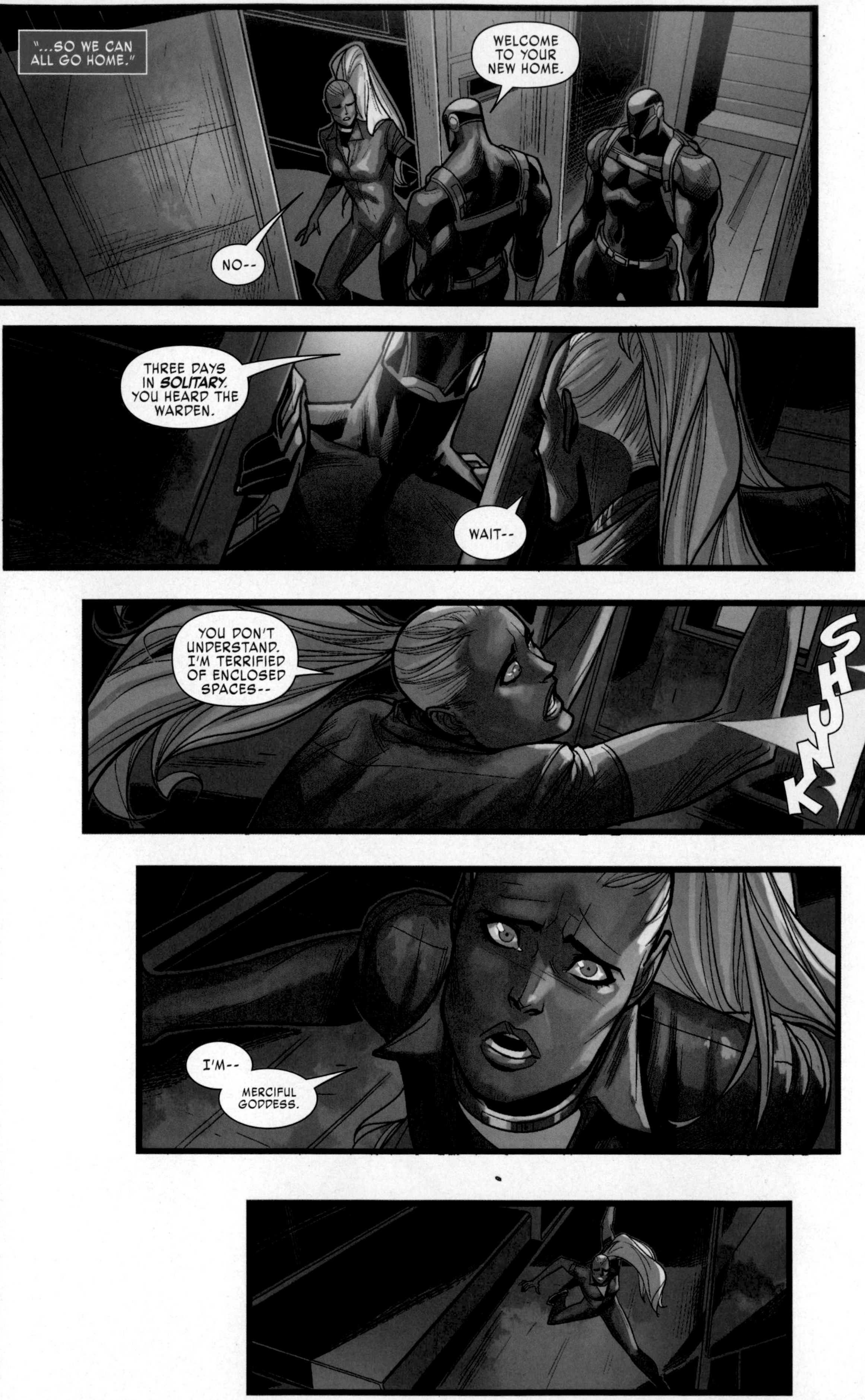
"...SO WE CAN ALL GO HOME."
WELCOME TO YOUR NEW HOME.
NO--
THREE DAYS IN SOLITARY. YOU HEARD THE WARDEN.
WAIT--
YOU DON'T UNDERSTAND. I'M TERRIFIED OF ENCLOSED SPACES--
SHUNK
I'M--
MERCIFUL GODDESS.

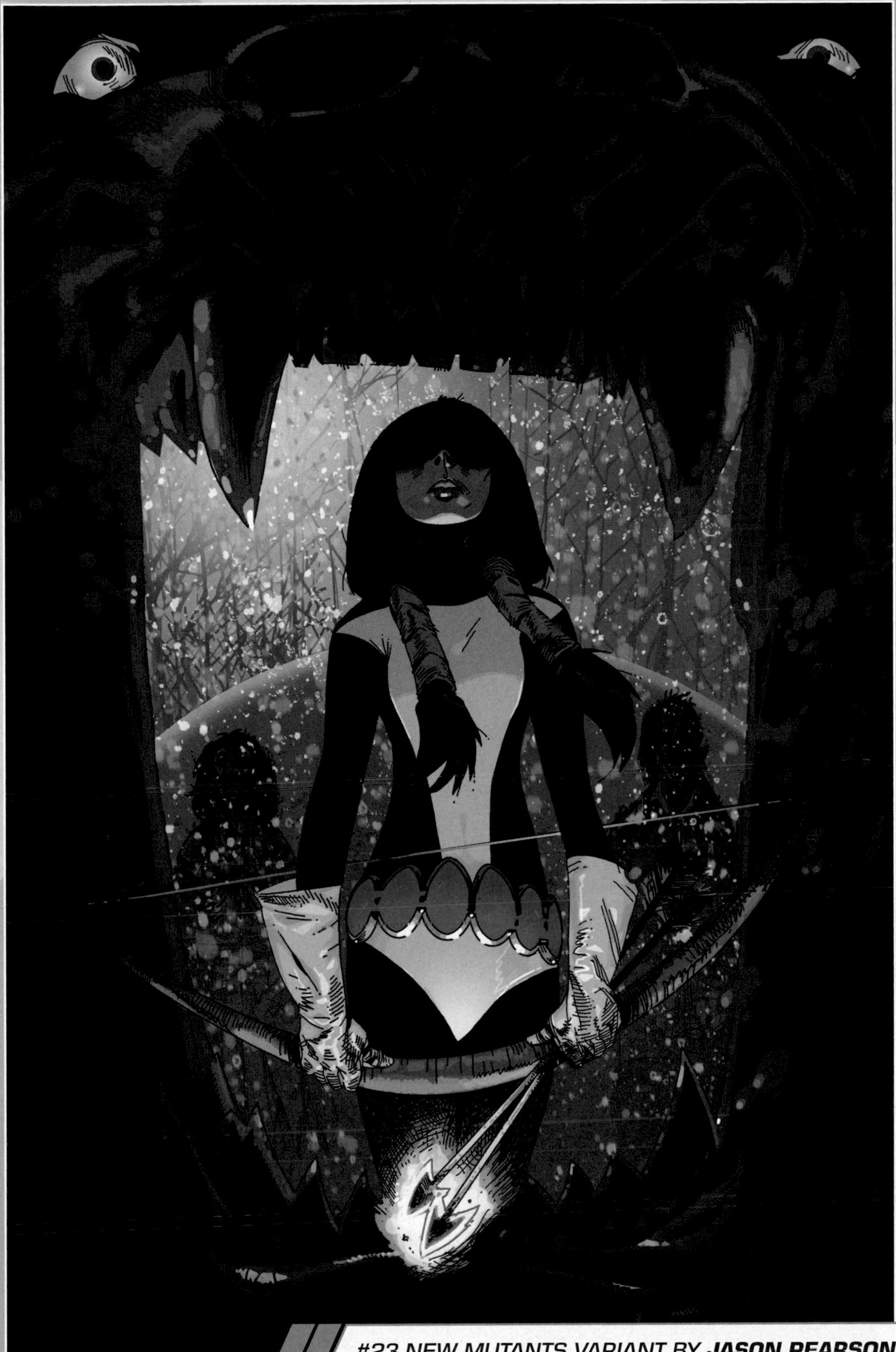

#23 NEW MUTANTS VARIANT BY **JASON PEARSON**

25

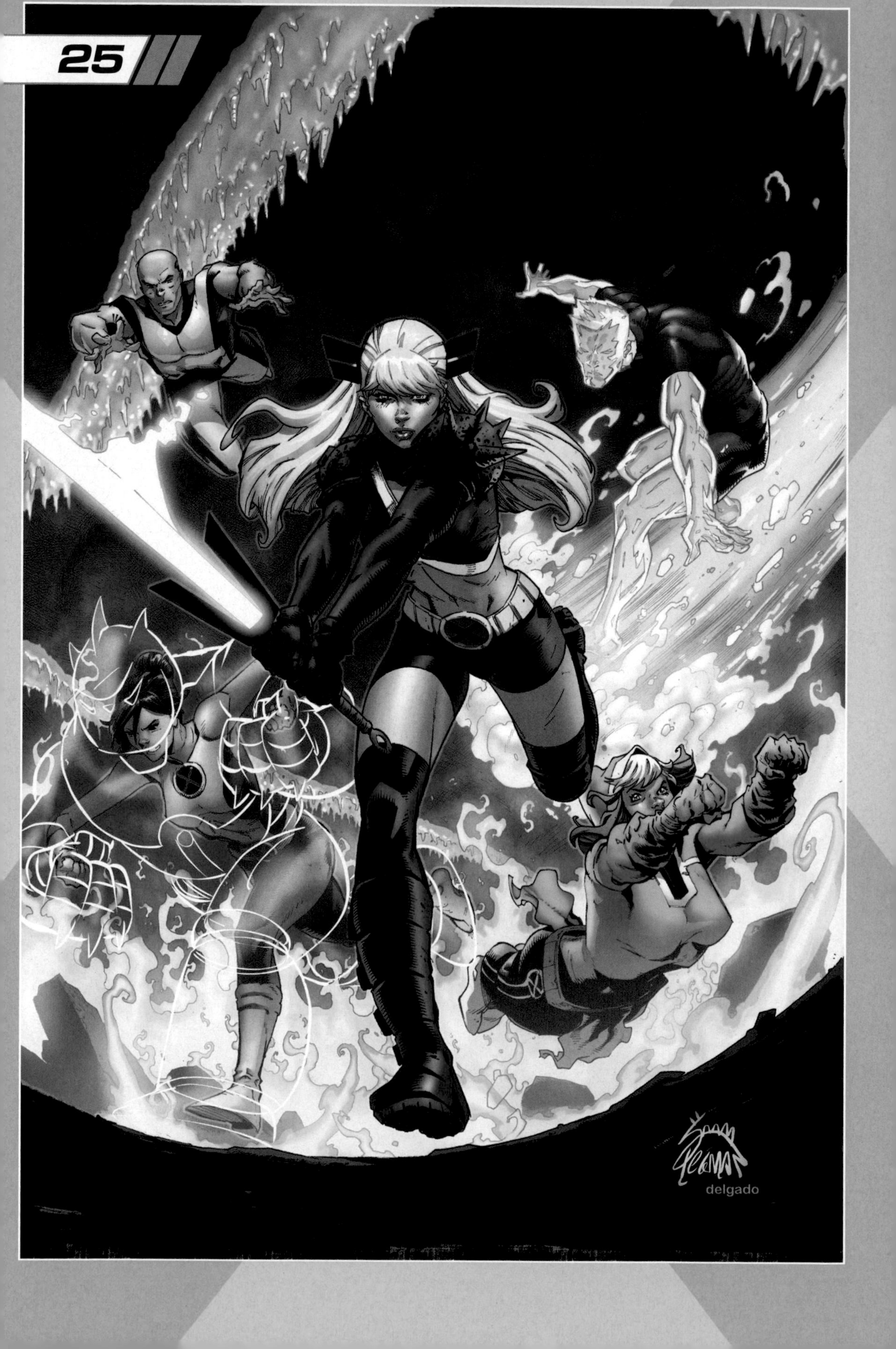
delgado

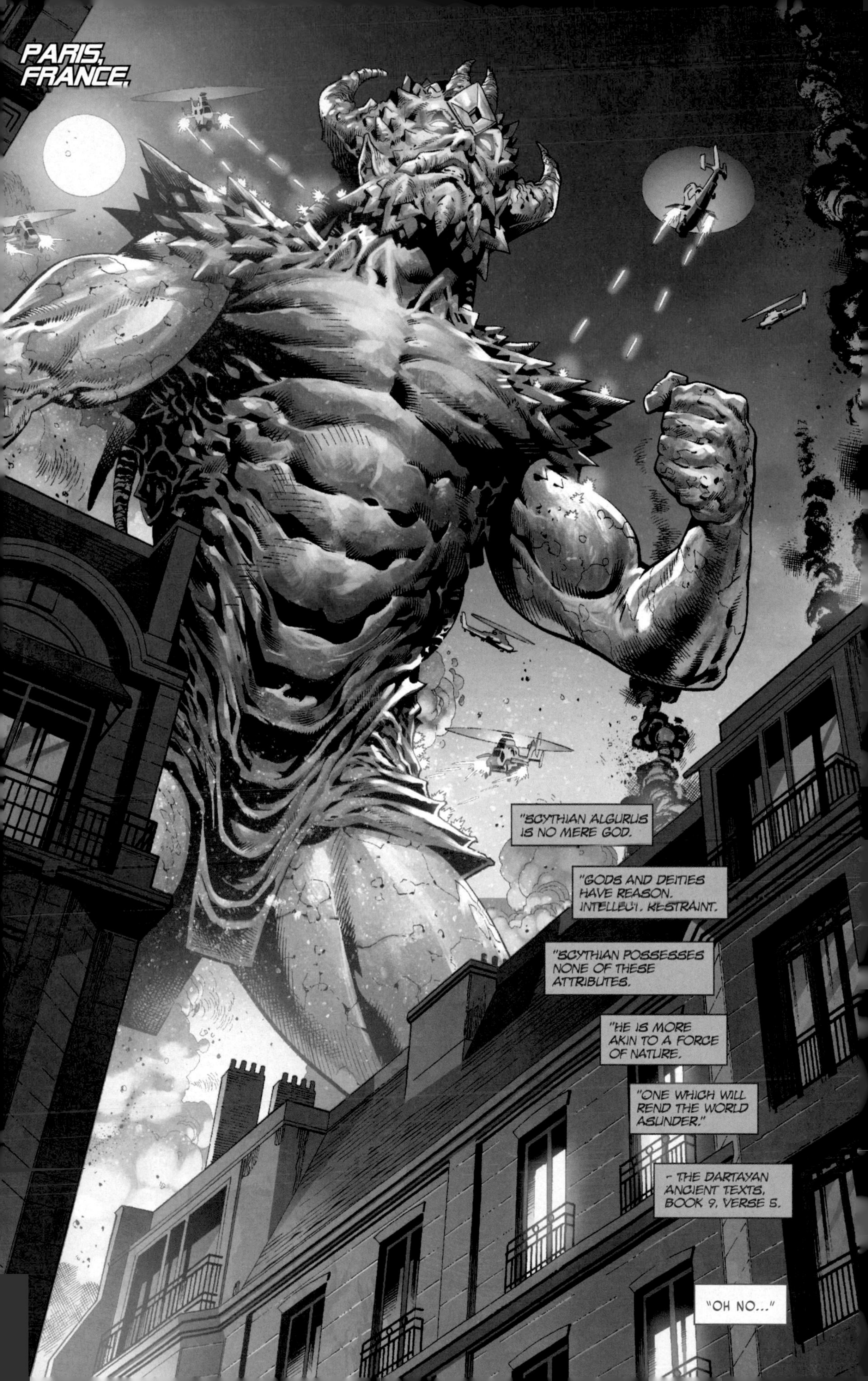
PARIS, FRANCE.
"SCYTHIAN ALGURUS IS NO MERE GOD.
"GODS AND DEITIES HAVE REASON. INTELLECT. RESTRAINT.
"SCYTHIAN POSSESSES NONE OF THESE ATTRIBUTES.
"HE IS MORE AKIN TO A FORCE OF NATURE.
"ONE WHICH WILL REND THE WORLD ASUNDER."
- THE DARTAYAN ANCIENT TEXTS, BOOK 9, VERSE 5.
"OH NO..."

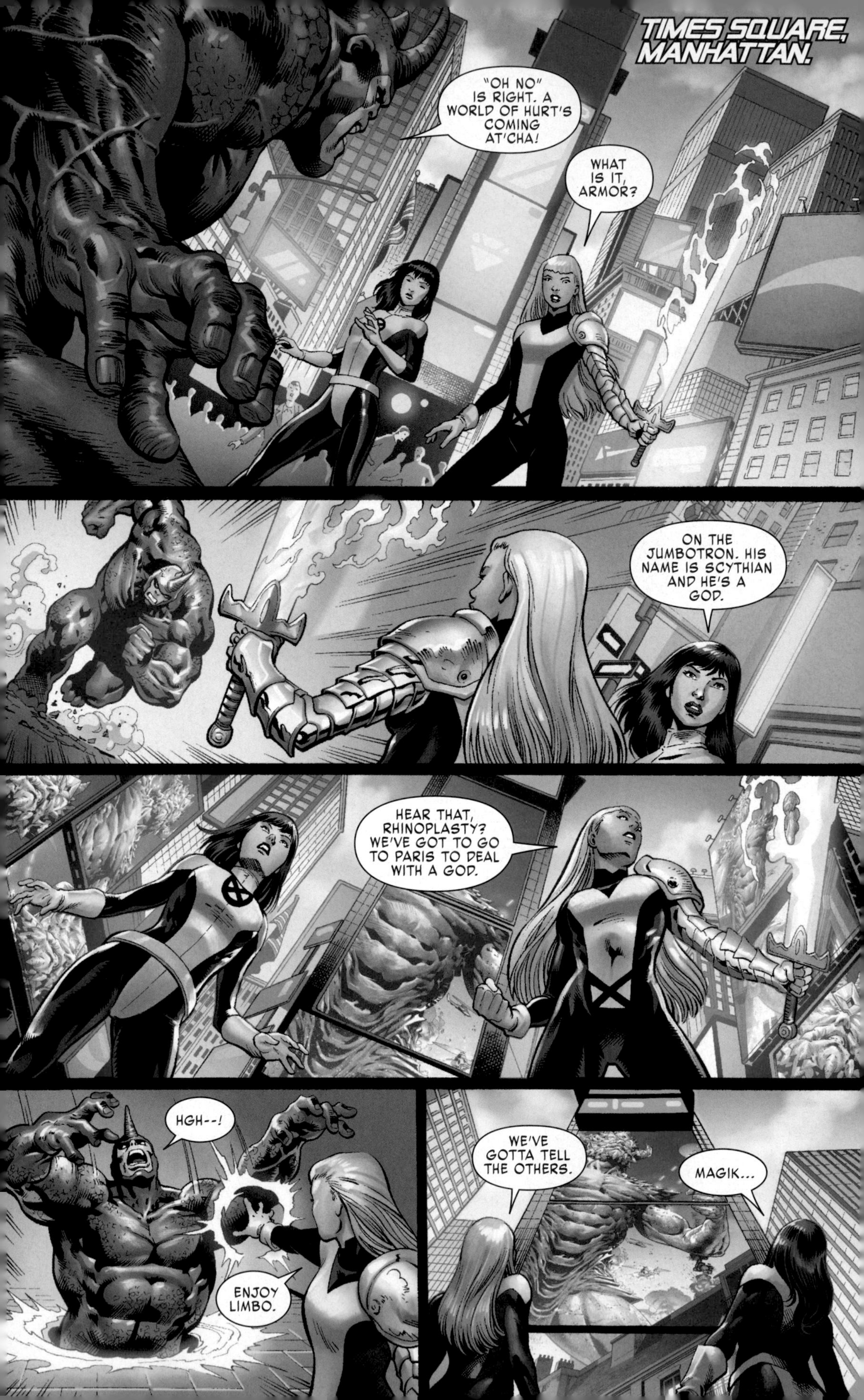
TIMES SQUARE, MANHATTAN.
"OH NO" IS RIGHT. A WORLD OF HURT'S COMING AT'CHA!
WHAT IS IT, ARMOR?
ON THE JUMBOTRON. HIS NAME IS SCYTHIAN AND HE'S A GOD.
HEAR THAT, RHINOPLASTY? WE'VE GOT TO GO TO PARIS TO DEAL WITH A GOD.
HGH--!
ENJOY LIMBO.
WE'VE GOTTA TELL THE OTHERS.
MAGIK...

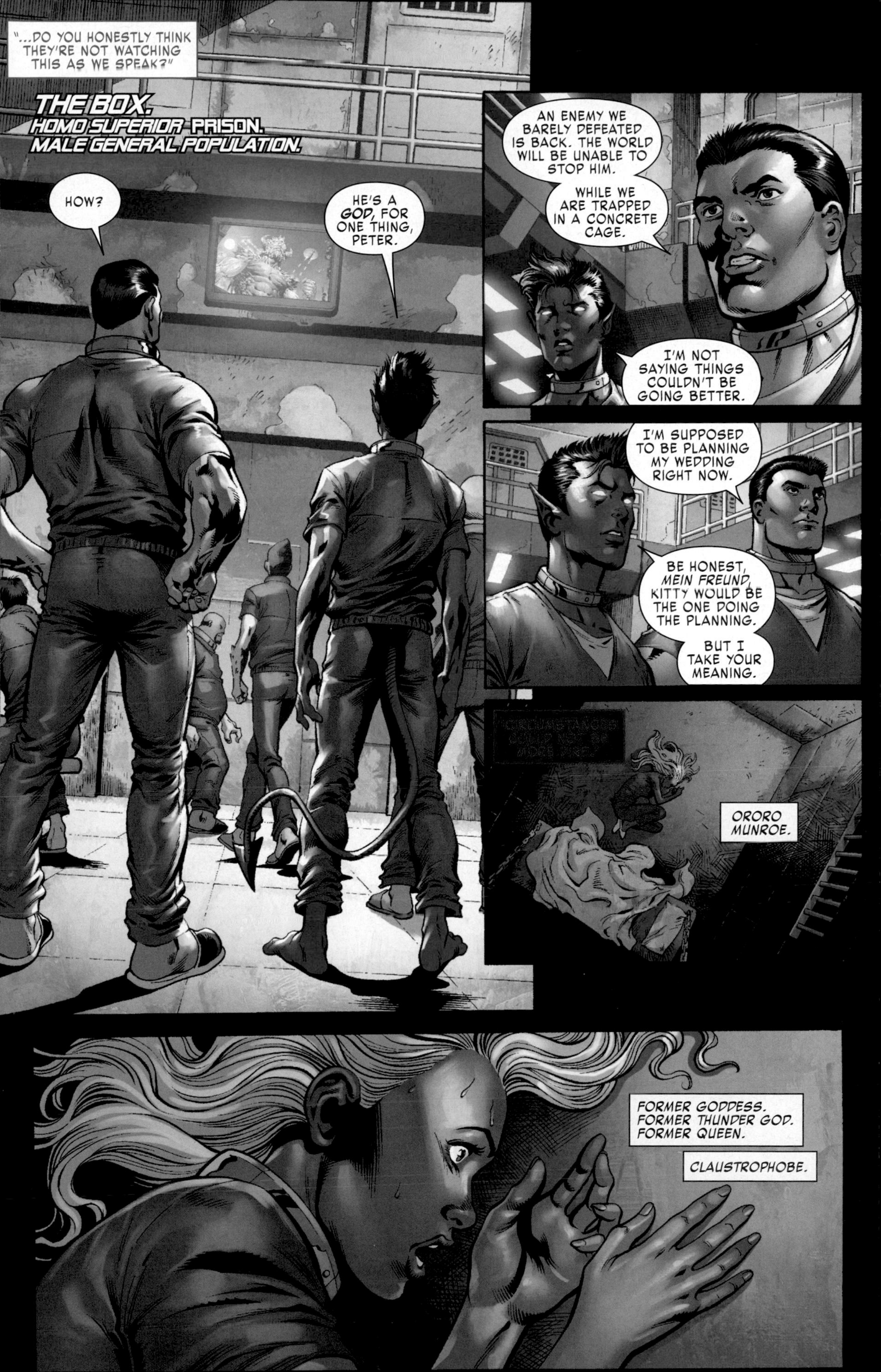
"...DO YOU HONESTLY THINK THEY'RE NOT WATCHING THIS AS WE SPEAK?"
THE BOX. HOMO SUPERIOR PRISON. MALE GENERAL POPULATION.
HOW?
HE'S A *GOD*, FOR ONE THING, PETER.
AN ENEMY WE BARELY DEFEATED IS BACK. THE WORLD WILL BE UNABLE TO STOP HIM.
WHILE WE ARE TRAPPED IN A CONCRETE CAGE.
I'M NOT SAYING THINGS COULDN'T BE GOING BETTER.
I'M SUPPOSED TO BE PLANNING MY WEDDING RIGHT NOW.
BE HONEST, *MEIN FREUND*, KITTY WOULD BE THE ONE DOING THE PLANNING.
BUT I TAKE YOUR MEANING.
CIRCUMSTANCES COULD NOT BE MORE DIRE.
ORORO MUNROE.
FORMER GODDESS. FORMER THUNDER GOD. FORMER QUEEN.
CLAUSTROPHOBE.

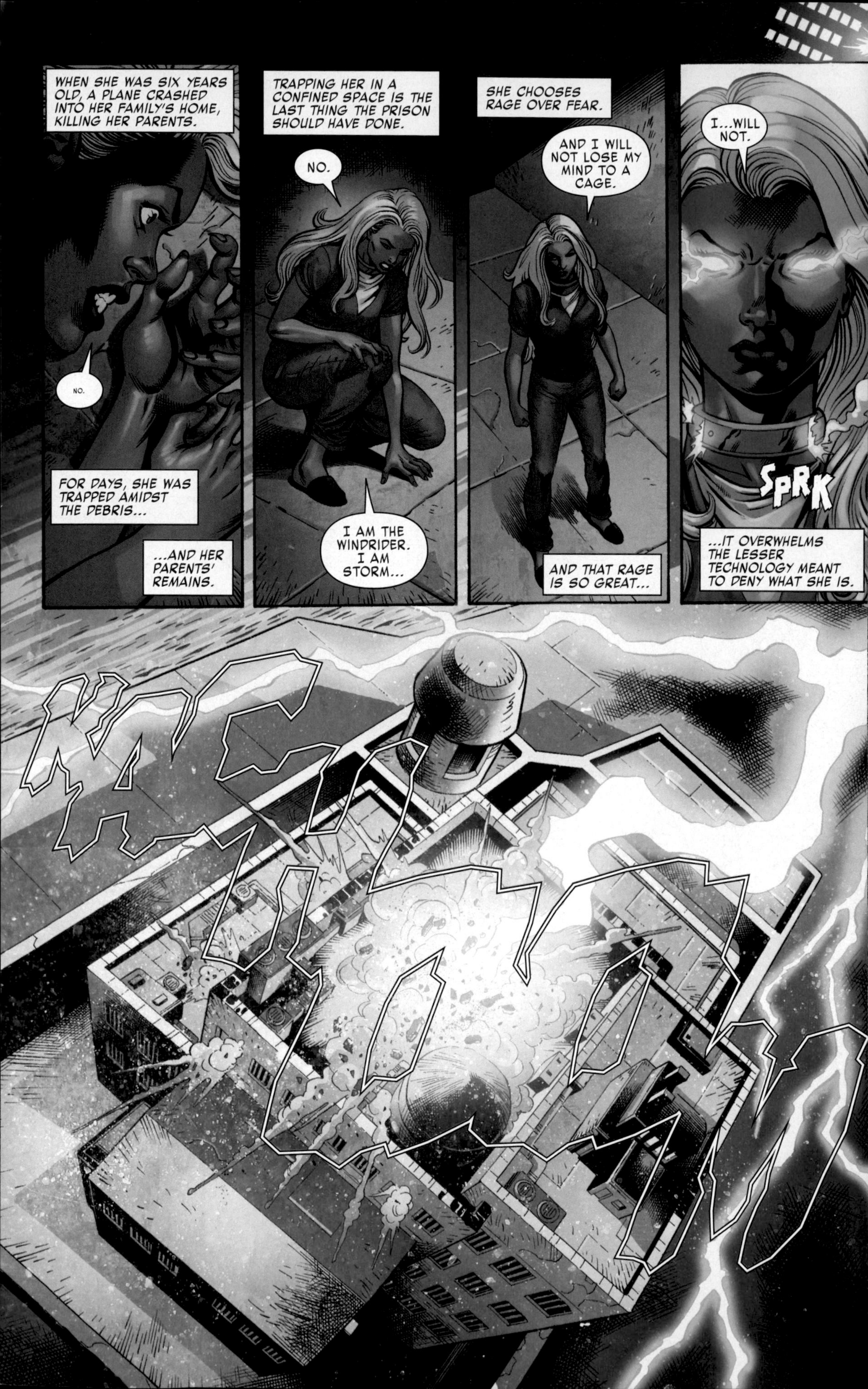
WHEN SHE WAS SIX YEARS OLD, A PLANE CRASHED INTO HER FAMILY'S HOME, KILLING HER PARENTS.
NO.
FOR DAYS, SHE WAS TRAPPED AMIDST THE DEBRIS...
...AND HER PARENTS' REMAINS.
TRAPPING HER IN A CONFINED SPACE IS THE LAST THING THE PRISON SHOULD HAVE DONE.
NO.
I AM THE WINDRIDER. I AM STORM...
SHE CHOOSES RAGE OVER FEAR.
AND I WILL NOT LOSE MY MIND TO A CAGE.
AND THAT RAGE IS SO GREAT...
I...WILL NOT.
SPRK
...IT OVERWHELMS THE LESSER TECHNOLOGY MEANT TO DENY WHAT SHE IS.

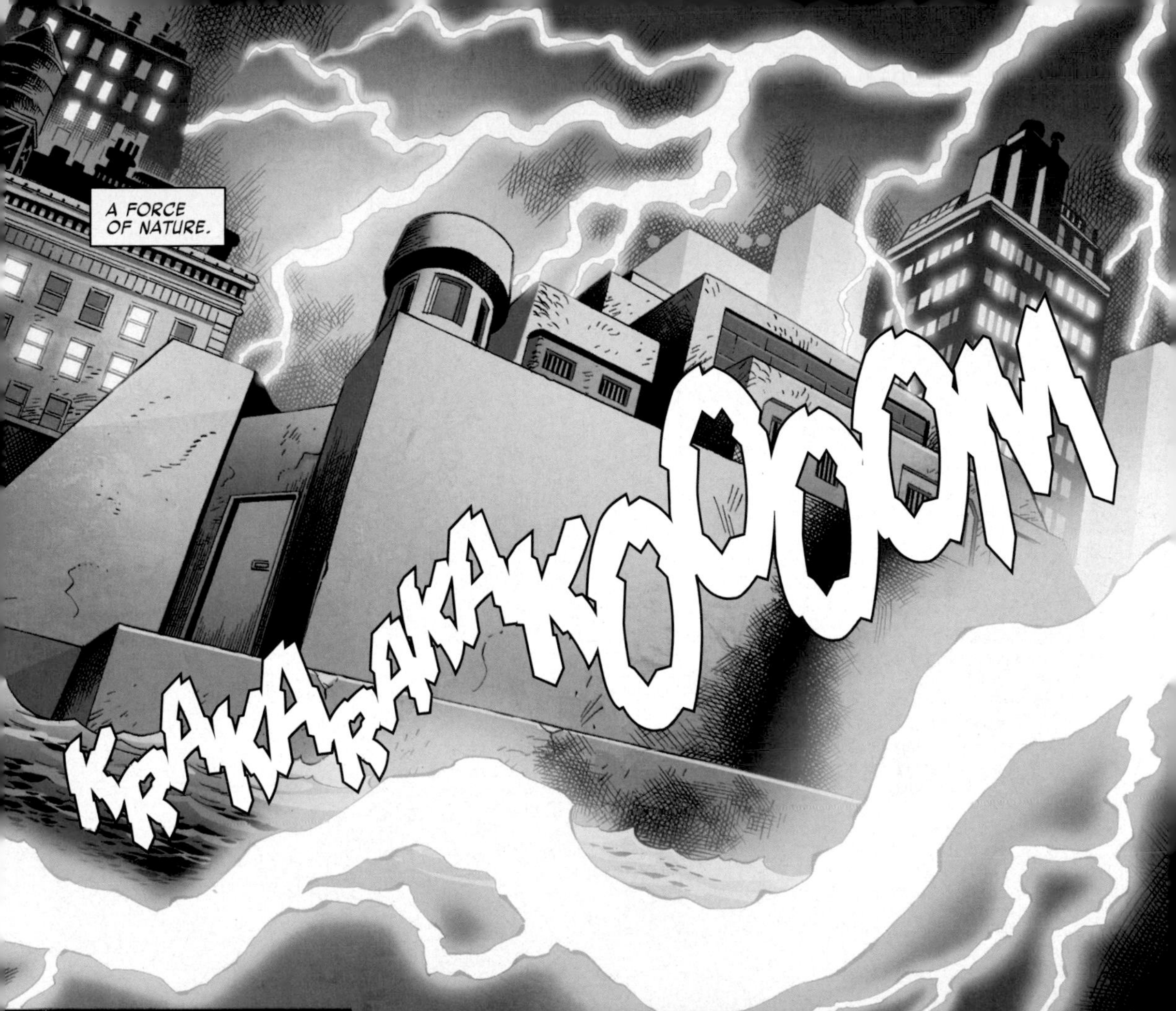
A FORCE OF NATURE.
KRAKARAKAKOOOOM
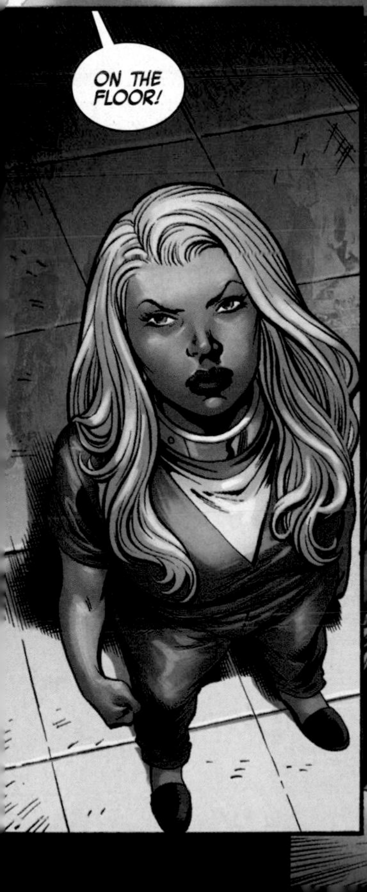
ON THE FLOOR!
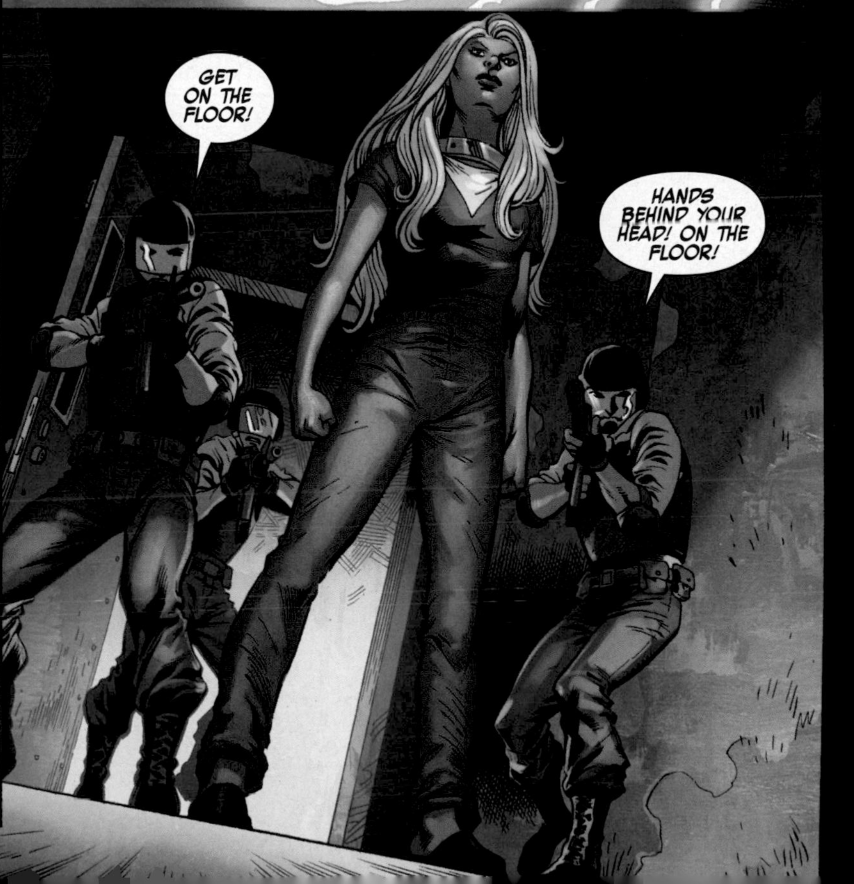
GET ON THE FLOOR!
HANDS BEHIND YOUR HEAD! ON THE FLOOR!

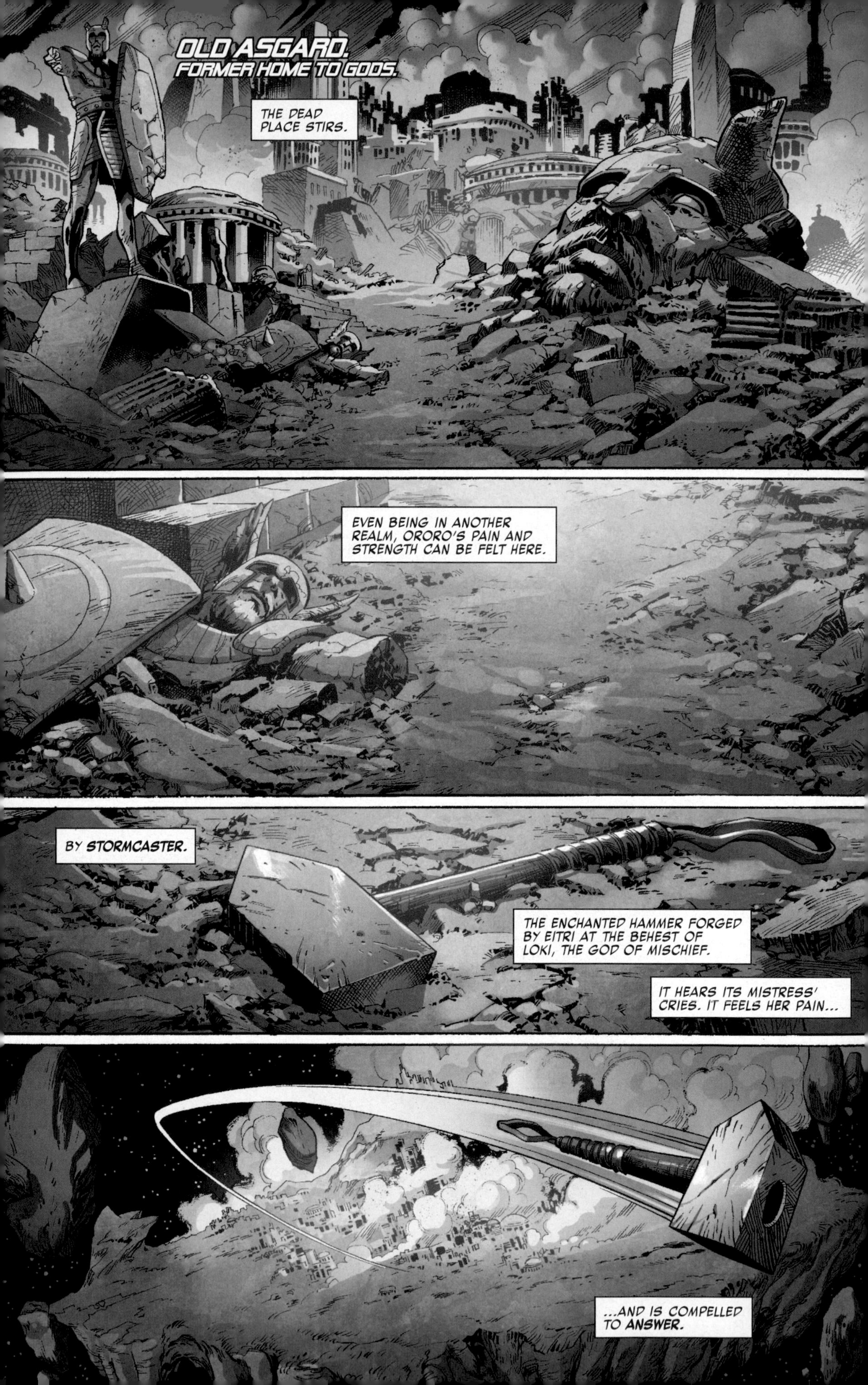
OLD ASGARD. FORMER HOME TO GODS.
THE DEAD PLACE STIRS.
EVEN BEING IN ANOTHER REALM, ORORO'S PAIN AND STRENGTH CAN BE FELT HERE.
BY STORMCASTER.
THE ENCHANTED HAMMER FORGED BY EITRI AT THE BEHEST OF LOKI, THE GOD OF MISCHIEF.
IT HEARS ITS MISTRESS' CRIES. IT FEELS HER PAIN...
...AND IS COMPELLED TO ANSWER.

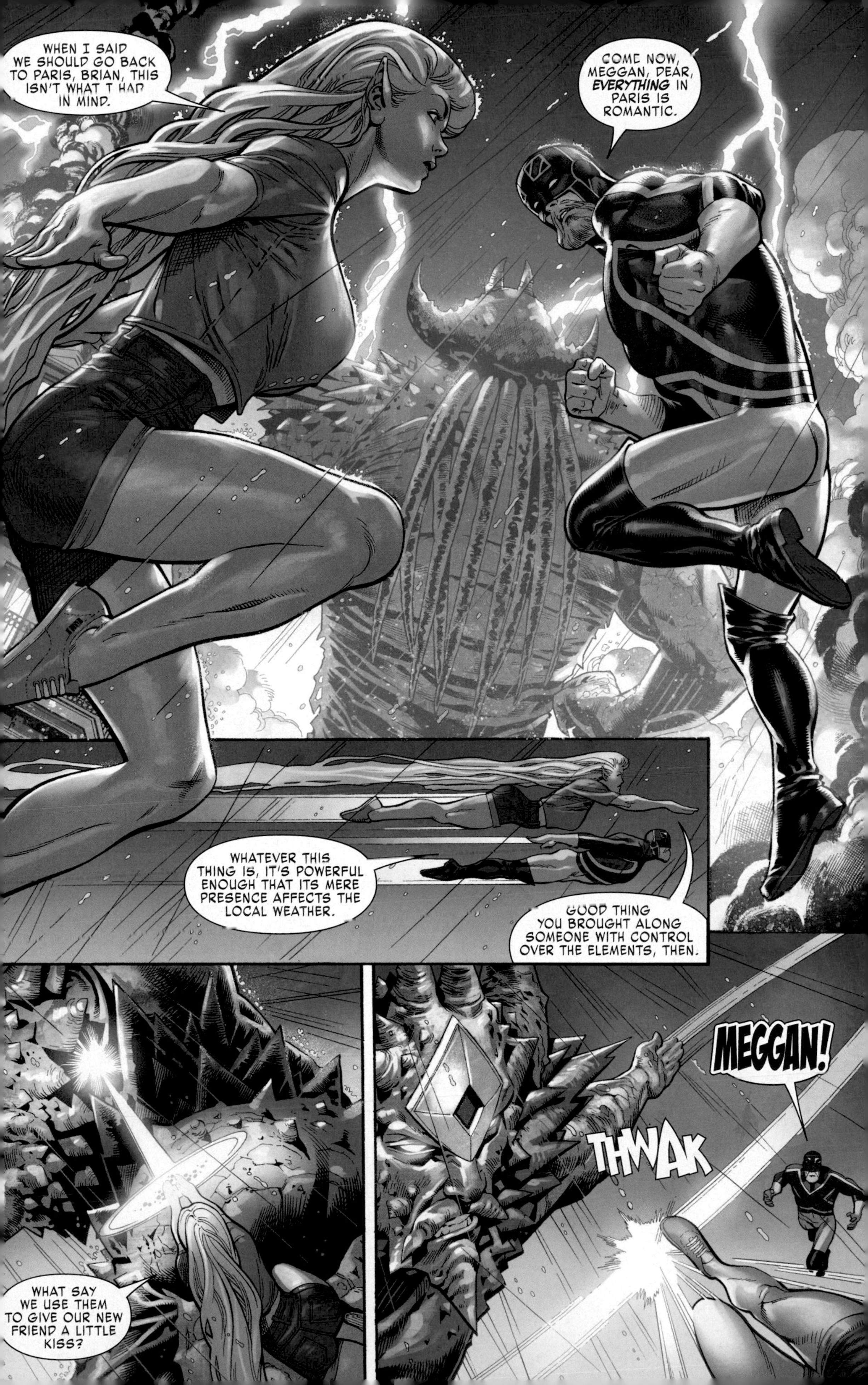
WHEN I SAID WE SHOULD GO BACK TO PARIS, BRIAN, THIS ISN'T WHAT I HAD IN MIND.
COME NOW, MEGGAN, DEAR, *EVERYTHING* IN PARIS IS ROMANTIC.
WHATEVER THIS THING IS, IT'S POWERFUL ENOUGH THAT ITS MERE PRESENCE AFFECTS THE LOCAL WEATHER.
GOOD THING YOU BROUGHT ALONG SOMEONE WITH CONTROL OVER THE ELEMENTS, THEN.
WHAT SAY WE USE THEM TO GIVE OUR NEW FRIEND A LITTLE KISS?
MEGGAN!
THWAK

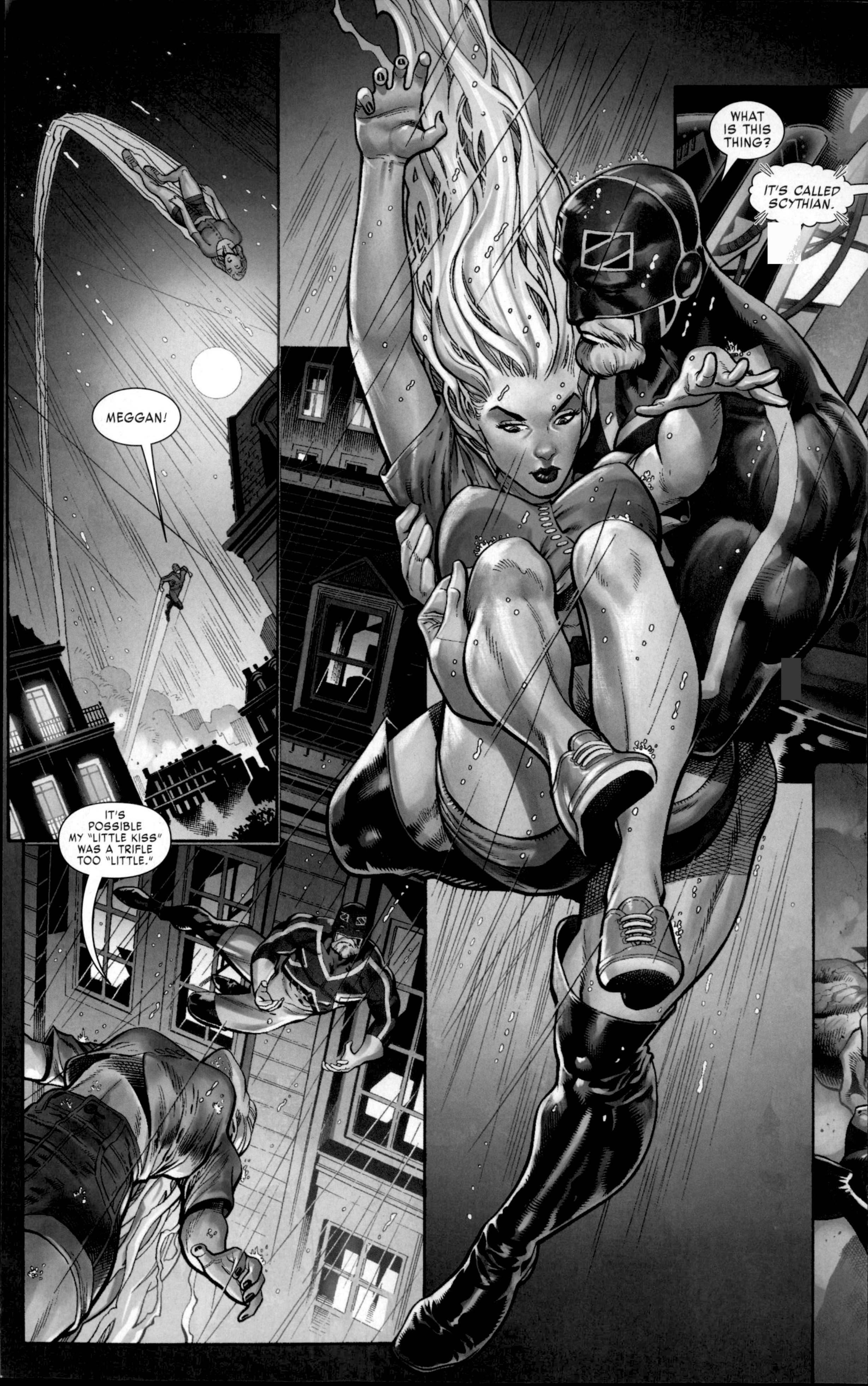
MEGGAN!
IT'S POSSIBLE MY "LITTLE KISS" WAS A TRIFLE TOO "LITTLE."
WHAT IS THIS THING?
IT'S CALLED SCYTHIAN.

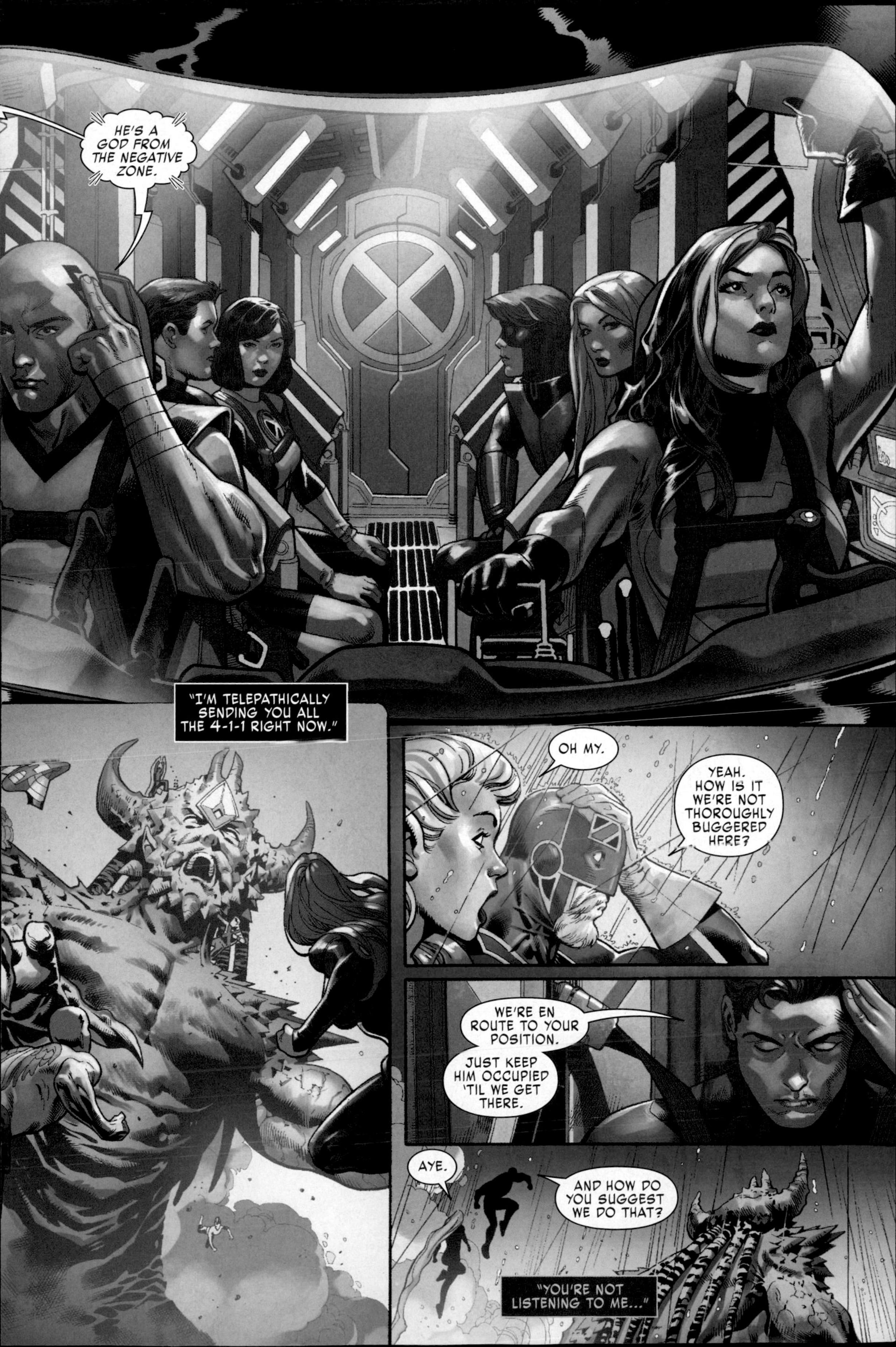
HE'S A GOD FROM THE NEGATIVE ZONE.
"I'M TELEPATHICALLY SENDING YOU ALL THE 4-1-1 RIGHT NOW."
OH MY.
YEAH. HOW IS IT WE'RE NOT THOROUGHLY BUGGERED HERE?
WE'RE EN ROUTE TO YOUR POSITION.
JUST KEEP HIM OCCUPIED 'TIL WE GET THERE.
AYE.
AND HOW DO YOU SUGGEST WE DO THAT?
"YOU'RE NOT LISTENING TO ME..."

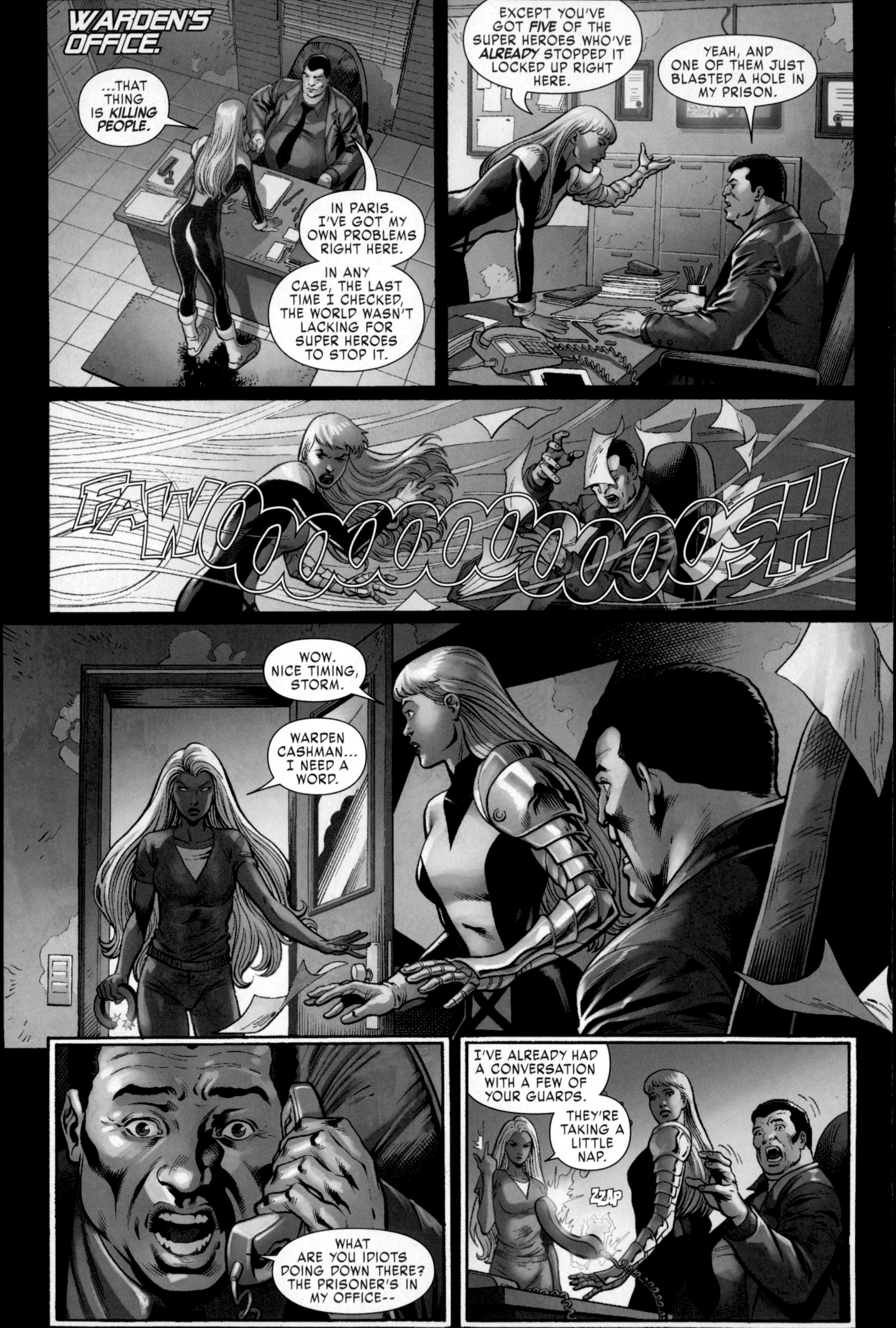
WARDEN'S OFFICE.
...THAT THING IS KILLING PEOPLE.
IN PARIS. I'VE GOT MY OWN PROBLEMS RIGHT HERE.
IN ANY CASE, THE LAST TIME I CHECKED, THE WORLD WASN'T LACKING FOR SUPER HEROES TO STOP IT.
EXCEPT YOU'VE GOT FIVE OF THE SUPER HEROES WHO'VE ALREADY STOPPED IT LOCKED UP RIGHT HERE.
YEAH, AND ONE OF THEM JUST BLASTED A HOLE IN MY PRISON.
FAWOOOOOOOOOOOSH
WOW. NICE TIMING, STORM.
WARDEN CASHMAN... I NEED A WORD.
WHAT ARE YOU IDIOTS DOING DOWN THERE? THE PRISONER'S IN MY OFFICE--
I'VE ALREADY HAD A CONVERSATION WITH A FEW OF YOUR GUARDS.
THEY'RE TAKING A LITTLE NAP.
ZZAP

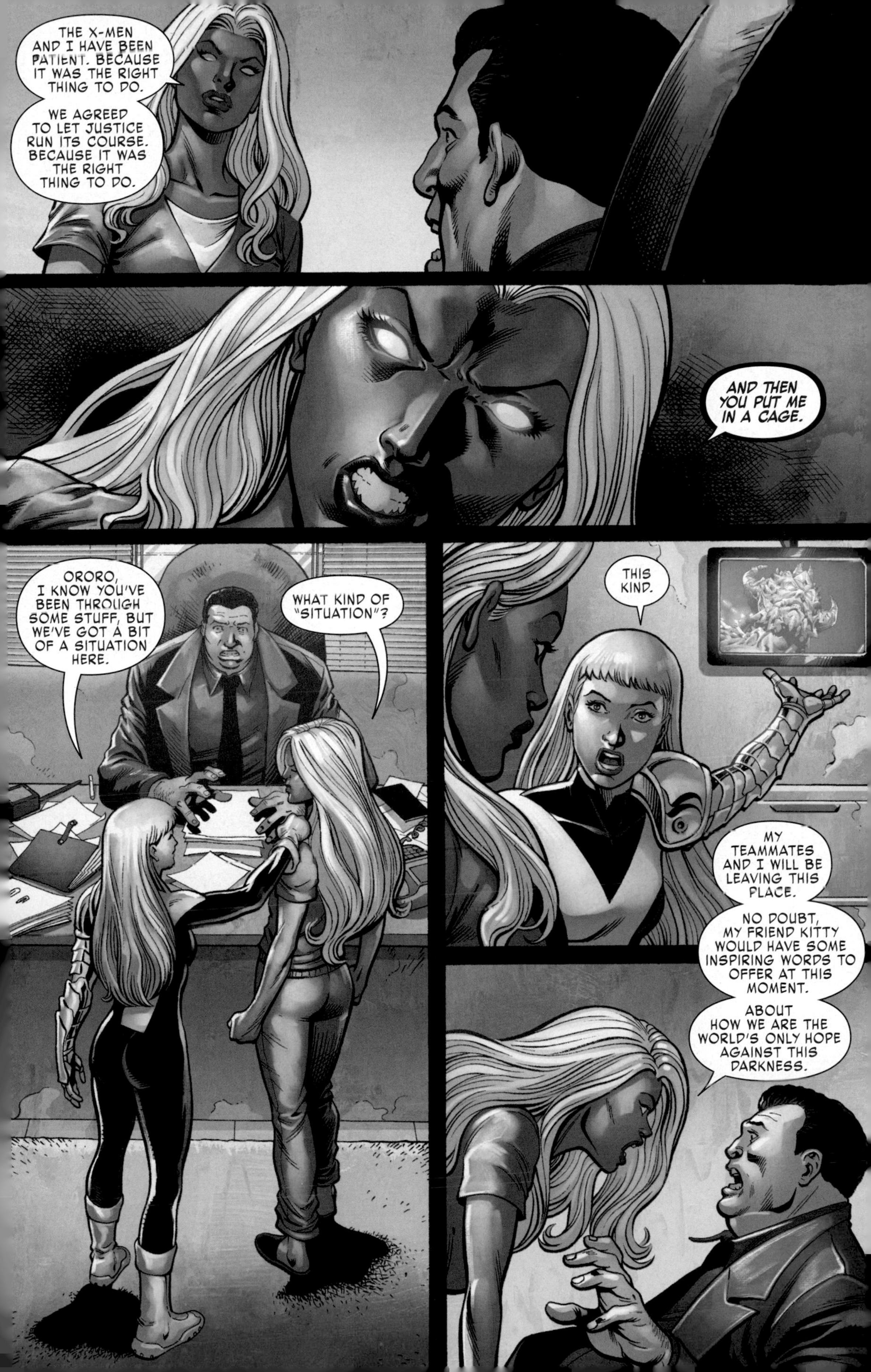
THE X-MEN AND I HAVE BEEN PATIENT. BECAUSE IT WAS THE RIGHT THING TO DO.
WE AGREED TO LET JUSTICE RUN ITS COURSE. BECAUSE IT WAS THE RIGHT THING TO DO.
AND THEN YOU PUT ME IN A CAGE.
ORORO, I KNOW YOU'VE BEEN THROUGH SOME STUFF, BUT WE'VE GOT A BIT OF A SITUATION HERE.
WHAT KIND OF "SITUATION"?
THIS KIND.
MY TEAMMATES AND I WILL BE LEAVING THIS PLACE.
NO DOUBT, MY FRIEND KITTY WOULD HAVE SOME INSPIRING WORDS TO OFFER AT THIS MOMENT.
ABOUT HOW WE ARE THE WORLD'S ONLY HOPE AGAINST THIS DARKNESS.

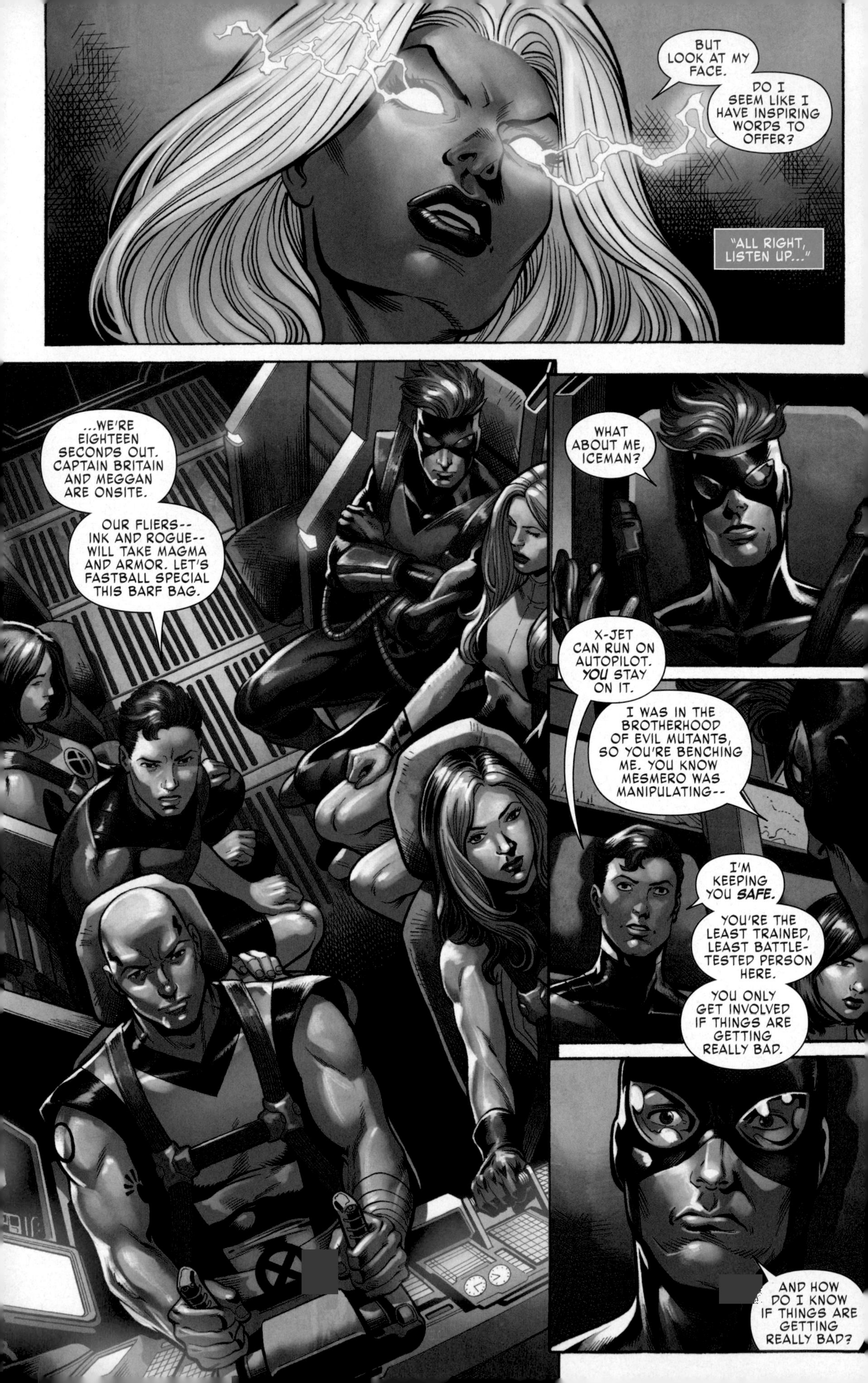

BUT LOOK AT MY FACE.
DO I SEEM LIKE I HAVE INSPIRING WORDS TO OFFER?
"ALL RIGHT, LISTEN UP..."
...WE'RE EIGHTEEN SECONDS OUT. CAPTAIN BRITAIN AND MEGGAN ARE ONSITE.
OUR FLIERS--INK AND ROGUE--WILL TAKE MAGMA AND ARMOR. LET'S FASTBALL SPECIAL THIS BARF BAG.
WHAT ABOUT ME, ICEMAN?
X-JET CAN RUN ON AUTOPILOT. *YOU* STAY ON IT.
I WAS IN THE BROTHERHOOD OF EVIL MUTANTS, SO YOU'RE BENCHING ME. YOU KNOW MESMERO WAS MANIPULATING--
I'M KEEPING YOU ***SAFE.***
YOU'RE THE LEAST TRAINED, LEAST BATTLE-TESTED PERSON HERE.
YOU ONLY GET INVOLVED IF THINGS ARE GETTING REALLY BAD.
AND HOW DO I KNOW IF THINGS ARE GETTING REALLY BAD?

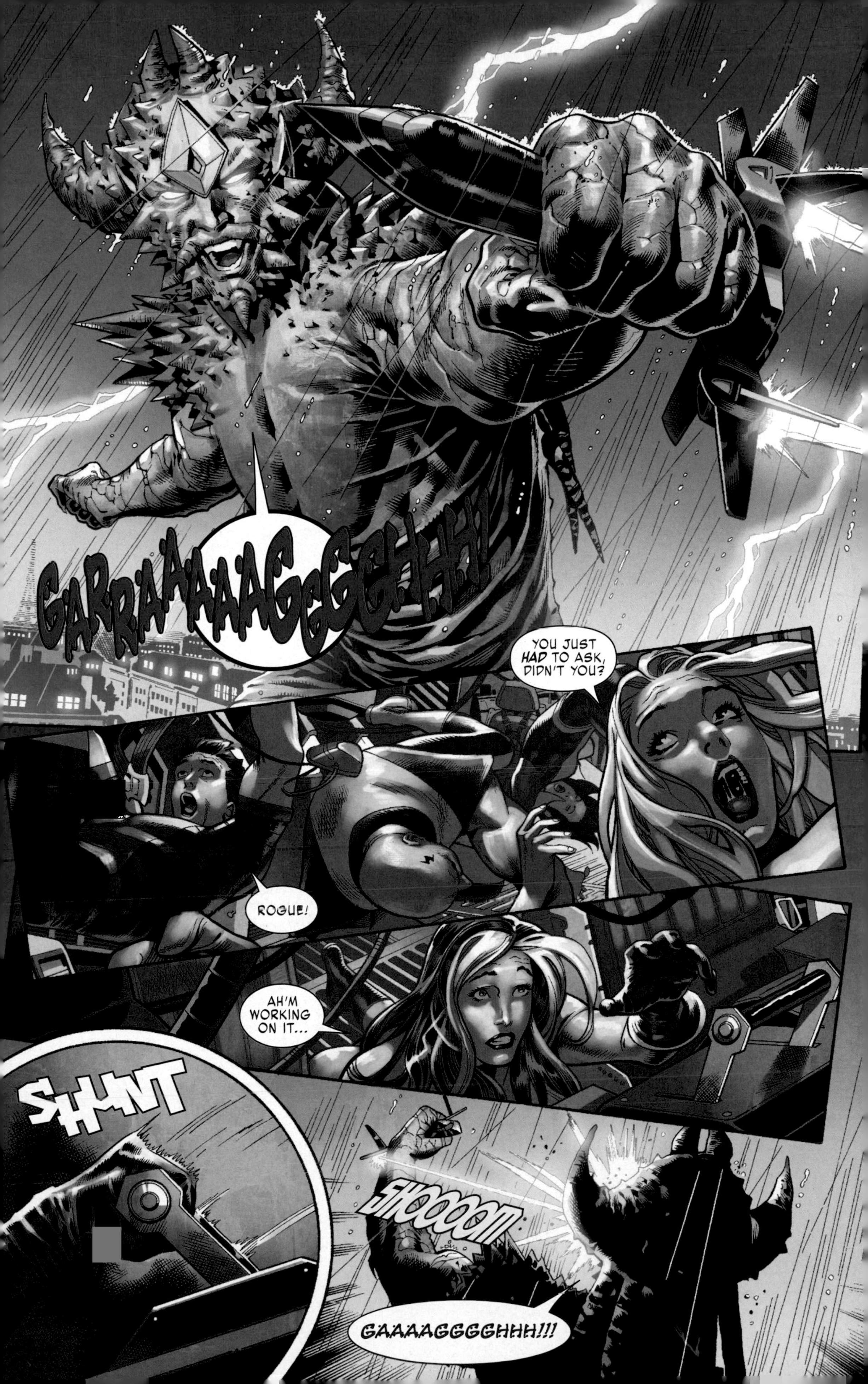
GARRAAAAAGGGHHH!
YOU JUST HAD TO ASK, DIDN'T YOU?
ROGUE!
AH'M WORKING ON IT...
SHUNT
SHOOOOM
GAAAAGGGGHHH!!!

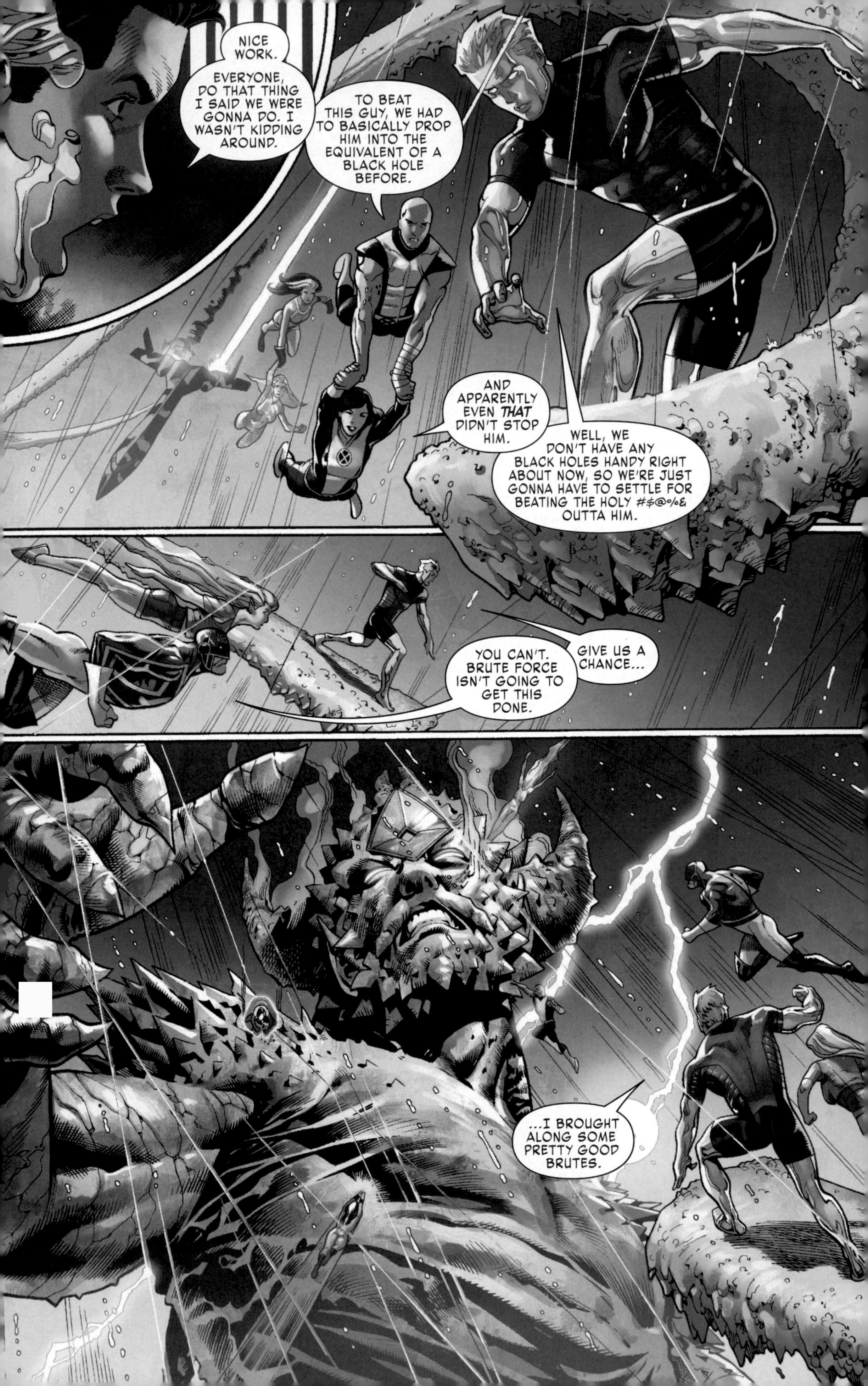
NICE WORK.
EVERYONE, DO THAT THING I SAID WE WERE GONNA DO. I WASN'T KIDDING AROUND.
TO BEAT THIS GUY, WE HAD TO BASICALLY DROP HIM INTO THE EQUIVALENT OF A BLACK HOLE BEFORE.
AND APPARENTLY EVEN *THAT* DIDN'T STOP HIM.
WELL, WE DON'T HAVE ANY BLACK HOLES HANDY RIGHT ABOUT NOW, SO WE'RE JUST GONNA HAVE TO SETTLE FOR BEATING THE HOLY #$@%& OUTTA HIM.
YOU CAN'T. BRUTE FORCE ISN'T GOING TO GET THIS DONE.
GIVE US A CHANCE...
...I BROUGHT ALONG SOME PRETTY GOOD BRUTES.

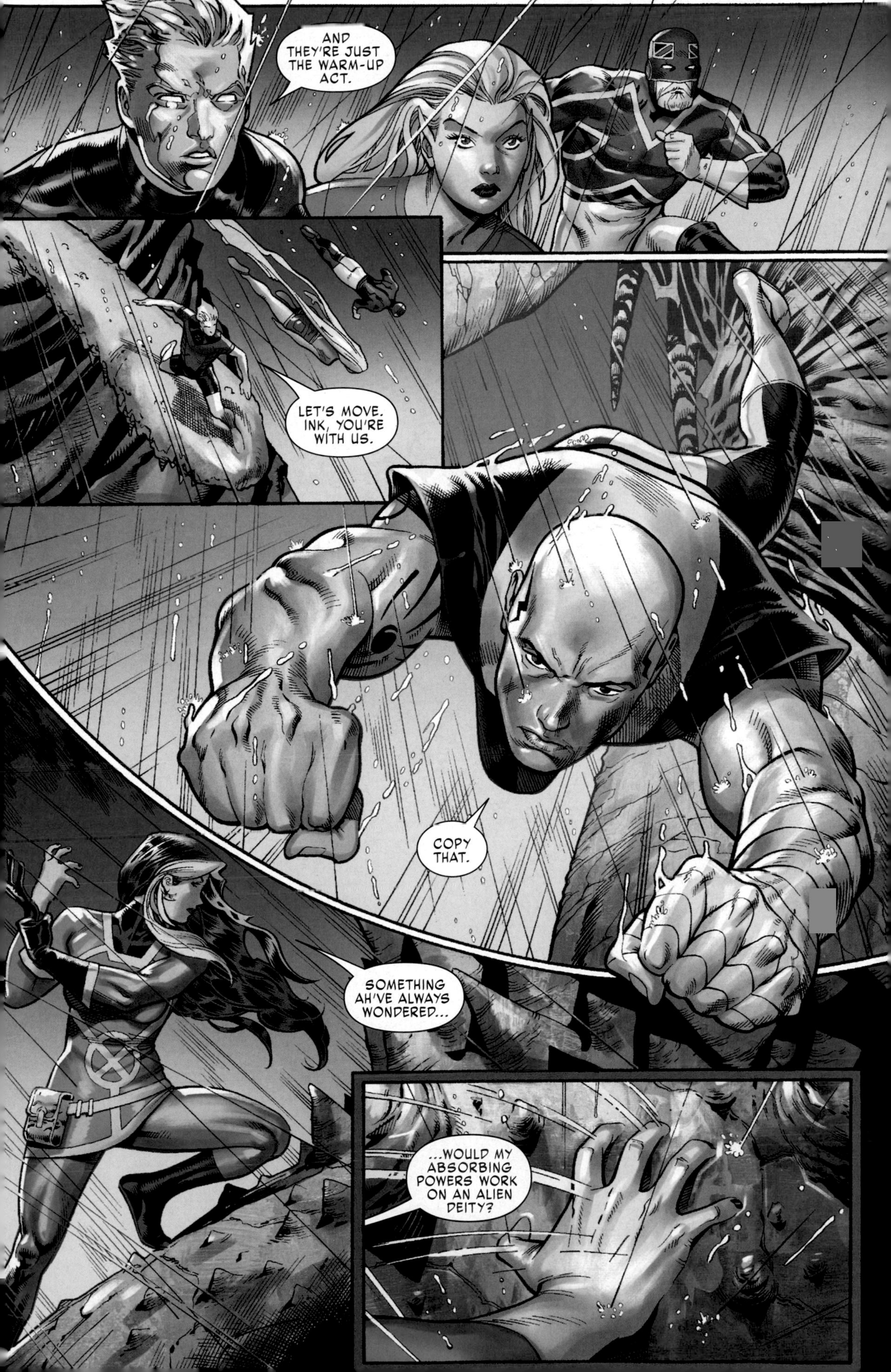
AND THEY'RE JUST THE WARM-UP ACT.
LET'S MOVE. INK, YOU'RE WITH US.
COPY THAT.
SOMETHING AH'VE ALWAYS WONDERED...
...WOULD MY ABSORBING POWERS WORK ON AN ALIEN DEITY?

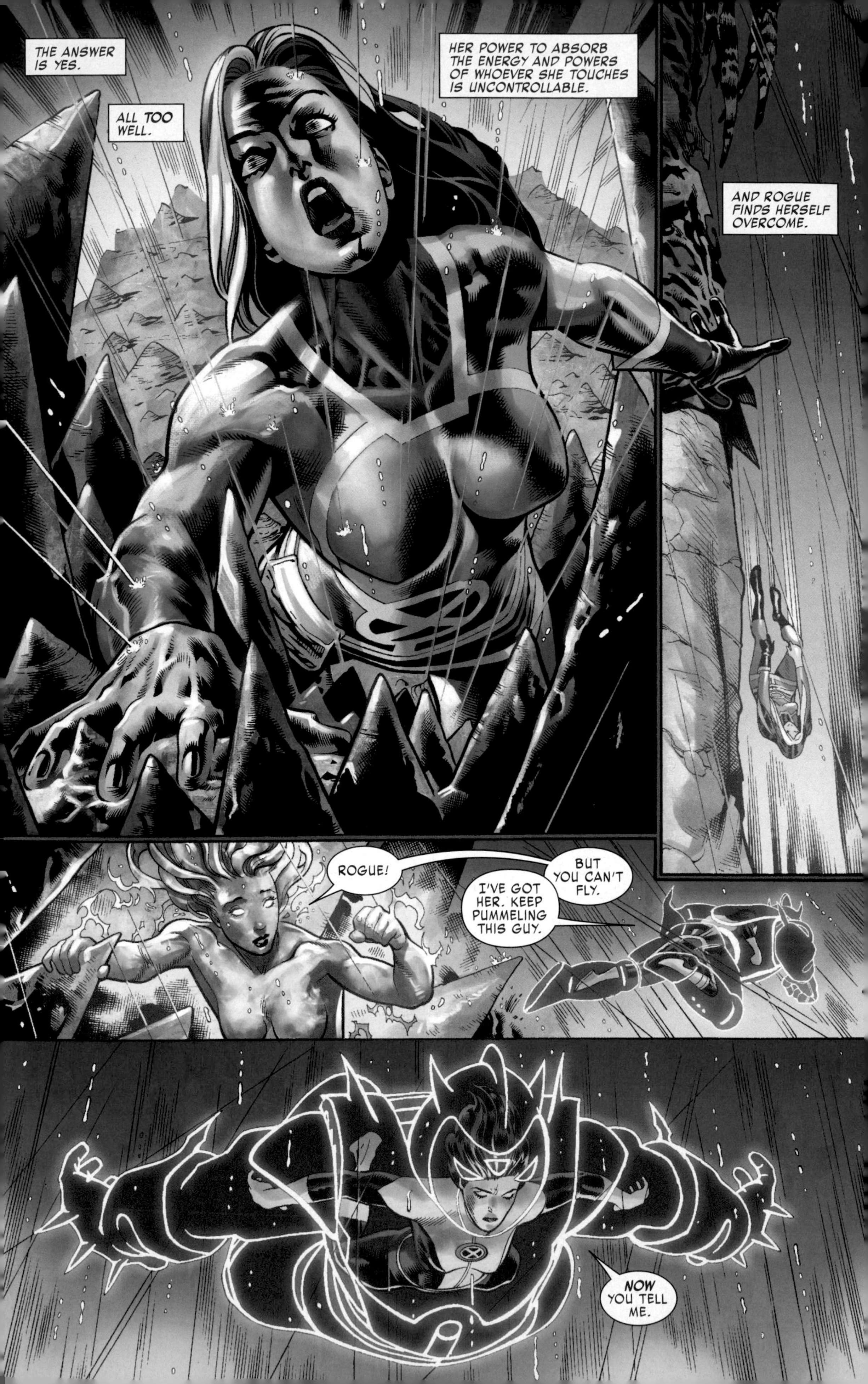
THE ANSWER IS YES.
ALL TOO WELL.
HER POWER TO ABSORB THE ENERGY AND POWERS OF WHOEVER SHE TOUCHES IS UNCONTROLLABLE.
AND ROGUE FINDS HERSELF OVERCOME.
ROGUE!
BUT YOU CAN'T FLY.
I'VE GOT HER. KEEP PUMMELING THIS GUY.
NOW YOU TELL ME.

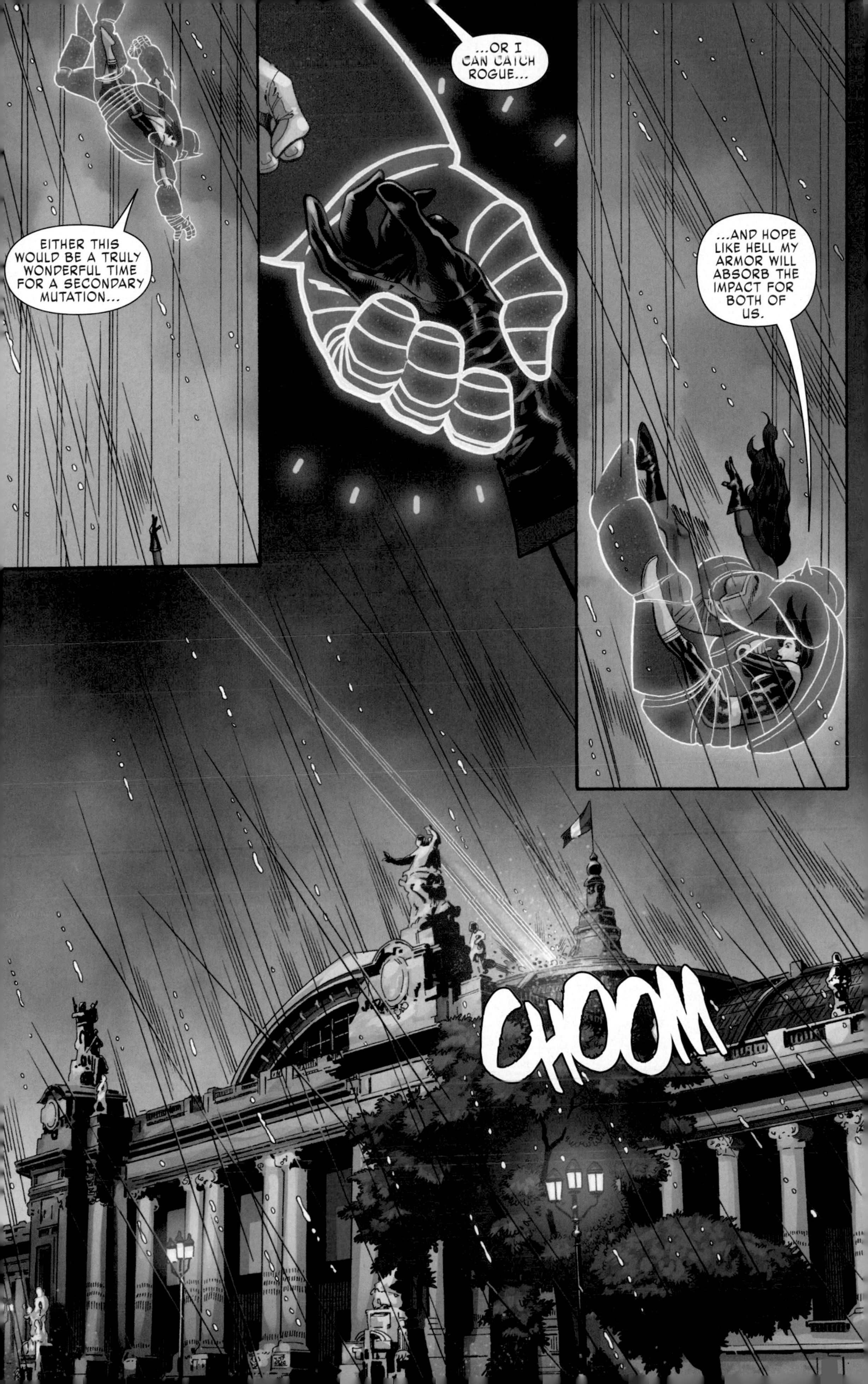
EITHER THIS WOULD BE A TRULY WONDERFUL TIME FOR A SECONDARY MUTATION...
...OR I CAN CATCH ROGUE...
...AND HOPE LIKE HELL MY ARMOR WILL ABSORB THE IMPACT FOR BOTH OF US.
CHOOM

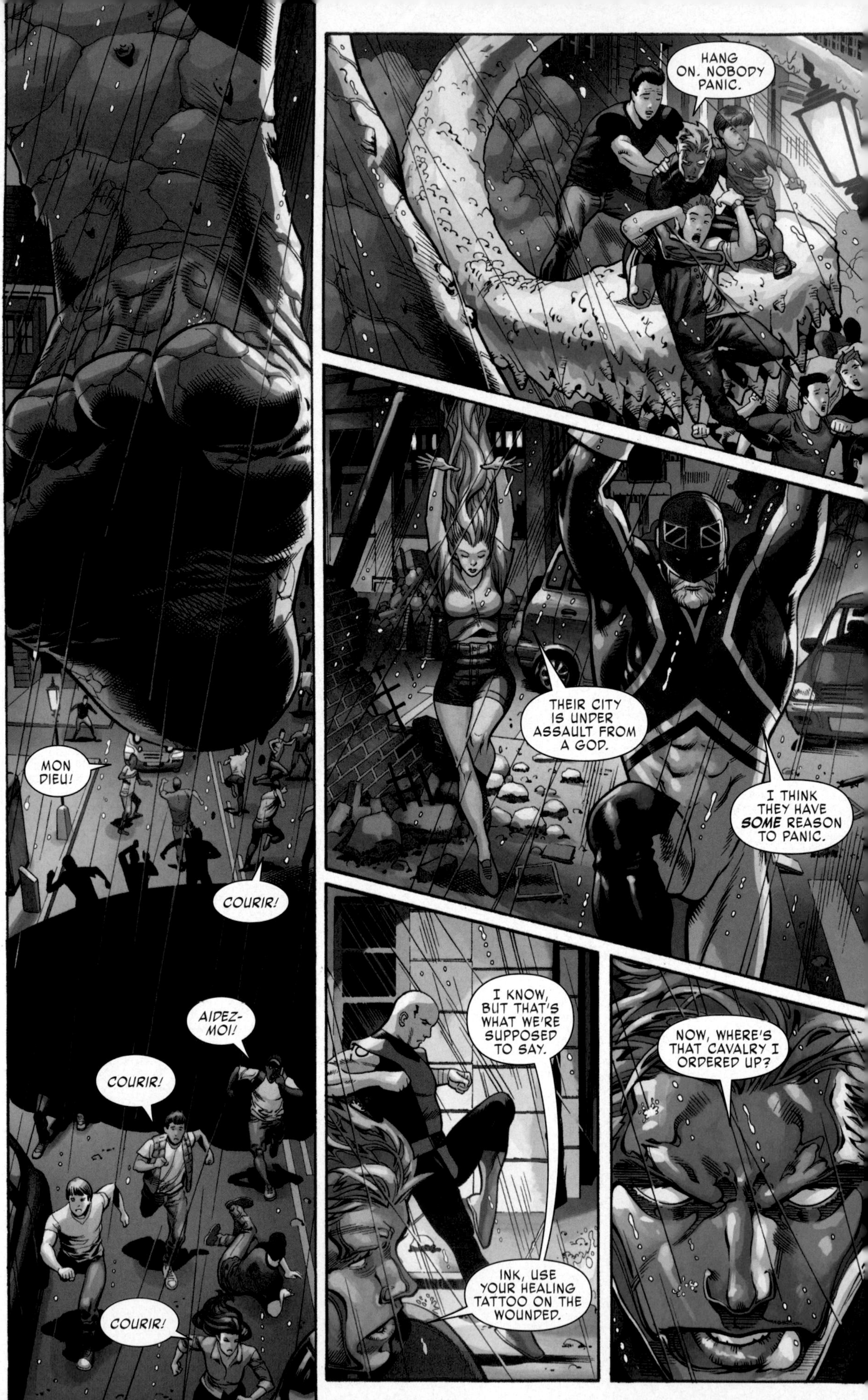
MON DIEU!
COURIR!
AIDEZ-MOI!
COURIR!
COURIR!
HANG ON. NOBODY PANIC.
THEIR CITY IS UNDER ASSAULT FROM A GOD.
I THINK THEY HAVE SOME REASON TO PANIC.
I KNOW, BUT THAT'S WHAT WE'RE SUPPOSED TO SAY.
INK, USE YOUR HEALING TATTOO ON THE WOUNDED.
NOW, WHERE'S THAT CAVALRY I ORDERED UP?

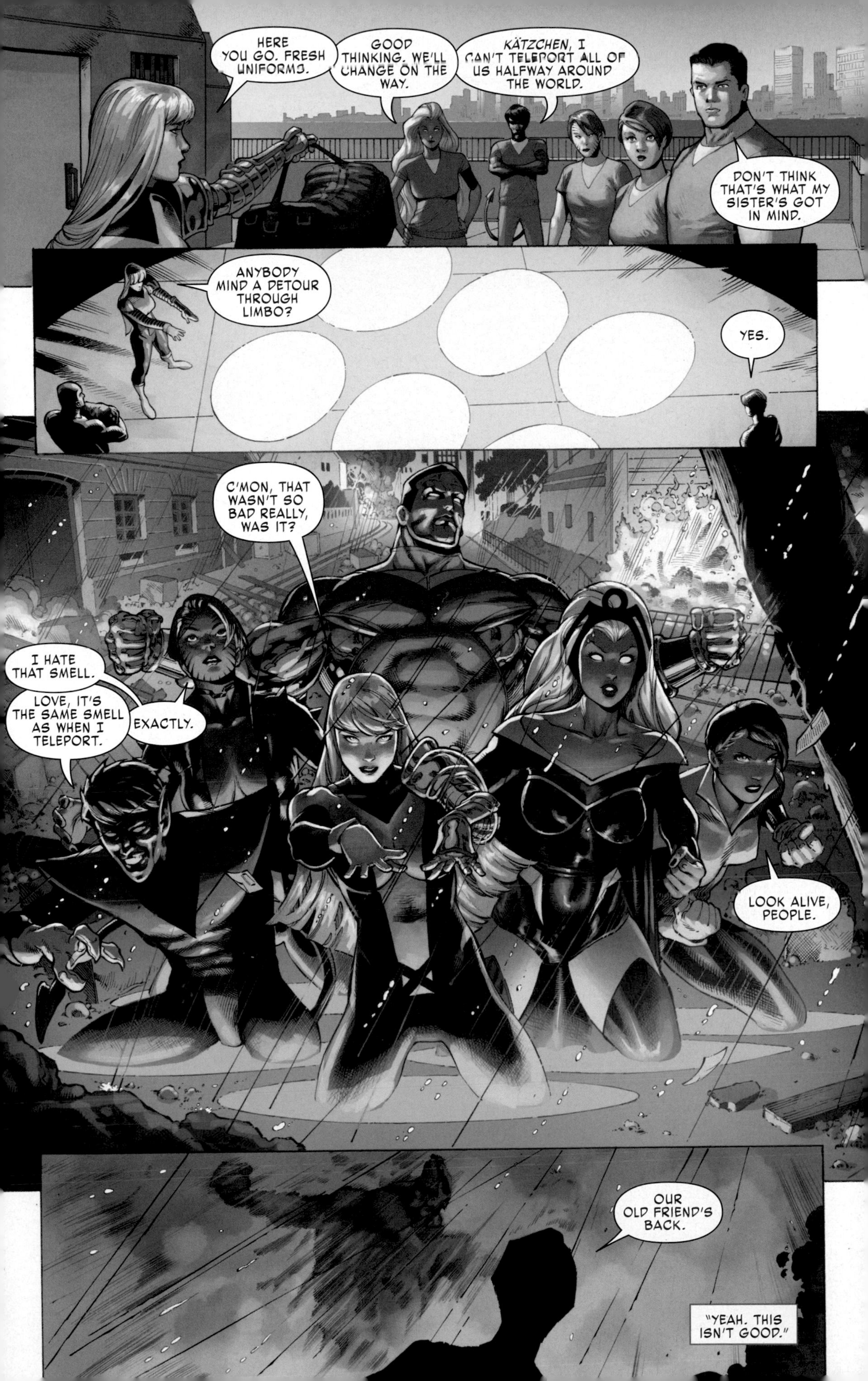
HERE YOU GO. FRESH UNIFORMS.
GOOD THINKING. WE'LL CHANGE ON THE WAY.
KÄTZCHEN, I CAN'T TELEPORT ALL OF US HALFWAY AROUND THE WORLD.
DON'T THINK THAT'S WHAT MY SISTER'S GOT IN MIND.
ANYBODY MIND A DETOUR THROUGH LIMBO?
YES.
C'MON, THAT WASN'T SO BAD REALLY, WAS IT?
I HATE THAT SMELL.
LOVE, IT'S THE SAME SMELL AS WHEN I TELEPORT.
EXACTLY.
LOOK ALIVE, PEOPLE.
OUR OLD FRIEND'S BACK.
"YEAH. THIS ISN'T GOOD."

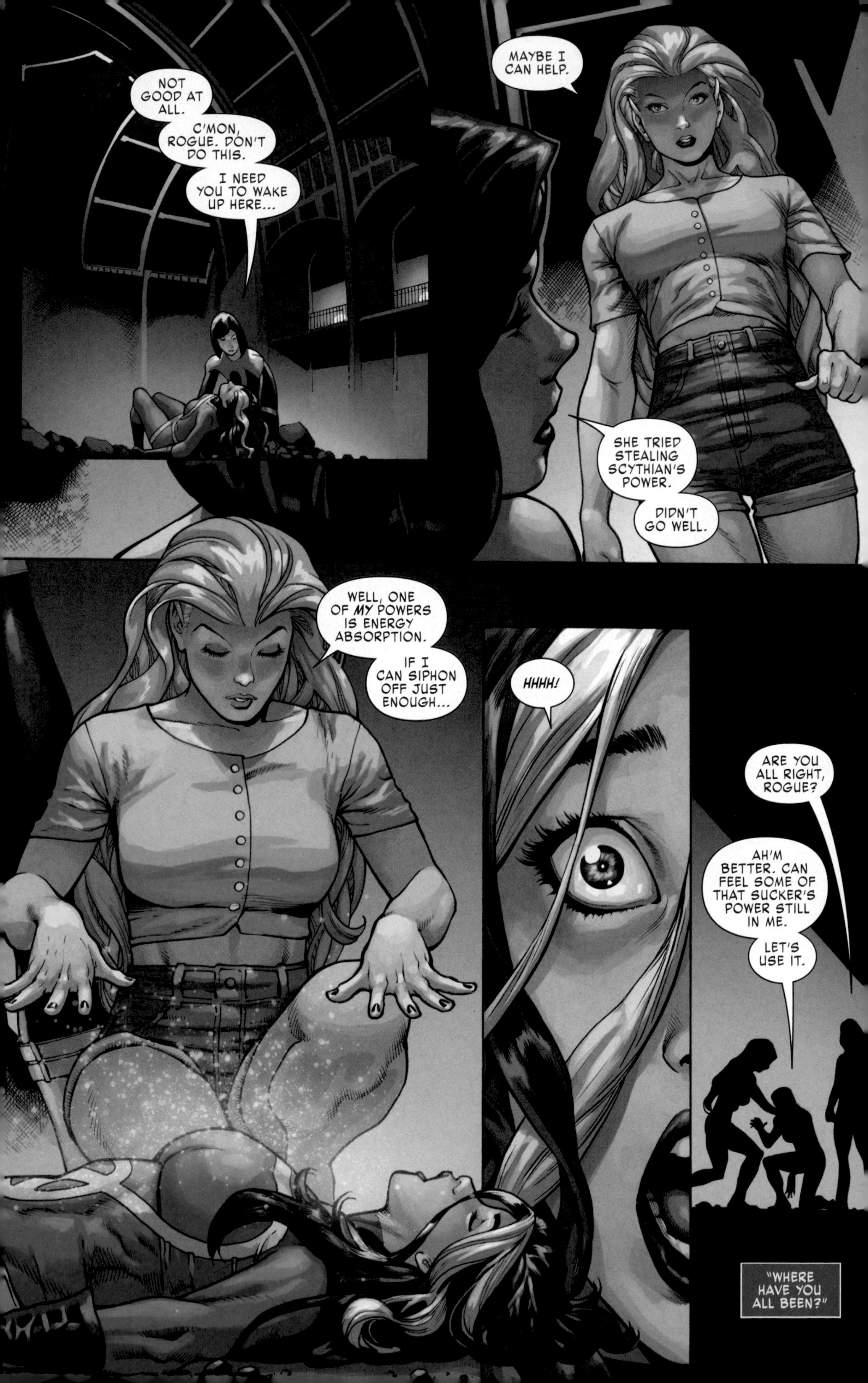
NOT GOOD AT ALL.
C'MON, ROGUE. DON'T DO THIS.
I NEED YOU TO WAKE UP HERE...
MAYBE I CAN HELP.
SHE TRIED STEALING SCYTHIAN'S POWER.
DIDN'T GO WELL.
WELL, ONE OF MY POWERS IS ENERGY ABSORPTION.
IF I CAN SIPHON OFF JUST ENOUGH...
HHHH!
ARE YOU ALL RIGHT, ROGUE?
AH'M BETTER. CAN FEEL SOME OF THAT SUCKER'S POWER STILL IN ME.
LET'S USE IT.
"WHERE HAVE YOU ALL BEEN?"

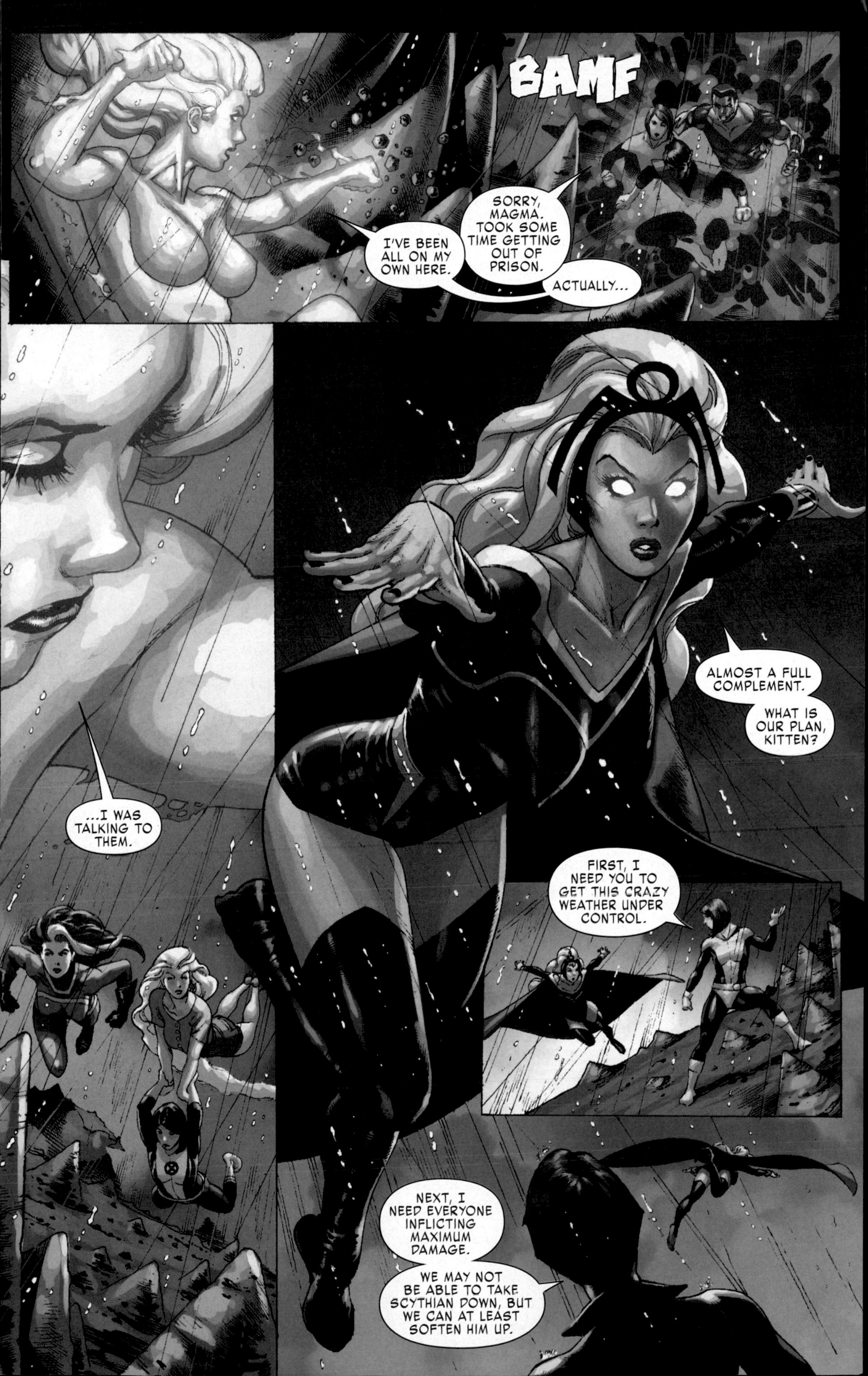
BAMF
I'VE BEEN ALL ON MY OWN HERE.
SORRY, MAGMA. TOOK SOME TIME GETTING OUT OF PRISON.
ACTUALLY...
...I WAS TALKING TO THEM.
ALMOST A FULL COMPLEMENT.
WHAT IS OUR PLAN, KITTEN?
FIRST, I NEED YOU TO GET THIS CRAZY WEATHER UNDER CONTROL.
NEXT, I NEED EVERYONE INFLICTING MAXIMUM DAMAGE.
WE MAY NOT BE ABLE TO TAKE SCYTHIAN DOWN, BUT WE CAN AT LEAST SOFTEN HIM UP.

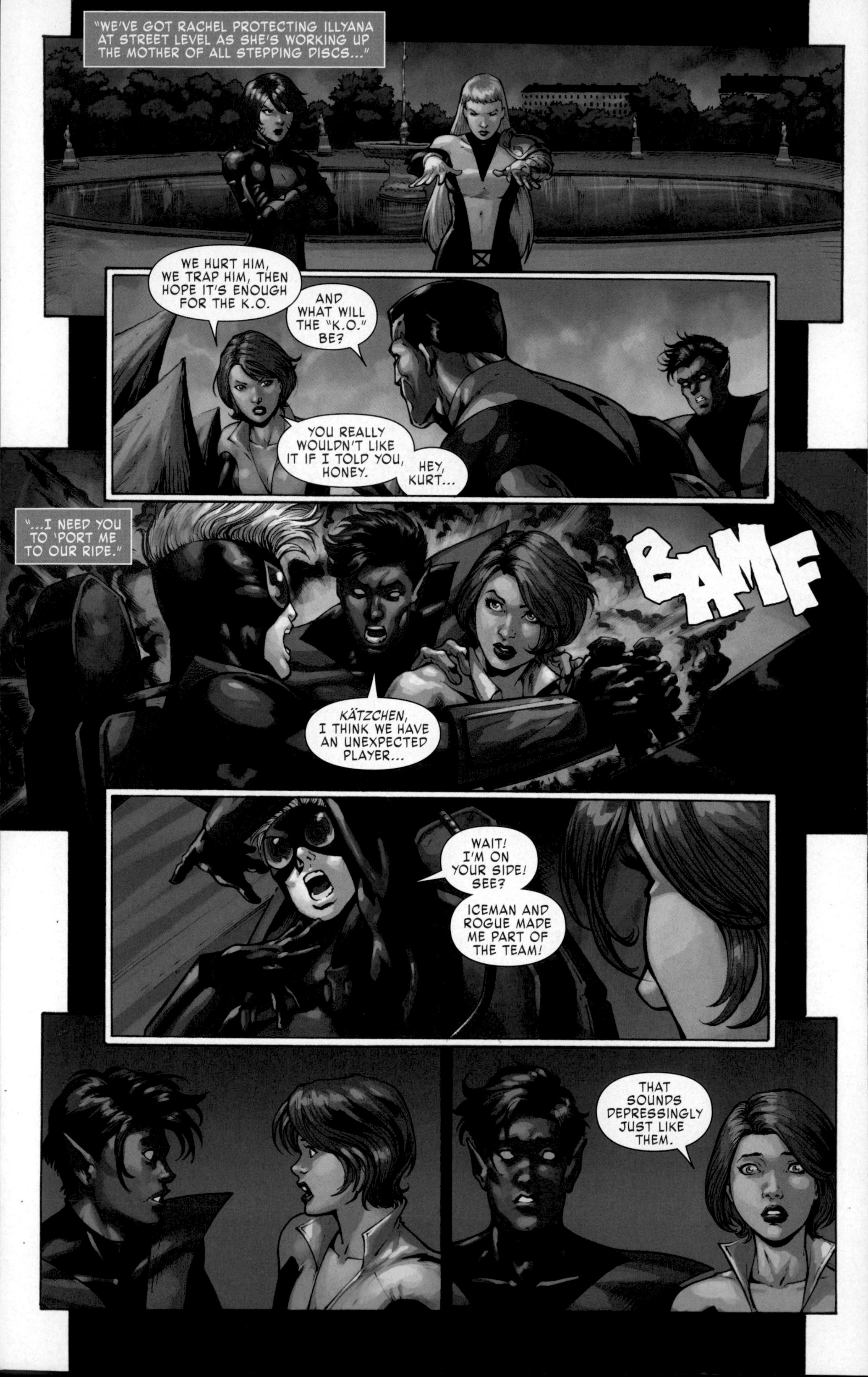
"WE'VE GOT RACHEL PROTECTING ILLYANA AT STREET LEVEL AS SHE'S WORKING UP THE MOTHER OF ALL STEPPING DISCS..."
WE HURT HIM, WE TRAP HIM, THEN HOPE IT'S ENOUGH FOR THE K.O.
AND WHAT WILL THE "K.O." BE?
YOU REALLY WOULDN'T LIKE IT IF I TOLD YOU, HONEY.
HEY, KURT...
"...I NEED YOU TO 'PORT ME TO OUR RIDE."
BAMF
KÄTZCHEN, I THINK WE HAVE AN UNEXPECTED PLAYER...
WAIT! I'M ON YOUR SIDE! SEE?
ICEMAN AND ROGUE MADE ME PART OF THE TEAM!
THAT SOUNDS DEPRESSINGLY JUST LIKE THEM.

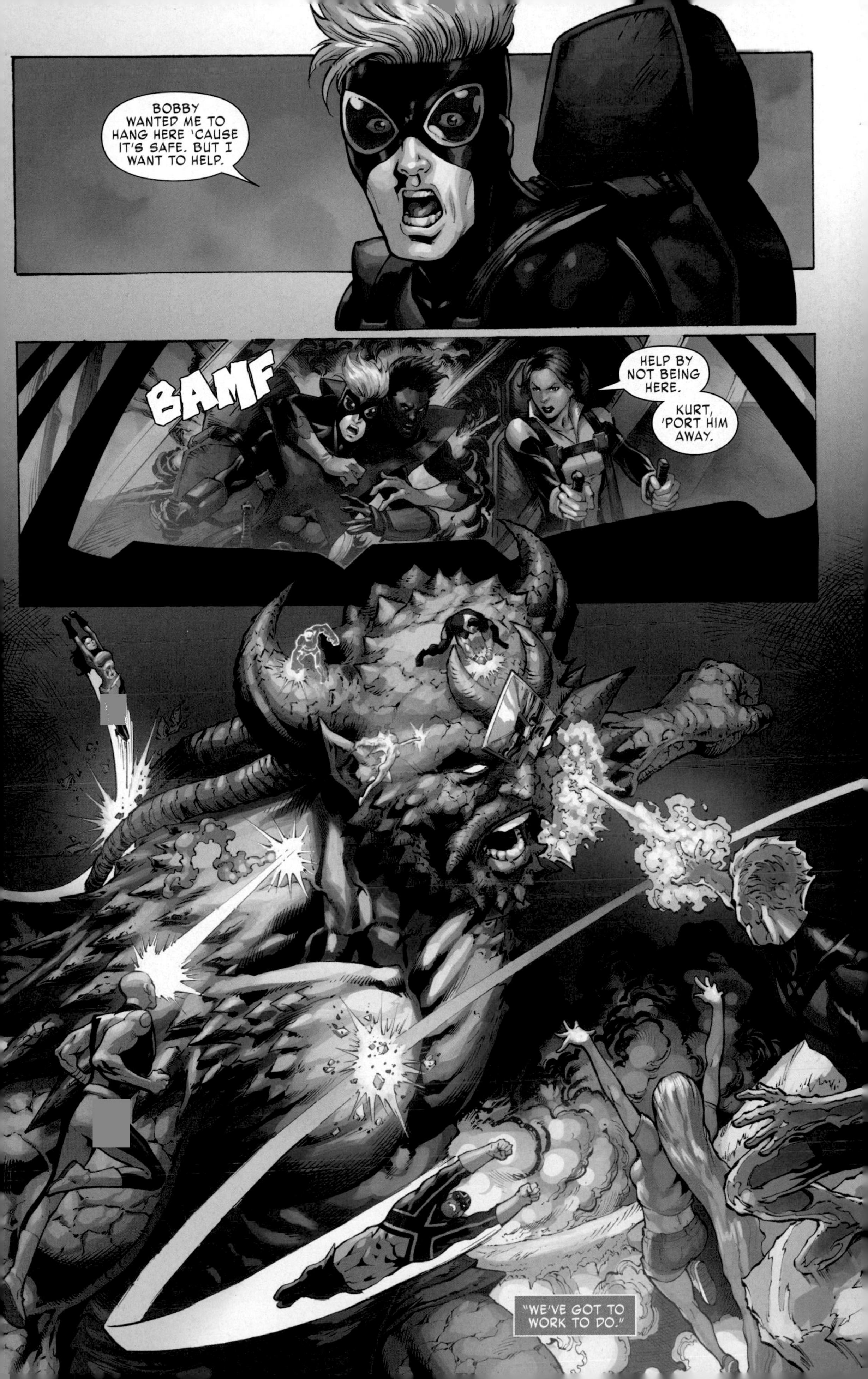
BOBBY WANTED ME TO HANG HERE 'CAUSE IT'S SAFE. BUT I WANT TO HELP.
BAMF
HELP BY NOT BEING HERE.
KURT, 'PORT HIM AWAY.
"WE'VE GOT TO WORK TO DO."

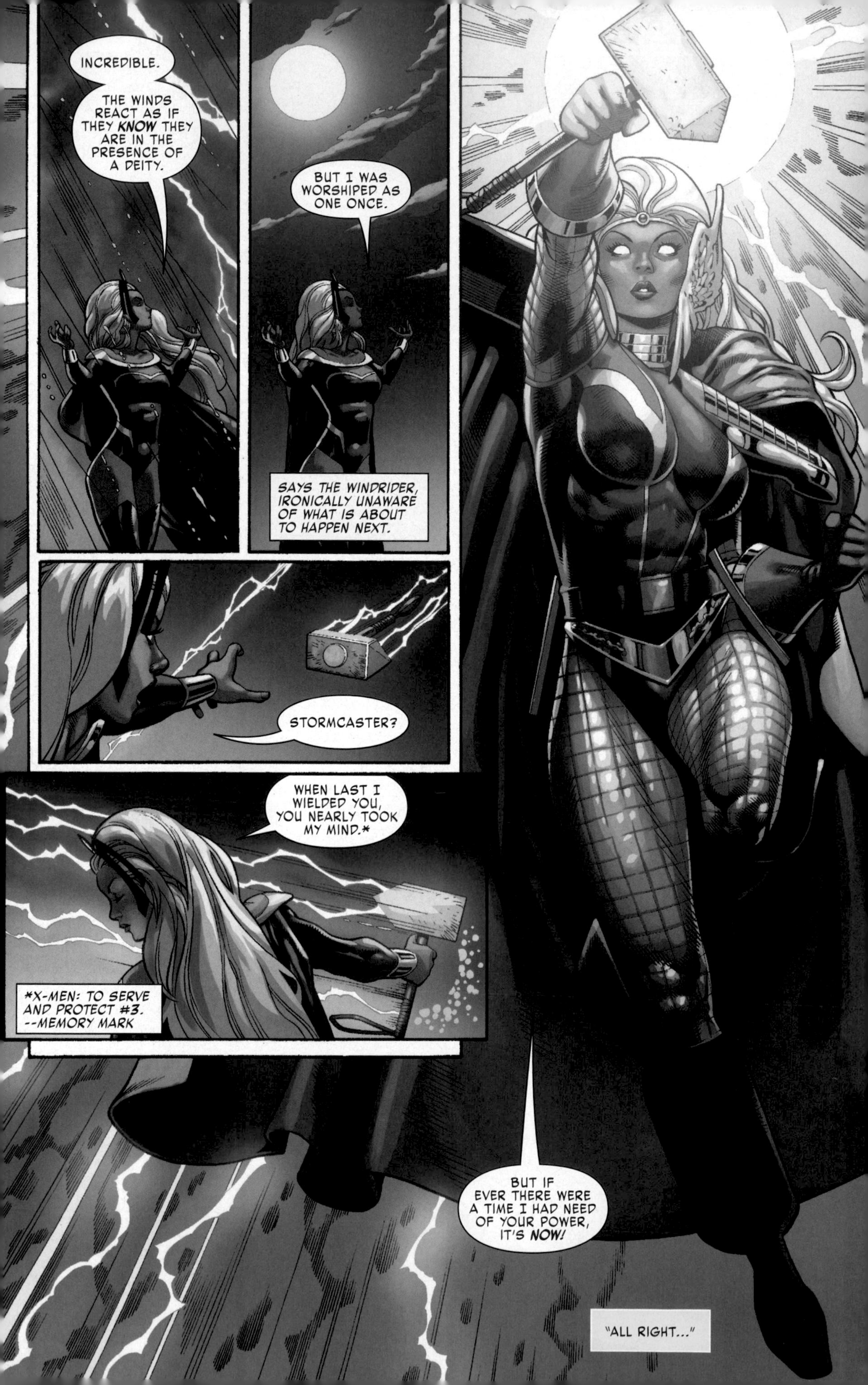
INCREDIBLE.
THE WINDS REACT AS IF THEY KNOW THEY ARE IN THE PRESENCE OF A DEITY.
BUT I WAS WORSHIPED AS ONE ONCE.
SAYS THE WINDRIDER, IRONICALLY UNAWARE OF WHAT IS ABOUT TO HAPPEN NEXT.
STORMCASTER?
WHEN LAST I WIELDED YOU, YOU NEARLY TOOK MY MIND.*
*X-MEN: TO SERVE AND PROTECT #3. --MEMORY MARK
BUT IF EVER THERE WERE A TIME I HAD NEED OF YOUR POWER, IT'S NOW!
"ALL RIGHT..."

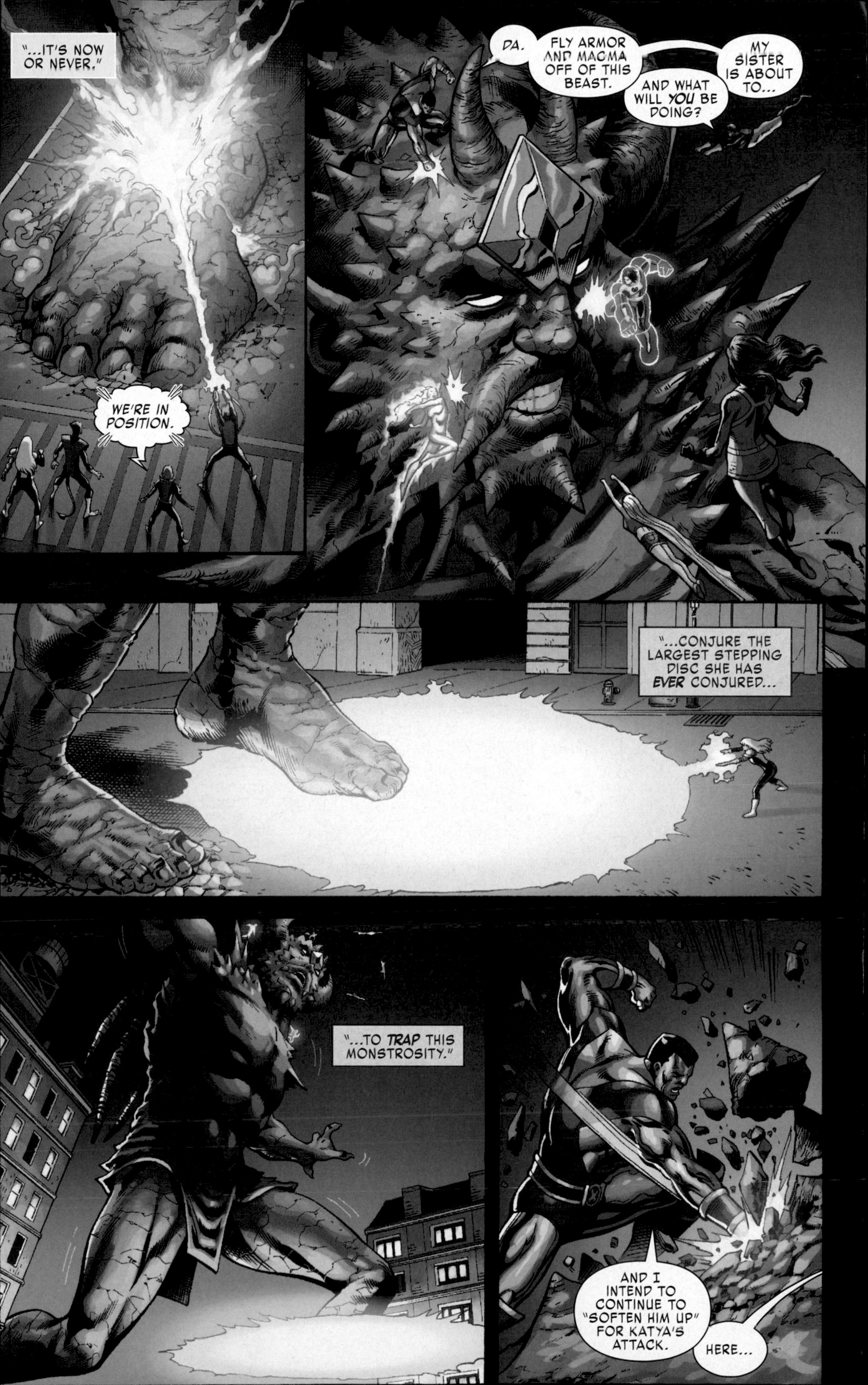
"...IT'S NOW OR NEVER."
WE'RE IN POSITION.
DA.
FLY ARMOR AND MAGMA OFF OF THIS BEAST.
AND WHAT WILL YOU BE DOING?
MY SISTER IS ABOUT TO...
"...CONJURE THE LARGEST STEPPING DISC SHE HAS EVER CONJURED...
"...TO TRAP THIS MONSTROSITY."
AND I INTEND TO CONTINUE TO "SOFTEN HIM UP" FOR KATYA'S ATTACK.
HERE...

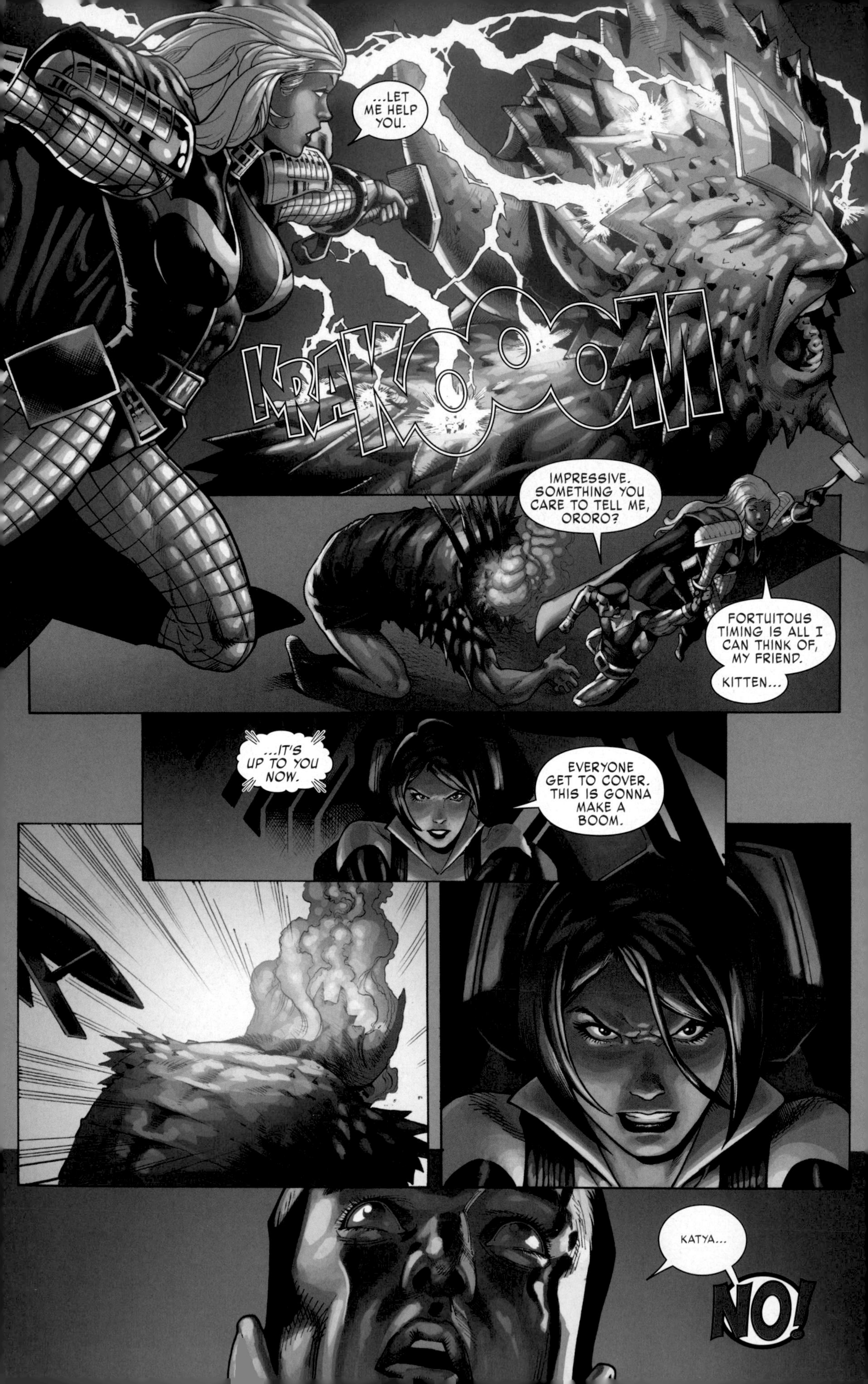
...LET ME HELP YOU.
KRAKOOOOM
IMPRESSIVE. SOMETHING YOU CARE TO TELL ME, ORORO?
FORTUITOUS TIMING IS ALL I CAN THINK OF, MY FRIEND.
KITTEN...
...IT'S UP TO YOU NOW.
EVERYONE GET TO COVER. THIS IS GONNA MAKE A BOOM.
KATYA...
NO!

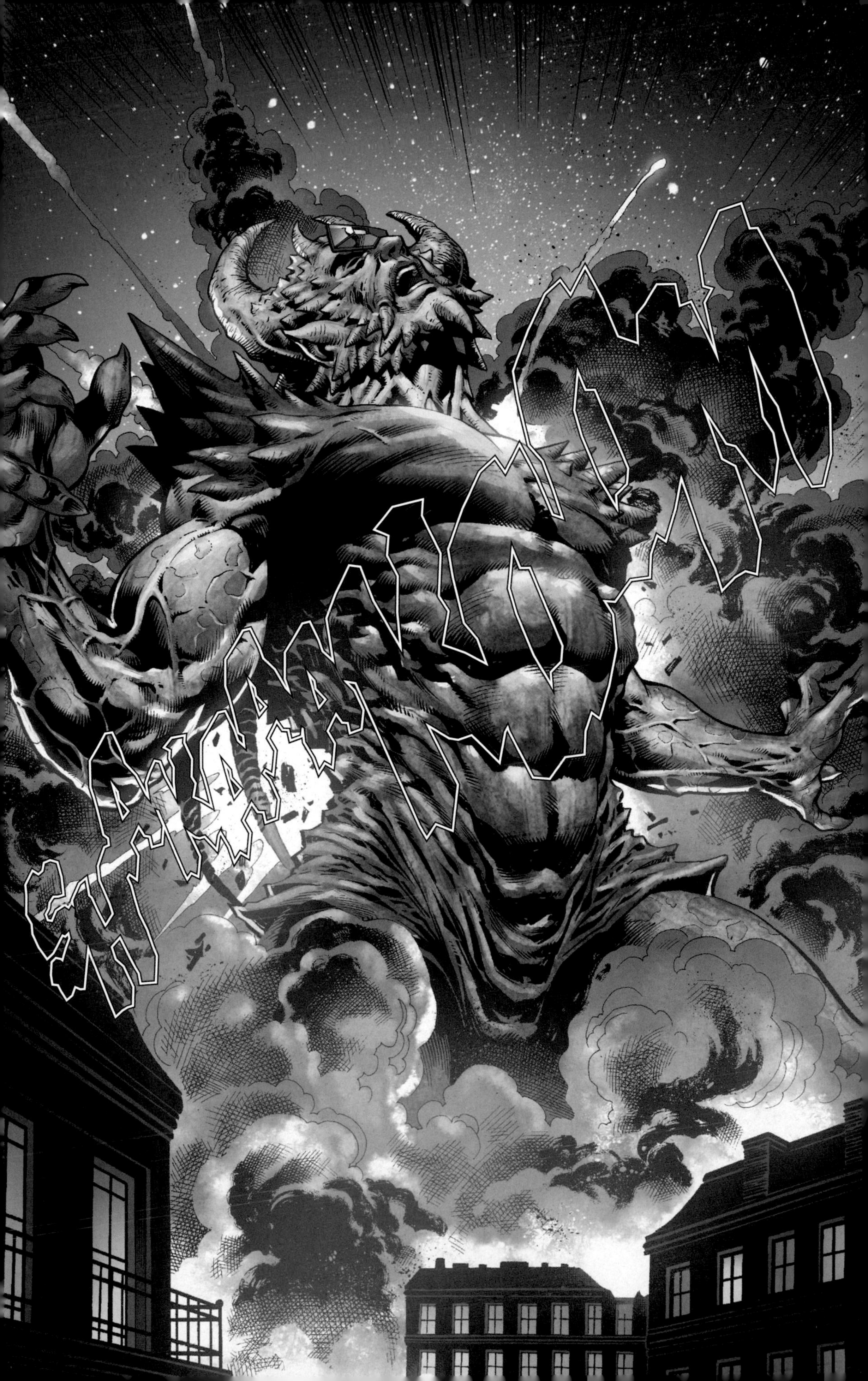

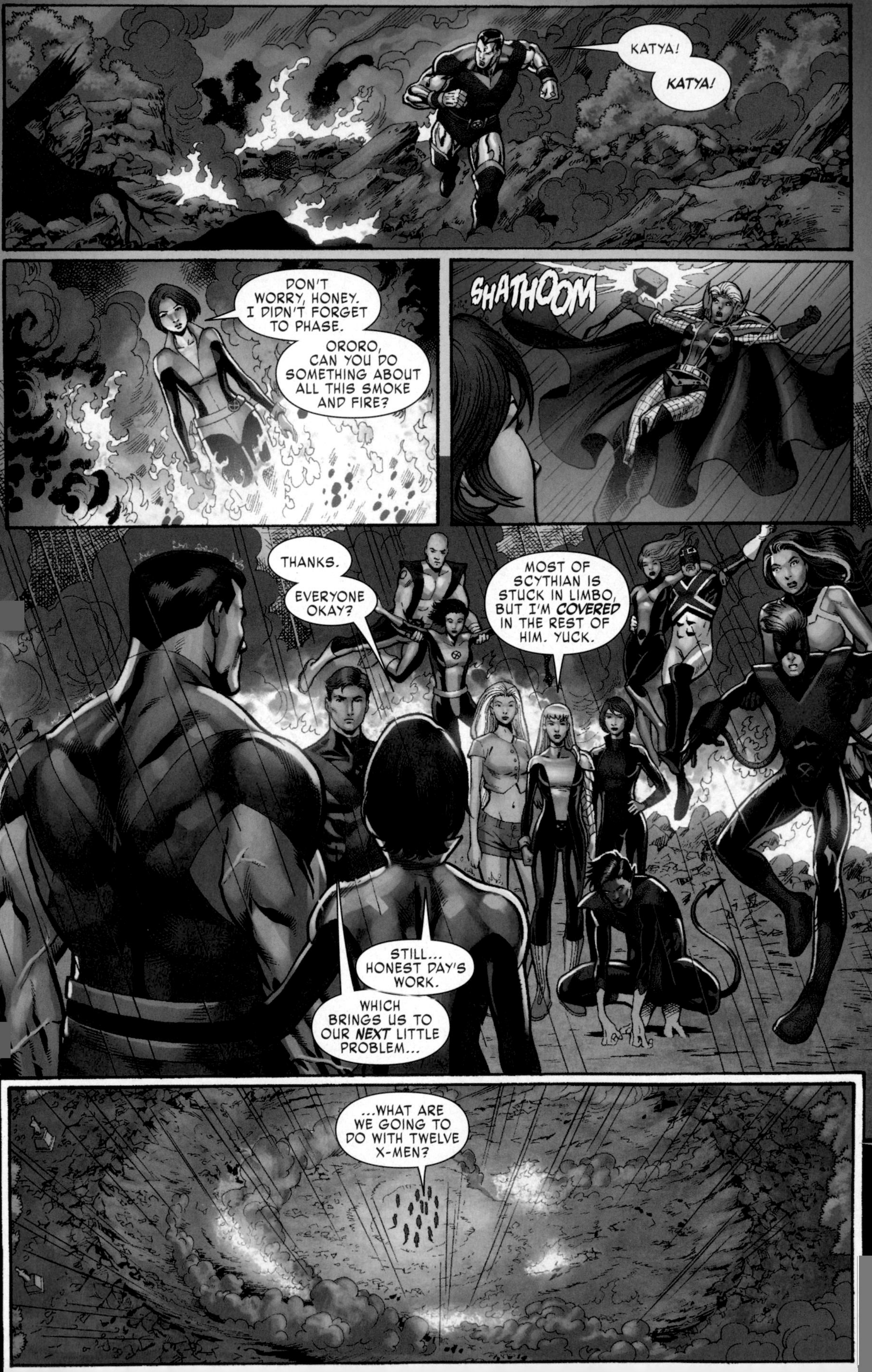
KATYA!
KATYA!
DON'T WORRY, HONEY. I DIDN'T FORGET TO PHASE.
ORORO, CAN YOU DO SOMETHING ABOUT ALL THIS SMOKE AND FIRE?
SHATHOOM
THANKS.
EVERYONE OKAY?
MOST OF SCYTHIAN IS STUCK IN LIMBO, BUT I'M COVERED IN THE REST OF HIM. YUCK.
STILL... HONEST DAY'S WORK.
WHICH BRINGS US TO OUR NEXT LITTLE PROBLEM...
...WHAT ARE WE GOING TO DO WITH TWELVE X-MEN?

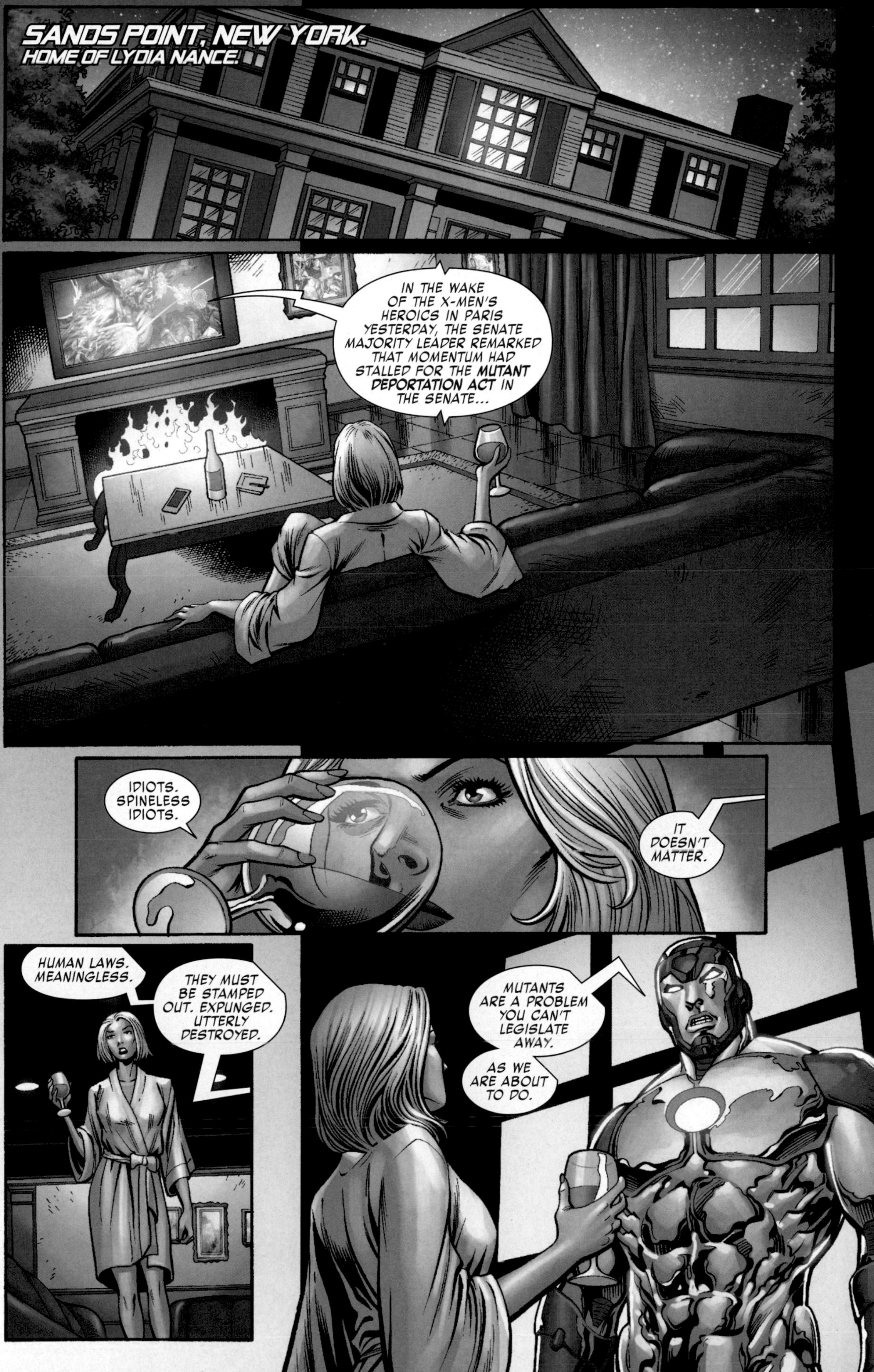
SANDS POINT, NEW YORK.
HOME OF LYDIA NANCE.
IN THE WAKE OF THE X-MEN'S HEROICS IN PARIS YESTERDAY, THE SENATE MAJORITY LEADER REMARKED THAT MOMENTUM HAD STALLED FOR THE MUTANT DEPORTATION ACT IN THE SENATE...
IDIOTS. SPINELESS IDIOTS.
IT DOESN'T MATTER.
HUMAN LAWS. MEANINGLESS.
THEY MUST BE STAMPED OUT. EXPUNGED. UTTERLY DESTROYED.
MUTANTS ARE A PROBLEM YOU CAN'T LEGISLATE AWAY.
AS WE ARE ABOUT TO DO.

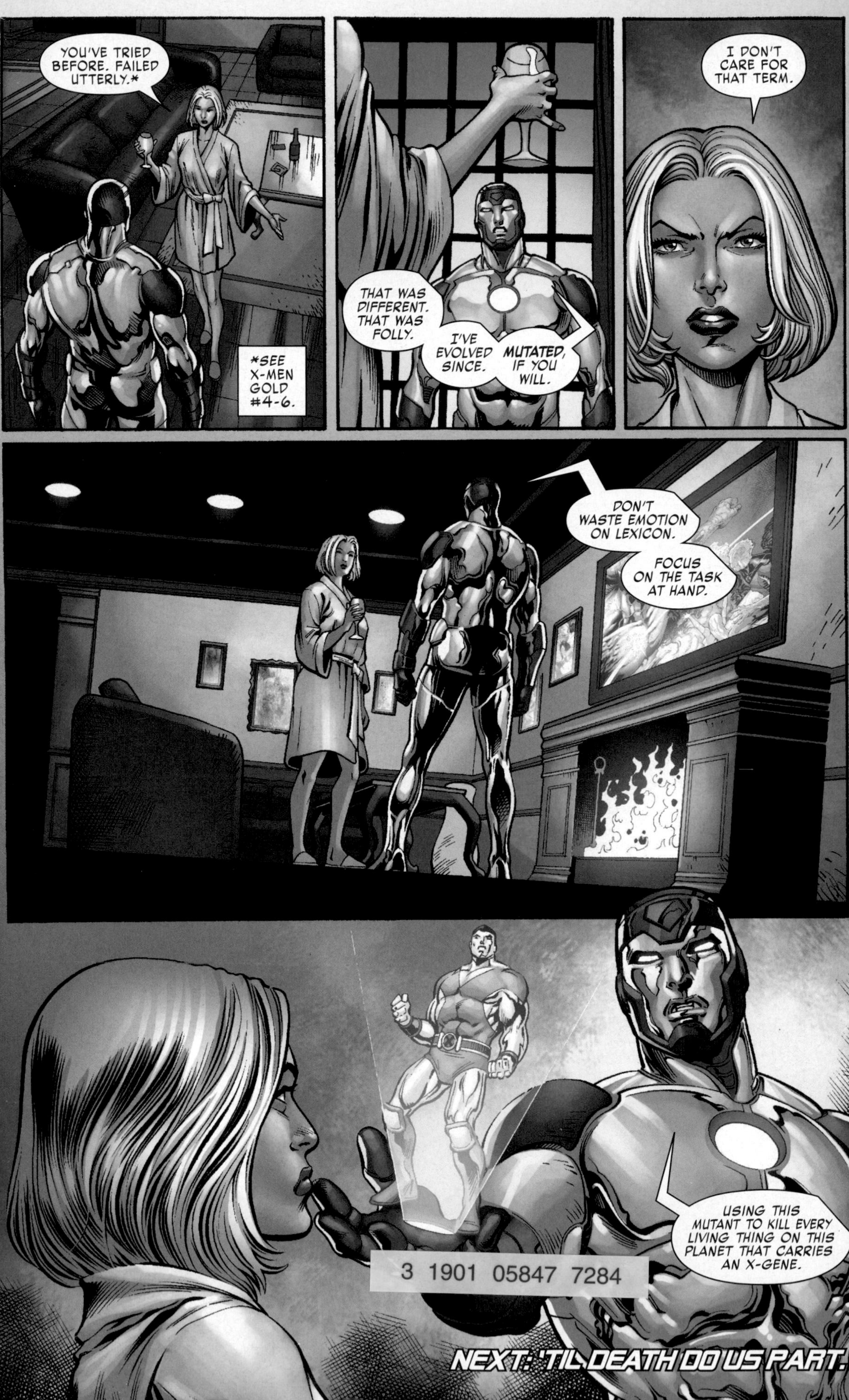
YOU'VE TRIED BEFORE. FAILED UTTERLY.*
*SEE X-MEN GOLD #4-6.
THAT WAS DIFFERENT. THAT WAS FOLLY.
I'VE EVOLVED SINCE.
MUTATED, IF YOU WILL.
I DON'T CARE FOR THAT TERM.
DON'T WASTE EMOTION ON LEXICON.
FOCUS ON THE TASK AT HAND.
USING THIS MUTANT TO KILL EVERY LIVING THING ON THIS PLANET THAT CARRIES AN X-GENE.
NEXT: 'TIL DEATH DO US PART.